24140   H-872

Somers
Presidential
agency: OWMR

DATE DUE

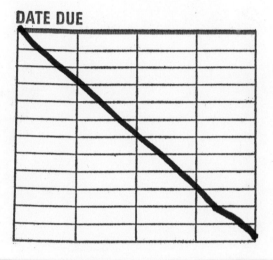

PRESIDENTIAL AGENCY

THE OFFICE OF WAR MOBILIZATION AND RECONVERSION

Herman Miles Somers

PRESIDENTIAL AGENCY

OWMR

THE OFFICE OF WAR MOBILIZATION AND RECONVERSION

GREENWOOD PRESS, PUBLISHERS
NEW YORK

For ANNE

ACKNOWLEDGMENTS

Most of the information for this study was gathered while I was a member of the staff of the Office of War Mobilization and Reconversion. My direct experience with the agency was confined to its latter-day history, but during this sixteen-month period I lived in constant association with participants in the earlier history and I obtained invaluable insights and data thereby. Officials of the agency cooperated generously throughout the study and the result owes much to their help.

In addition to daily conversations with staff members, I had many interviews with past officials of the Office and with high officers of other agencies whose responsibilities had brought them into close working relationship with OWM and OWMR. I talked with many of the leading actors in the events described in the following pages. Without the cooperation of these busy people who gave up many hours to supply information not otherwise available, this would have been a much less accurate study. I regret that the list of my creditors is too long to permit individual acknowledgment. I hope they may find some partial repayment in my effort to interpret faithfully the valuable knowledge they passed on to me.

All or parts of the manuscript have been read in various stages of preparation by a number of persons, too many to acknowledge individually, who were in a position to check the validity of fact and interpretation. A few deserve special mention. My friend, teacher, and colleague, Professor W. Y. Elliott of Harvard, formerly Vice Chairman for Civilian Requirements, War Production Board, guided and encouraged this effort through its most difficult stages and I borrowed much from his scholarship and administrative experience. Professor Lincoln Gordon of Harvard, former Program Vice Chairman, War Production Board, devoted many hours to discussion with me of difficult points and read the manuscript with painstaking care. His superb intimate knowledge of and insights into the affairs discussed here served as a constant bulwark. Professor William Haber of the University of Michigan, a War Manpower Commission and OWMR executive during the war, and an OWMR consultant in the postwar period, shared with me his rich personal experience and gave me constant and invaluable help.

Dean Paul H. Appleby of Syracuse University, Professor V. O. Key of Yale, Professor Kenneth Hechler of Princeton, Dr. Don K. Price, Associate Director of the Public Administration Clearing House, Dr. Harold Stein, Director of the Committee on Public Administration Cases and former Deputy Director of OWMR, and Professor Paul Ylvisaker of Swarthmore all read and made valuable suggestions on portions of the manuscript which saved me from errors of emphasis or interpretation. Dr. J. Donald Kingsley, now Director of the International Refugee Organization, made the original suggestion causing me to undertake this study, and lightened my tasks while he was Deputy Director of OWMR. Professor Carl J. Friedrich gave me useful counsel during the initial stages of the undertaking.

I owe a different kind of debt to my friend, Professor John M. Gaus of Harvard. Many years ago he awakened in me an appreciation for the deep significance of public service and the art of public administration. His active interest in this work gave me the faith to complete a job I was ready to give up on several occasions.

Beatrice G. Reubens rendered able and creative assistance in research and editorial work. My long-time secretary, Shirley Harris Goldblum, contributed competent and selfless hours far beyond the call of duty. To the skilled and experienced editorial hand of my wife, Anne Ramsay Somers, the book owes such compactness and clarity as it may contain.

I am indebted to the American Philosophical Society for a grant which made possible completion of the work.

My thanks are extended to Harcourt, Brace and Company for permission to quote extensively from Donald M. Nelson's *Arsenal of Democracy*. The unpublished letters and memoranda cited are now public documents on file in the National Archives with other OWM and OWMR records.

H. M. S.

Haverford College
Haverford, Pennsylvania
August 15, 1949

CONTENTS

Contents   xi

ABBREVIATIONS

AAF	Army Air Forces
ANMB	Army and Navy Munitions Board
APUC	Area Production Urgency Committee
ASF	Army Service Forces (successor to the Services of Supply)
BEW	Board of Economic Warfare
CMP	Controlled Materials Plan
Colmer Committee	House Special Committee on Postwar Economic Policy and Planning
CPA	Civilian Production Administration (successor to WPB)
E.O.	Executive Order
JCTB	Joint Contract Termination Board
JPSC	Joint Production Survey Committee
JCS	Joint Chiefs of Staff
Lend-Lease	Office of Lend-Lease Administration
NDAC	National Defense Advisory Commission
NEC	National Emergency Council
NHA	National Housing Agency
NRPB	National Resources Planning Board
OCR	Office of Civilian Requirements, WPB (successor to Office of Civilian Supply)
OCS	Office of Contract Settlement
ODT	Office of Defense Transportation
OES	Office of Economic Stabilization
OPA	Office of Price Administration (successor to OPACS)
OPACS	Office of Price Administration and Civilian Supply
OPM	Office of Production Management
OWI	Office of War Information
OWM	Office of War Mobilization
OWMR	Office of War Mobilization and Reconversion (successor to OWM)
OWM–OWMR	OWM and OWMR considered as one continuous Office
PAW	Petroleum Administration for War

PEC	Production Executive Committee, WPB
PRC	Production Readjustment Committee, WPB
RRA	Retraining and Reëmployment Administration
RFC	Reconstruction Finance Corporation
SOS	Army Services of Supply
SPAB	Supply Priorities and Allocations Board
SSS	Selective Service System
Tolan Committee	House Select Committee Investigating National Defense Migration
Truman Committee	Senate Special Committee Investigating the National Defense Program
USES	United States Employment Service
WFA	War Food Administration
WLB (or NWLB)	National War Labor Board
WMC	War Manpower Commission
WPB	War Production Board

The terms "departments" and "agencies" are used interchangeably, except when referring to a specific unit of government.

LABOR MARKET AREAS

In discussion of manpower controls, the following WMC classifications are used to indicate the labor supply condition of the different labor market areas:

Group I   Severe current labor shortage
Group II   Labor shortage anticipated
Group III   Balanced supply and demand
Group IV   Labor surplus

PRESIDENTIAL ASSISTANCE:
A PROBLEM IN WAR AND PEACE

*O*n *May 27, 1943, the President of the United* States issued an executive order which provided an unprecedented delegation of executive authority. The order, creating an Office of War Mobilization, gave its director authority over virtually all domestic phases of the wartime government.

About sixteen months later, in October 1944, Congress reaffirmed and extended these powers in an act which rechristened the agency, the Office of War Mobilization and Reconversion. It is considered the broadest grant of power ever legislated by Congress, creating for the first time by statute a superdepartmental director over the whole range of home-front executive activities for war and reconversion—powers so great that some critics questioned the constitutionality of such a grant to anyone short of the President.

OWM–OWMR[1] thus acted as the highest governmental authority, short of the President, in the total field of industrial and civilian mobilization and reconversion. For this reason alone its administrative experience, to which most of this book is devoted, is an important subject for study.

Such study soon reveals, however, that the significance of the OWM–OWMR experience is even broader. Beyond its importance as a super war agency, lies the fact that this was a significant experiment in staffing the Presidency. In addition to its direct authority it was a notable, although improvised, attempt to equip the President with a strong staff arm for executive policy and program coördination, as distinguished from administrative man-

[1] The continuity of these agencies was such that they may, for most purposes, be considered one. When referring to the entire span of the agency, it will be called OWM–OWMR. When activities prior to October 1944 are the subject, only the designation OWM will be employed. For activities after October 1944, it will be called OWMR.

agement and fiscal control. In setting up OWM, President Roosevelt appears to have had in mind creation of a civilian "chief of staff" with jurisdiction almost as broad as his own, except for military strategy and diplomatic operations.[2]

While the long-range interest of this unique experiment for wartime organization of the government will probably not be questioned, its significance for ordinary peacetime administration could easily be overlooked because of its association with a crisis condition. Examination readily reveals that the conditions which prompted the need for the Presidential assistance provided by OWM–OWMR did not originate with the war—although the war emphasized and influenced the character of the problem—nor did the end of war terminate such need.

Almost every twentieth-century American President has publicly declared his distress at the organizational difficulties of coping with his job. Although general recognition of the central problem is relatively recent, it is now widespread. Today it is almost platitudinous to say that the job of the American President has grown to superhuman proportions and that full performance borders on the impossible. It is also well recognized that expansion of executive authority and responsibility continues more rapidly than provision of the Presidency with the tools required for the job.

During recent years some significant steps have been taken in an effort to provide the President with some of these tools— central control and coördinating instrumentalities. The growth and recognition of the Executive Office of the President, the remarkable development of the Bureau of the Budget, establishment of an over-all economic planning staff, and other implementations of the Presidency have all been salutary. Yet it is a source of concern that there remains a pronounced void in the institutional staffing of the President's office. There is no regular pro-

---

[2] The congressional intent in OWMR was a complex of political factors, but the Committee which drafted the model for the OWMR Act said later, perhaps with some hindsight, that "the clear intent of this legislation was to have the Office of War Mobilization and Reconversion act for the President as a general staff empowered not only to formulate plans, but through its other powers to see that those plans were carried out by appropriate agencies." (79th Cong., 2nd Sess., House, Special Committee on Postwar Economic Policy and Planning, *Eleventh Report*, December 1946, p. 21.)

vision for the central task of day-to-day program and policy coördination. How best to fill this vacuum is a subject on which students of administration have speculated and debated.

The administrative story of OWM–OWMR is a valuable case study in this area. It is evident that the experience contains significant lessons for the organization, methods, and functions of such a staff unit, in both war and peace. The Office's experience took place in an unusual period and in an unusual social and political environment. Its role, techniques, and effectiveness were deeply influenced by such considerations, and evaluation of results must be tempered accordingly. The character and role of such an office will vary in emergency periods from other times. Yet it seems clear that in many administrative fundamentals the war situation was not unique but rather a dramatic demonstration of the problem of governance in an increasingly complex and interdependent industrial society. The OWM–OWMR experience presents an impressive addition to the evidence of continuing need for an institutional staff to perform for the President many of the functions which the Office handled during the war crisis.

The treatment of this study is neither chronological nor comprehensive. Chapter 1 contains a résumé of efforts to coördinate war organization before OWM, including an attempt to classify and appraise the various approaches. Chapters 2 and 3 present broad summaries of the functions, organization, and general activities of the Office during its two phases. Chapters 4, 5, and 6 review in detail the role of the Office in three selected crucial problem areas. The final chapter, the seventh, offers a proposal for a permanent Office of Program Coördination and attempts to distill some pertinent principles from the OWM–OWMR experience which have general administrative interest and may also serve as guideposts for the establishment of such a new office.

Most of the book is, of course, concerned with the role and the methods of OWM–OWMR. This focus results in an apparent understatement of the parts played by other agencies in the episodes described. The purpose is not to overplay the contributions of OWM–OWMR; this is simply the story of a particular office and not a war history.

Similarly, this study does not attempt to appraise the merits of the disputes the Office was called upon to resolve. It is primarily a study in public administration and thus confines itself largely to description and appraisal of the functions served by OWM–OWMR, its techniques, strategy, scope, and place in the administrative process, and its implications for the future development of the Executive Office of the President.

CHAPTER 1

COÖRDINATION OF WAR PROGRAMS BEFORE OWM

*C*reation of the Office of War Mobilization came relatively late in the war mobilization drive. The United States had been formally at war for eighteen months, and the industrial war effort was at least three years old. Industrial production had risen remarkably. But the coming of the new Office was generally applauded. Why was this step so welcome to a nation which normally dislikes to "change horses in mid-stream"? President Roosevelt demonstrated in both his peace and war administrations a decided reluctance to delegate broad authority. Yet there were no loopholes or qualifications in the executive order creating OWM. Congress ordinarily resents any sweeping transfer of authority to an appointed official, but hardly a murmur of dissent came from the halls of Congress.

To understand all this—the circumstances which led to creation of OWM and the role it was expected to play—we must review briefly the high points in the history of war mobilization. While OWM represented the last major organizational change, it was not part of a preconceived plan but rather an outgrowth of developments of the previous four years.

Changing world conditions following the outbreak of war in Europe in 1939 dictated a greatly expanded role for government in the economic life of the nation. The new administrative responsibilities were enormous. Yet the mechanisms for meeting them developed slowly. The lag of public opinion, reluctant to face the possibility of American involvement in the war, the extended period of peaceful defense preparation, the exigencies of the national political campaign of 1940, are important clues to an understanding of the United States' slow and faltering mobilization before 1942 and its cumbersome administrative machinery. On the long road which led to OWM, milestones were marked by the short-lived War Resources Board, the National Defense

Advisory Commission, the Office of Production Management, the Supply Priorities and Allocations Board, and the War Production Board.

WAR RESOURCES BOARD

Shortly before a state of limited national emergency was declared on September 8, 1939, the first civilian agency to consider problems of wartime industrial mobilization was established. On August 9, 1939 the War and Navy Departments, with the President's approval, announced formation of a civilian advisory committee to the Army and Navy Munitions Board. This group, known as the War Resources Board, consisted of four prominent industrialists, a banker, the head of an economic research organization, and a scientist.[1]

The Board's job was to report on further revisions of the Industrial Mobilization Plan, already successively revised in 1931, 1933, 1936, 1939.[2] The "M-Day" plan was to be put into effect at the outset of emergency to insure sufficient munitions for the military, essentials for the civil population, and to provide general economic stability. It contemplated speedy enactment of the full range of legislation required to permit a War Resources Administration to control or coördinate all elements necessary for industrial war organization, including prices, profits, wages, labor allocation, Selective Service, imports and exports. The plan had been repeatedly attacked as a scheme to push the United States into war and to place undue control of the economy in the hands of the military.

The Army and Navy Munitions Board had in mind that the War Resources Board should ultimately become the War Resources Administration contemplated by the plan.[3] This expec-

---

[1] E. R. Stettinius, Jr., Chairman of the Board of U. S. Steel Corporation; Karl T. Compton, President of Massachusetts Institute of Technology; Walter S. Gifford, President of American Telephone and Telegraph Company; John Lee Pratt, a director of General Motors Corporation; General Robert E. Wood, Chairman of Sears, Roebuck and Company; Harold G. Moulton, President of Brookings Institution; and John Hancock, a Lehman Brothers partner. The Board received widespread criticism as being chiefly representative of "big business," with no representation of labor or consumers.

[2] For the 1939 plan see, 76th Cong., 2nd Sess., *Senate Document No. 134,* October 24, 1939.

[3] Civilian Production Administration, *Industrial Mobilization for War,* U. S. Government Printing Office, 1947, p. 8.

tation was never realized. The War Resources Board had a short life. Rumors of its dissolution broke out as early as September even before its report had been submitted. The report itself was classified top secret and was not released until 1946, despite great pressure in the early war days to make it public.

In dissolving the Board in November, the President implied that it had recommended its own dissolution. It was generally rumored at the time, however, that far from seeking termination the Board had drafted orders for the President's signature giving it authority over various executive departments and agencies for purposes of industrial mobilization.

Evidence released after the war indicates that the Board, after receiving a warning from the President that he was not interested in any plan delegating full and centralized authority over the civilian economy, agreed to work out "an organization plan that would be more in line with the ideas of the President." The Board's report contained two alternative proposals. The first suggested a super-agency with "almost complete control of the economic life of the Nation." The second proposed establishing seven war agencies, each exercising a delegated war power and reporting directly to the President. They were to coördinate among themselves. The Board recommended the second alternative.[4]

The Industrial Mobilization Plan had wide support and was frequently cited whenever war administration seemed to falter. However, even if the plan had been suitable after the nation was actually at war, an issue still widely disputed, it certainly was unrealistic in the days before Pearl Harbor. Its assumption of an "M-Day" when full war mobilization and organization could be undertaken at one time was academic. Roosevelt was completely unready to delegate such authority to another individual. Not only did he require personal control of the delicate first moves in the defense program, but he had not yet tested any group of men to discover whom he might entrust with such vast responsibility.

While the President did not undertake the direct moves recom-

[4] *Industrial Mobilization for War*, pp. 9–11. The recollection of one of the Board's members differs from the official version. General Robert E. Wood told the press that the Board's report recommended that the war agencies all be under the complete direction of a War Resources Administration. (*N. Y. Times*, January 21, 1946.)

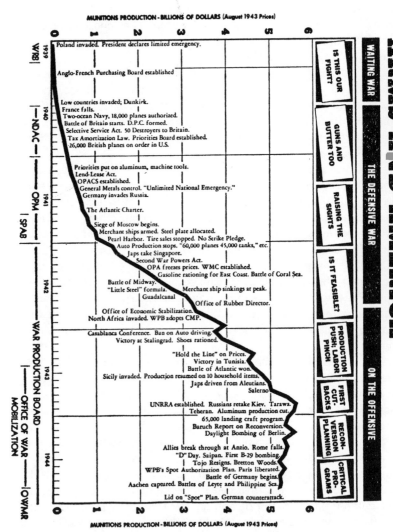

Source: Office of War Mobilization and Reconversion.

mended by the War Resources Board, his early war organizational steps resembled in many ways the administrative framework it had suggested.

NATIONAL DEFENSE ADVISORY COMMISSION

The abrupt end of the "sitzkrieg" in the Spring of 1940 and the rapid sweep of German armies over western Europe finally aroused the public to the necessity of an American rearmament program. While developments drew us closer to the anti-axis powers, the defense program at home was mushrooming. The central problem was to coördinate the foreign armaments program with the domestic defense program. Although munitions production was not great during 1940, the preliminary steps— appropriations by Congress, awarding of contracts, and construction of new facilities—were boldly taken.[5]

Ordinary peacetime procedures were swept aside by a great flood of legislation which introduced peacetime military conscription for the first time in American history, fixed rules to prevent excessive profits on defense contracts, mobilized the National Guard and Army reserves for a year, encouraged expansion of facilities by a short-term tax amortization policy, permitted the government to requisition materials placed under export embargo, authorized the President to order priority for deliveries under Army and Navy contracts, and empowered RFC to use its great financial resources to promote expansion of defense production. With vast increases in congressional appropriations for production facilities and materiel, and initiation of the "cash and carry" system for foreign purchase of munitions, the existing administrative machinery of the government became totally inadequate to ease the transition from a peace to a war economy.

Some business and political leaders suggested that the War Resources Board be recalled.[6] Establishment of a Board of Mobilization of Industries Essential to the National Preparedness, authorized by a 1916 statute, was urged by the Treasury De-

[5] In the last half of 1940 nearly $10.5 billions in contracts were awarded; this sum was nine times the total expenditures for military purposes of both Army and Navy for the fiscal year 1937. (Bureau of the Budget, *The United States at War*, Government Printing Office, 1946, p. 29.)

[6] *N. Y. Times*, May 18, 1940. In this group, Alfred M. Landon, Thomas Dewey, and Frank E. Gannett were prominent.

partment. The War Department indicated that it could handle the program for a time, using the Army and Navy Munitions Board to channel contracts and determine requirements, and the Department's business advisory committees to cushion the impact on industry. Some people thought expansion of existing agencies, the Departments of Commerce and Labor, for example, would be sufficient to take care of the defense effort. Wayne Coy, wartime assistant to President Roosevelt, offers an interesting explanation for rejecting that approach, sound though it may have seemed from an administrative point of view:

as our defense effort got underway, the question soon presented itself whether the emerging civilian control functions should be vested in the permanent departments or in agencies set up for this specific purpose. There were technical pros and cons for either alternative. The weightiest consideration, it seemed to me, was essentially political. Establishment of special war agencies promised not only a welcome influx of fresh blood and outside talent, but also a desirable opportunity for drawing into the government both representatives of important interests and exponents of the political opposition.[7]

In May 1940, the President announced his decision regarding the new administrative organization. As a preliminary step, the Office for Emergency Management, previously authorized by executive order of September 8, 1939, was formally established in the Executive Office of the President where it was to act as a holding company for future defense agencies.[8] He then took his first important step toward coördination of the economy for defense purposes. Under authority of a national defense statute, passed during World War I and never repealed, the President revived the Advisory Commission to the Council of National Defense.

The Council itself, composed of six Cabinet officers—the Secretaries of War, Navy, Interior, Agriculture, Commerce, and Labor —agreed at its first session to meet and act only at Cabinet meetings, in effect reducing itself to inactivity. On the other hand, the Advisory Commission, appointed by the Council with the Presi-

[7] Wayne Coy, "Basic Problems," *American Political Science Review*, December 1946, p. 1127.

[8] Administrative Order, May 25, 1940. OEM was to serve as liaison between the President and the defense agencies and as a framework for creation of stronger organizations than were then authorized by law.

dent's approval, was intended to be active under the President's direction. Each of its seven members was directed to take charge and be responsible to the President for investigation, research, and coördination in his field.[9]

The President's decision to reëstablish the National Defense Advisory Commission was based on an evaluation of many factors: the ease of setting it up under an old statute at a time when he was reluctant to open the issue with Congress while the latter was considering selective service legislation; his interest in directing the program himself and unreadiness to delegate broad power;[10] imminence of the 1940 political campaign and the strong isolationist sentiment in certain areas; and reluctance to propose a super-agency at a time when piecemeal powers and action were the most that public opinion could be expected to support.[11] The NDAC type of organization had several positive advantages in the spring of 1940. The President was able to retain full control over the defense effort while observing the performance of potential candidates for the position of "Industrial Mobilizer." As a legally powerless body, NDAC could not embarrass the President in the preliminary stages of mobilization. As a group it was far more representative of the various interests in the nation than the War Resources Board had been and was helpful in gaining popular support for the President's program.

[9] E. R. Stettinius, Jr.—responsible for industrial materials; William S. Knudsen, President of General Motors—industrial production; Sidney Hillman, President of the Amalgamated Clothing Workers of America—employment policies; Chester C. Davis, Member of the Federal Reserve Board—farm products; Ralph Budd, Chairman of the Board, Chicago, Burlington & Quincy Railroad—transportation; Leon Henderson, Member, Securities and Exchange Commission—prices; Harriet Elliott, Dean of Women, University of North Carolina—consumer interests. William H. McReynolds, long-time Federal employee and a presidential secretary, was named head of OEM and secretary of the Council and of the Advisory Commission. A month later, Donald M. Nelson, Executive Vice-President, Sears, Roebuck & Company, was appointed Coördinator of National Defense Purchases and joined the group as an equal.

[10] A few months later, in response to persistent demands for a single top authority, the President said the Constitution did not permit him to create a second President and that the President could delegate authority but not ultimate responsibility. (*The Public Papers and Addresses of Franklin D. Roosevelt*, 1940 vol., Macmillan, 1941, p. 623.)

[11] *The United States at War*, p. 33; Donald M. Nelson, *Arsenal of Democracy*, Harcourt, Brace, 1946, p. 89.

At the time of its appointment the Commission was expected to act only in an advisory capacity. However, members preferred to think of themselves as commissioners and soon had proceeded beyond the advisory stage to actual administrative responsibility.[12] As the defense program grew, individual members acquired new functions and staffs, the core of many of the later war agencies.

NDAC's most significant power was authority to clear contracts, vested in William Knudsen and Donald Nelson. By agreement, the job was divided so that Knudsen cleared ordnance and "hard goods" contracts and Nelson handled quartermaster items and "soft goods." Working with the Quartermaster General, Nelson and his staff changed the buying habits of the Services. Negotiated contracts replaced sealed bids and orders were placed off-season rather than immediately after appropriations were made. Nelson's group drew up a set of principles on purchasing which was approved by the armed forces, the President, and Congress. NDAC also had limited powers in other areas: review of applications for accelerated tax amortization on defense facilities, priorities, stockpiling of critical materials and estimating requirements. The "five-year amortization plan" was developed and pushed through Congress by Nelson and Leon Henderson who also persuaded Reconstruction Finance Corporation to adopt similar procedures for its subsidiary Defense Plant Corporation.

Henderson and Nelson went to work on the priorities issue in the summer of 1940. On October 21, the President set up in NDAC a Priorities Board, composed of Knudsen as Chairman, Stettinius, Henderson, and Nelson as Administrator. However, NDAC soon found, according to Nelson, that it could not work a priorities system without an allocation system and that no priorities could be effected by an agency without authority.[13]

On the all-important production front, Knudsen depended almost entirely on exhortation and encouragement. NDAC had so few real powers that the commissioners frequently learned of developments affecting them after they had occurred. Estimates

[12] Donald Nelson thought that NDAC went "beyond the advisory function without any real authority to do so, and that the nation is lucky the commissioners had the fortitude to exceed—at least in a measure—their vaguely stipulated powers." (*Arsenal of Democracy*, p. 87.)
[13] *Arsenal of Democracy*, p. 112.

of requirements were still in a very rudimentary stage. Only a small inroad was made on this basic problem. The Industrial Materials Division under Stettinius listed 14 strategic and 15 critical materials, but actual stockpiling was slow. Only 10 million of the 100 million dollars appropriated by Congress in 1939 for stockpiling critical materials had been spent by mid-1940 and the program lagged despite pressure from above.

Because the nation was not yet at war and many people thought that we could and should keep out, the NDAC period was anomalous and difficult. Businessmen were reluctant to invest money in enterprises whose futures were uncertain; some firms would not accept contracts because it meant sacrifice of civilian trade for something they did not expect to last. Basic industries hesitated and in some cases vigorously resisted efforts to expand for fear of a glut at the end of the defense period; labor was wary lest the rearmament program he used to deprive it of rights. NDAC, reflecting within its own membership the diverse views of the nation, ran into serious internal controversies on such questions as expansion of capacity, dealing with organized labor, and curtailment of nonessential production.

The more deeply the Commission became involved in operations, the more it felt the awkwardness of its uncoördinated structure and its difficult liaison with other agencies. Lack of synchronization and overlapping of functions and activities, due in part to the absence of a chairman, and the lack of stipulated authority were probably NDAC's most significant defects.[14] It has been called, not without justice, an "administrative stop-gap." [15]

Demand for a single administrator with "power to coördinate

[14] Donald Nelson's comments on NDAC are illuminating: "It was an unusually sturdy and well balanced array of talent. But note that no one was designated to act as chairman. I believe that this was a serious mistake, and that the Board's most critical weakness stemmed from this omission. This weakness I was able to spot later when I sat in with the Commission and saw how aimless an organization without a directing and integrating force can become. Every member of the Commission was, in his own orbit, energetic and conscientious, and had definite notions about how to do his job, but there was no one to synchronize and guide the combined efforts of this group of strong individuals. There was no one to settle the arguments and quarrels which are inevitable when determined, able and well intentioned persons have different ideas as to how to reach the same goal." (*Arsenal of Democracy*, pp. 82–83.)
[15] *The United States at War*, p. 25.

the coördinators" arose on every side.[16] For its part, labor was demanding greater representation and influence in decisions. As the end of 1940 approached, public dissatisfaction with NDAC was reinforced by the new administrative needs created by Lend-Lease.

Despite its amorphous pattern, NDAC was important in shaping the future course of wartime agencies. The Commission contained, in embryo, virtually every important agency which was later to be created. It contained, within itself, possibilities for two divergent patterns of development. It would have been possible to give it a new name, a single responsible head, and expanded functions and staff. In short, a War Resources Administration could have been established with the centralized control and integrated approach characteristic of that type of organization. It was equally possible to break up NDAC into its component parts and strengthen the individual units so that they formed independent organizations.

The latter was the choice the President made, starting with the most urgent jobs, that of production, priorities, and procurement. He removed from NDAC the portions of its work handled by Knudsen, Hillman, and Nelson, and set up the Office of Production Management. Separation of OPM from NDAC was the first of a series of surgical operations which ultimately did away with NDAC. While never officially terminated, it held its last meeting on October 23, 1941.

OFFICE OF PRODUCTION MANAGEMENT

The new agency was established the day after the President delivered his important "all-out aid to the democracies" message. Two top NDAC men, Knudsen and Hillman, were designated Director General and Associate Director General, respectively. They were to have joint authority in direction of the defense program, much like partners in a law firm, the President explained to

[16] On November 21, 1940, Senator Taft announced that he would introduce a bill to create a War Resources Board under a single administrator. (*N. Y. Times*, November 22, 1940.) On the same day Alfred P. Sloan, Jr., Chairman of the Board of General Motors, demanded that the National Defense Board should be under the direction of one man. A few weeks later, at the convention of the National Association of Manufacturers, President H. W. Prentis, Jr. made a strong plea for a single civilian boss for NDAC. (*N. Y. Times*, December 13, 1940.)

dubious press representatives.[17] Along with Knudsen and Hillman, the Secretaries of Navy and War were named to an OPM Policy Council to lay down general principles on which the Director General and Associate would act.

OPM's powers were more definite than those of NDAC. The executive order delegated to it authority to:

Formulate and execute in the public interest all measures needful and appropriate in order (1) to increase, accelerate, and regulate the production and supply of materials, articles, and equipment and for provision of emergency plant facilities and services required for the national defense, and (2) to insure effective coördination of those activities of the several departments, corporations, and other agencies of the government which are directly concerned therewith.[18]

Moreover, the power to place compulsory orders, given to the President by the Selective Service and Training Act of 1940, was delegated to OPM. The requisitioning power provided by an Act of October 10, 1940 was also assigned to it and proved an important means of forcing compliance.

Nevertheless, the President retained many powers which the codirectors needed in order to exert full jurisdiction over a mobilization program. There were significant omissions in OPM authority: determination of military or other requirements and placement of contracts or purchasing of supplies. OPM could only "survey, analyze and summarize" the requirements submitted by the Army, Navy, and other agencies "for purposes of coördination." In the same way, OPM could do no more than coördinate "the placement of major defense orders and contracts," and advise "with respect to the plans and schedules of the various departments and agencies for the purchase of materials, articles, and equipment required for defense." Until August 1941 OPM had no more power over priorities than NDAC had had at the end of 1940.

So wary was the President of permitting OPM independence that he specified its internal organization in the executive order.

[17] The President said, "I have a single, responsible head; his name is Knudsen and Hillman." (*The Public Papers and Addresses of Franklin D. Roosevelt*, 1940 vol., p. 684.) Donald Nelson wrote: "The new machine was to operate with co-pilots . . . which apparently meant that the boss would be Super-Director General, just as he had been with NDAC." (*Arsenal of Democracy*, p. 117.)

[18] E.O. 8629, January 7, 1941.

OPM's three major divisions—production, purchases, and priorities—operated autonomously, much as they had under NDAC.

Absence of a strong programing group was noted by John Biggers, head of production, who proposed a Production Planning Board to fill this gap. Although Biggers wanted the Board attached to OPM at the topmost level, Knudsen organized it in February 1941 as an adjunct of Biggers' Division. This Board received particular attention because of the membership of Harry L. Hopkins, then known as the President's closest adviser. The other members were private citizens, representing various interest groups. The Production Planning Board was able to do a few important things in its limited capacity. It took a leading role in formulating the first comprehensive statement of over-all defense and foreign-aid needs.

OPM's attempt to maintain control over all vital defense industries of the country was undermined when the President designated Secretary of the Interior Ickes as Petroleum Coördinator for National Defense in May 1941. Although OPM had an oil unit, it did not have an industry branch and it gave up authority for a basic industry which should have been meshed with its production program. In setting up the first "czar" agency, an organization concerned with a particular commodity, the President set a precedent for a continuing practice which resulted in lasting confusion and conflict for the general functional agencies, such as OPA, OPM, and WPB.[19]

Protracted disputes with old-line agencies, with specific powers, were a frequent result of the efforts of the new defense agency. When OPM challenged the authority of the Federal Power Commission by controlling electric power for defense purposes, the old agency maintained it was the only department with statutory authority to allocate electric power.

The armed services presented a far greater problem to OPM. The War and Navy Departments were not eager to concede much power. When it appeared inevitable that OPM would exercise some authority, the Services asked to sit on OPM policy-making bodies, in addition to the central council. For its part, OPM found

[19] The "czar" agencies usually had policy accountability to OPM, and later to WPB, in theory, but in practice they acted autonomously.

military estimates of requirements unrealistically small, inadequately calculated, and internally inconsistent.

Duplication of effort between OPM and the armed services was a major problem. The Navy proposed that the OPM Priorities Board include representatives of the Army and Navy and other government agencies. This proposal was reiterated in February 1941 by Secretary Knox when he suggested that the priorities functions of the Army and Navy Munitions Board be transferred to OPM's Board.[20] This transfer did not occur due to Army opposition, and representatives of the Army and Navy ultimately gained seats on the OPM Board. But the latter had a small, weak staff and no field organization for the priorities job. ANMB gradually took over its priorities functions.

The Services also challenged OPM on contract clearance and contract distribution. The Navy proposed at the outset that OPM should not clear contracts for facilities but limit its interest to the site location. Soon after OPM was created, Donald Nelson, in charge of purchases, had his authority challenged by the Army and Navy. Although Nelson asked only to be in charge of planning and coördination of military purchases, the armed forces rejected even this. The President settled the dispute by designating Donald Nelson to clear all Army and Navy defense contracts. This early conflict and the positive position taken by Nelson is noteworthy in view of the fact that throughout his later tenure of office in the War Production Board he was most frequently criticized for letting the military usurp his authority.

The declaration of an unlimited emergency on May 27, 1941 caused reëxamination of the relations between OPM and ANMB. The Industrial Mobilization Plan had called for a merger of the two groups in such an event. Closer integration was achieved, however, only on a small scale. Army and Navy liaison officers were assigned to the Priorities Division, and W. S. Harrison, then Director of the Production Division, was assigned to represent OPM at meetings of the ANMB Executive Committee. During 1941 OPM began to distinguish between strictly military production and other defense production. The Services were given responsibility for production as well as planning of purely military

[20] *Industrial Mobilization for War*, p. 117.

items like ordnance. Some OPM staff units were moved bodily to the Army in order to make this transfer final.

Complex and troublesome as the OPM-military conflicts were, it was OPM's difficulties with another civilian agency that caused some of the loudest clashes. After OPM was created, demand for a separate price control agency, on a par with OPM, was met by establishment of the Office of Price Administration and Civilian Supply in April 1941. With the advent of OPACS, a fundamental policy dispute which had been raging backstage came fully into focus. Donald Nelson has described the basic conflict thus:

there were those who were convinced that total war was ahead for the United States, and that we were arming not only to help the nations with which we sympathized but to preserve our own country by strong, aggressive action. They were sometimes called "expansionists" or "all-outers." They were for the quick conversion of industry, a longer-range policy for the accumulation of raw-material stockpiles, a firmer and deeper organization of the economy for war. . . .

Opposed to this group were men . . . who thought that we could avoid a shooting war and that there was no need to shake our economy apart in anticipation of an emergency which would probably not occur. . . . The majority opinion in RFC advocated bargaining and going slow in the expenditure of the kind of money which would have been necessary. In OPM itself this school of thought not only retarded the importation of certain materials which were necessary in the processing of vital products such as steel and aluminum, but it also pursued a cautious course in the expansion of our manufacturing facilities.[21]

In addition to the deep policy disagreements, the two agencies were in conflict as to scope of operations. Having made the initial decision to separate price control from production control, a decision which was to plague the war effort continually, the line of demarcation was further blurred by assigning civilian supply functions to OPACS. OPACS was given part of the priority powers; after OPM assigned priorities for essential defense production, OPACS could tell OPM how the remaining supply should be distributed among competing civilian demands. This splitting of the priority power and OPACS' lack of authority to enforce any of its recommendations made the system administratively unworkable.

---

[21] *Arsenal of Democracy*, pp. 125–126. OPACS was a leader among the "all-outers," while OPM was regarded in the other camp. At this stage, Nelson was clearly in the former group.

In May 1941 the President signed a law imposing mandatory priorities of wartime scope on all industry. Previously, the government could give mandatory priorities only for contracts placed by the Army and Navy. Now it acquired the right to decide in all cases what production should come first, whether in the armaments or domestic civilian supply field. Both OPM and OPACS fought for the expanded priorities power and the issue was finally resolved by shuffling the functions of the two agencies and creating a superstructure, the Supply Priorities and Allocations Board,[22] to coördinate and centralize high power decisions.

OPM was largely reduced to an operating agency. It was declared the center of administration for all types of priority action, under general policies of SPAB, but OPM's Council was made subordinate to the new Board.

It was more than the conflict over priorities between OPM and OPACS that stimulated creation of SPAB. All through 1941 external events had been pressing the country closer toward war and full military production. Lend-Lease, to which the Soviet Union had been added in June, plus enormously increased defense orders, placed additional strain on essential war materials and brought to the fore conflicts between military production and civilian consumption, created the need for a mandatory priorities system, pushed prices upward, and made it necessary to expand facilities predominantly through public financing.

OPM was in no position to meet these challenges. Its limited powers, creation of other defense agencies of coördinate rank, resentment of established agencies against the intruder, internal conflict over "all-out defense" versus "business as usual," and the trials and errors of a preparatory period spelled its downfall after a year of complex operations and reorganizations.

On the legislative side, more power was given to the President and new laws brought the country closer to a war footing. Declaration of an "unlimited national emergency"—a step the Chief Executive may take only if he believes war to be imminent—gave the President many new powers derived chiefly from laws passed just before and during the first World War. The precise extent of these powers was not known but it was assumed that the Presi-

[22] E.O. 8875, August 28, 1941.

dent could take almost complete control over the national economy. He created several new agencies.

But in the administrative hierarchy there was no one short of the President himself with enough weight to make a major decision and to force its execution. Both Bernard Baruch and Harold Smith, Director of the Budget, began to urge that a single agency be given priority authority and control over all production, military and civilian.

SUPPLY PRIORITIES AND ALLOCATIONS BOARD

In deciding to set up SPAB, made up of a group of coördinate agency heads, the President undoubtedly was swayed by a desire not to make his decision a clear victory for any individual, group, or point of view. The Board consisted of the four members of the OPM Council, which thereafter ceased to have a function, plus three additions, Messrs. Hopkins, Henderson, and Wallace, all known as "all-outers." In addition to industry and labor, symbolized by the two heads of OPM, each of the claimants on the nation's resources was represented: the armed forces by the Secretaries of War and Navy; foreign needs by Wallace, Chairman of the Economic Defense Board; Lend-Lease by Hopkins, Special Assistant to the President; civilian supply by Henderson, Price Administrator and Director of Civilian Supply in OPM.[23] Donald Nelson was made Executive Director. Later Jesse Jones, Secretary of Commerce, who directed RFC and its subsidiaries, was added as a member.

The personnel of SPAB was a less conservative group and more in sympathy with the President's aims than the OPM Council. SPAB was more inclined to break precedents in mobilizing industry and to favor planning in order to balance requirements against supply.[24]

The functions of SPAB were to:

(a) Determine the total requirements of materials and commodities needed respectively for defense, civilian, and all other purposes; establish policies for the fulfilment of such accomplishments, and, where necessary, make recommendations to the President relative thereto.

[23] The executive order creating SPAB also transferred the civilian supply functions of OPACS to OPM where a Division of Civilian Supply was created. This converted OPACS to OPA.

[24] *Industrial Mobilization for War*, p. 110.

(b) Determine policies and make regulations governing allocations and priorities with respect to the procurement, production, transmission or transportation of materials, articles, power, fuel, and other commodities among military, economic defense, defense aid, civilian, and other major demands of the total Defense Program.

Once again the President made clear that he was retaining a considerable amount of authority in his own hands. The White House press release, which accompanied the executive order, emphasized that the Board would follow general policies enunciated by the President. The statement declared: "The Board, of course, will have no power to determine the division of finished materials—such as planes or guns or ships. Its jurisdiction will extend only to the materials, parts, machine tools, etc. required for their manufacture." [25]

Several limitations of SPAB stood out immediately. The Board itself could hardly be anything more than advisory on general policy since all of its members already had other heavy responsibilities. Its chairman was not only presiding officer of the Senate, but also chairman of the Economic Defense Board, a full-time job. Thus it appeared the key man in the new setup would be Donald Nelson, the Executive Director. But Nelson had no direct authority except through specific actions of the Board. His relationship to Knudsen, his boss in OPM, where Nelson was Director of Priorities, was unclear. [26] A similar question surrounded Leon Henderson. As Price Administrator, he sat equal with Knudsen on the Board and held an equal vote. But, as director of the Division of Civilian Supply in OPM, he reported to Knudsen.

Bernard Baruch, chairman of the War Industries Board of the first World War, [27] told the press that he regarded the creation of

[25] *White House Press Release,* August 28, 1941.

[26] Speculation was rife as to who outranked whom. In *The N. Y. Times Magazine* of September 28, 1941, R. L. Duffus stated that Nelson probably outranked Knudsen. "Let us suppose that Nelson wants to make an important change in the priorities system. He goes to his Board—SPAB—and gets the step approved. Then, as Managing Director of SPAB, he can direct Knudsen to order him, Nelson, to carry out the new policy."

[27] The alleged parallel in experience between Mr. Baruch's job in World War I and the job facing the nation in World War II is questionable. In World War I the United States made little effort to mobilize industry until after war had actually been declared, and curtailment of nonessential industries was not suggested until six months after the opening of hostilities. It proceeded on a piecemeal basis and it was not until a month before the Armistice that curtailment of production was decreed for a number of civilian

SPAB as "a faltering step forward." "You have seven excellent men there, anyone of whom is capable of doing a swell job, but none has the final word." [28]

It took about a week for the general press to be deflected from the prestige of Wallace's title as chairman and to recognize that in so far as the Board had any person resembling a top man it was Nelson, to whose leadership was due most of SPAB's successful activity.

In spite of limitations of authority and organization SPAB made some notable achievements during its three months' existence.[29] These were attributed to its position as a top-level planning and policy group not hampered by operating responsibilities. A central planning viewpoint emerged for the first time. With OPM, OPA, and other agencies subsidiary to it, SPAB was able to act as a central authority handing down decisions to be executed by the operating agencies. SPAB relied on OPM for staff functions such as research and administrative services.

The new agency started dramatically with some well-publicized and impressive steps which captured the public imagination. On September 10, it announced the undertaking of an over-all study of the needs of Lend-Lease, defense, and civilians. It proposed to compile and organize for the first time, a schedule of requirements in terms of labor, raw materials, and machinery. This attempt to assemble total requirements and to replace priorities

---

goods industries. The state of industrial mobilization reached at the end of the first war was probably not as far advanced as in the period immediately preceding Pearl Harbor.

[28] *N. Y. Times*, September 5, 1941. On the same day, Arthur Krock wrote that as Baruch and Judge Rosenman had originally planned and charted the new agency, it was to be headed by a single administrator with full power flowing from the President. Baruch was sharply disappointed in the change. It was elsewhere commonly accepted that the President had not yet found a person emerging from the group he had brought into the war effort whom he felt he could completely trust. Nelson was gradually emerging to this status.

[29] It won praise from two of the official histories of the period—*The United States at War* (pp. 80–85) and *Industrial Mobilization for War* (pp. 109–111). Donald Nelson said, "SPAB was certainly an administrative anomaly, even for Washington, yet it worked surprisingly well, and during its brief life it took, in a number of vitally important, far-reaching cases, action which made possible the amazingly successful war production program that came into being after Pearl Harbor." (*Arsenal of Democracy*, p. 156.)

with an allocations system was an important contribution, as was SPAB's emphasis on all-out mobilization of the economy.

SPAB also laid down a policy for the civilian economy. It agreed that the necessary productive equipment for such basic civilian industries as agriculture must be assured and provision made for enough repair materials to keep the civilian economy going. Curtailment of "less essential" portions of the civilian economy was undertaken by SPAB and the expansion of steel-producing capacity was recommended to OPM.

Despite such progress, SPAB's lack of sufficient authority and cumbersome structure called attention to its inadequacies, and considerable dissatisfaction was expressed by the public and in Congress. The day before Pearl Harbor, Senator Kilgore proposed legislation to centralize administration of the defense program under a new Cabinet officer. The plan, calling for establishment of a Department of Defense Coördination and Control, with jurisdiction over all defense purchases and the utilization of industrial resources under one responsible head, had received strong support from other Senators. Simultaneously, Senator Truman announced that the Senate Defense Investigating Committee would urge President Roosevelt to appoint a "defense works czar." "Unless a man of full authority is placed at the head of the program it will be swamped by waste and small business will crack up." [30]

WAR PRODUCTION BOARD

With American entrance into the war it was apparent not only that the production effort faced a great speed-up, but that the inadequate system of controls and the war organization required complete remodeling. Executive action came five weeks after Pearl Harbor, after alternatives were proposed and sharply debated.

Following upon the heels of a well-publicized Senate report charging waste, inefficiency, self-interest, and failure in the national defense program and calling for reorganization of authority in a single head,[31] the President announced establishment of a War Production Board, whose chairman, Donald M. Nelson,

[30] *N. Y. Times*, December 7, 1941.
[31] 77th Cong., 2nd Sess., Senate, Special Committee Investigating the National Defense Program, *Report No. 480*, Pt. 5, January 15, 1942.

would have authority to make final decisions on procurement and production and to head the entire armaments program.[32] The executive order was considered Roosevelt's greatest delegation of power since 1933.[33]

SPAB was immediately abolished, OPM a week later, and all their powers transferred to WPB. The chairman was given authority to determine all policies and procedures of all agencies in respect to war procurement and production "including purchasing, contracting, specifications and construction; and including conversion, requisitioning, plant expansion, and the financing thereof; and issue such directives in respect thereto as he may deem necessary or appropriate." The Army and Navy Munitions Board was instructed to report to the President through the chairman of WPB. "The Chairman may exercise the powers, authority, and discretion conferred upon him by this order through such officials or agencies and in such manner as he may determine; and his decisions shall be final." On April 7, Nelson was delegated the power over allocation which Title III of the Second War Powers Act had given to the President.

Nelson's executive order was broad enough to include virtually every aspect of the domestic war effort, except price control in which he could nevertheless exercise considerable influence.[34] There seemed little doubt in January of 1942 of the President's intention: the actual authority granted to Nelson appeared adequate and unreserved. In some respects it was not much less than the authority which later went to the director of OWM. But the authority and the power were soon diluted and diffused. In less

[32] E.O. 9024, January 16, 1942. Two subsequent orders broadened and defined WPB powers: E.O. 9040, January 24, 1942, and E.O. 9125, April 7, 1942.

[33] *N. Y. Times,* January 14, 1942. Conflicting versions on the drafting of the order are given in Donald M. Nelson, *op. cit.,* p. 196, and James F. Byrnes, *Speaking Frankly,* Harper, 1947, pp. 15–16.

[34] The general approval which greeted the new organization also fostered some debate on Senator Kilgore's proposal that Nelson's post ought to be in the Cabinet. Baruch answered this suggestion by pointing out that the chairman of the new WPB should have power and status which Cabinet rank could only dilute, since that would put Cabinet members on equal terms with him and therefore "final say" would again be the President's daily chore. In the light of his own experience Baruch said the individual status was the workable one. (*N. Y. Times,* January 16, 1942.) The wisdom of this approach became clearer in later days when OWM was established.

than a year, the head of WPB was no longer supreme head of the economy.

WPB was greeted by an utterly unenviable situation in January 1942. The circumstances had within them almost insuperable odds against success. After the devastating blow at Pearl Harbor, the full extent of which was not revealed to the public until much later, both American and Allied military fortunes were discouraging throughout 1942. The war production chief was inevitably in line for criticism, since the need for arms appeared unlimited and production goals were set almost beyond attainable limits. Indeed, through most months of 1942 output failed to meet schedules. In early 1943, when military victories began to cheer the public, the competing demands of various production programs on the economic resources of the nation reached a level incapable of achievement due to the simultaneous enormous expansion of the synthetic rubber, high octane, landing craft, and heavy bomber programs. The man responsible for each of these programs felt that his own cause was most crucial and did not hesitate to feud publicly with the others. At best such a period of war mobilization would have been stormy.

Nelson firmly avowed his belief that a war production agency should have a single administrator, that authority should be vested in the administrator, and that the priority power must be indivisible—lessons derived from his valuable experience with NDAC, SPAB, and OPM. Although he won a complete victory on each of these points in his original grant of authority from the President, within a short time he had lost the substance, if not the form, of each of these principles. By early 1943 he had created a deputy chairman, Charles E. Wilson, and turned over virtually the entire WPB job to him, so that the question of who was really WPB boss was a common subject for Washington gossip. He had been granted full authority, but he had given away many functions, allowed the creation of several coördinate agencies in essential fields over which he should have retained authority, and permitted many inroads on WPB's power to make final decisions. WPB was soon regarded as a war agency on an equal plane with other agencies. He tried to protect his priority power most of all.[35] But even here Nelson did not exhibit the firm authority necessary to prevent a considerable dilution in that power. Effective authority is not necessarily what is legislated, but rather what is asserted and effectuated by agency action. WPB learned this too late.

Nelson, in stripping himself of various powers and giving them to others, encouraged creation of a host of new agencies with overlapping authority and interests.[36] There were already in existence the Board of Economic Warfare, the Office of Lend-Lease Administration, the Office of Defense Transportation, RFC's various defense corporations, the National War Labor Board, the Office of Price Administration, and numerous lesser agencies. The War Shipping Administration and National Housing Agency were created shortly after WPB. A quick and firm exhibition by Nelson that he intended to follow fully his broad directive to "exercise general direction over the war procurement and production program" and that he understood literally the President's order that "federal departments, establishments, and agencies will comply with the policies, plans, methods and procedures, in respect to war procurement and production as determined by the chairman," would have given him policy jurisdiction over all these agencies, with the possible exception of those concerned with economic stabilization.

[35] When the President, listening more and more to other voices as 1942 wore on, undercut Nelson's priority powers by empowering the Food Administrator to make allocations of certain raw materials, Nelson fought hard to retain these powers. In the field of shipping, WPB retained its priority power throughout. Nelson regarded the Army's onslaught on his priority powers as a maneuver in its attempt "to gain control of the national economy" and "to make an errand boy of WPB." (*Arsenal of Democracy*, p. 366.)

[36] Nelson wrote: "As interpreted and executed by me, it was not the one man job conceived by the President when the Board was created. The economic power vested in me at that time was potentially greater than that ever held by any other civilian, except a wartime President. The records will show that of my own initiative I shed controls and authorities not directly germane to my principal function (which was war production) as rapidly as I could be sure that they had been placed in competent hands. This was done not to escape responsibility, but to allocate responsibility in such a way that the administrative capacity of no one person—including myself—would be spread so thin that it would lose its tensile strength." (*Arsenal of Democracy*, pp. xi–xii.)

One of the first powers Nelson gave away was his authority over rationing which he transferred to OPA in January. He retained control over the commodities and quantities to be rationed and the principles to govern rationing. Although this was probably a sound division of duties between the agencies, even here Nelson did not avoid trouble, since OPA regarded the Division of Civilian Supply, which acted for Nelson on rationing programs, as a competing operating agency.

His most damaging errors took place in connection with the setting up of a "czar" for manpower and a "czar" for the rubber program.[37] On April 18 the President issued an executive order establishing a War Manpower Commission with responsibility for deciding and carrying out programs and policies "to assure the most effective mobilization and maximum utilization of the Nation's manpower in the prosecution of war." Various government agencies concerned with labor supply were transferred to WMC. The President had offered Nelson the opportunity to have the manpower control agency placed under his supervision but Nelson rejected the suggestion and allowed WMC to become a completely separate and independent organization.[38] In view of the fact that labor controls were so clearly a key factor in production programing and that manpower would inevitably become the ultimate bottleneck, Nelson's decision was baffling even to his associates. This error was to cause WPB as much difficulty as its disputes with the military.[39]

Conflicts in the synthetic rubber program also resulted in damage to WPB. After well-publicized friction over production delays, Congress overwhelmingly passed in the summer of 1942 a bill which would have stripped WPB of authority over the manufacture of synthetic rubber from alcohol drawn from agricultural products. The President vetoed the bill and established a fact-

[37] There was also considerable difficulty with WFA and with Ickes and his "czar" agencies, which included PAW and the Solid Fuels Administration for War.

[38] *Industrial Mobilization for War*, p. 228.

[39] Critics of WPB did not miss the implications of these organizational problems. For example, in November, before the Senate Education Committee, top labor representatives blamed manpower shortages on malutilization and lack of a coördinating agency. They criticized lack of coördination between production and manpower. (*N. Y. Times*, January 1, 1943.)

finding committee to investigate the entire rubber situation.[40]
The committee reported the situation so dangerous that unless
vigorous corrective measures were taken immediately the country
would face both military and civilian collapse due to rubber
scarcity.

As a result the President established an Office of the Rubber
Director with William M. Jeffers, President of the Union Pacific
Railroad, as "czar." Technically the Office was placed within
WPB. However, Nelson stated that the new director would be
vested "with all the authority of the Chairman of the War Production Board over the rubber program and all its phases," and
that Jeffers would himself issue directives to all government
agencies concerned with rubber.[41] Nelson now found himself
with an independent "czar" within the confines of his own organization and it was not clear how much authority the WPB chairman retained. Moreover, the entire episode was clearly taken by
the public as a reflection of WPB failure and a vote of "lack of
confidence" by Congress.

There was a crying need for a coördinating and central policy-
making body, but WPB shied away from any supervisory relation
to other agencies, even though the latter might actually be concerned with an area which overlapped WPB's sphere or might
be closely related to WPB's main problem. Nelson's apparent failure to distinguish between operating and policy responsibilities
proved crucial. Had he never assumed for WPB general operating
responsibilities, he might have succeeded in retaining recognition
and acceptance of his over-all policy authority. He ignored a
lesson from WPB's predecessor, SPAB, one of whose greatest
assets had been freedom from operating responsibilities. It is
noteworthy that the original order setting up WPB provided for
the transfer of SPAB to WPB, but did not dispose of OPM. OPM,
with broader powers, could have remained the operating agency
WPB turned out to be, if Nelson's concept of the job had been
that of a top coördinator.

When the lower echelon officials of WPB were in day-to-day
negotiations and squabbles with other agency officials on opera-

[40] It was comprised of Bernard Baruch, chairman; Dr. James B. Conant,
President of Harvard University; and Dr. Karl T. Compton, President of
Massachusetts Institute of Technology.
[41] WPB General Administrative Order 2–62, October 20, 1942.

tional matters, it was only natural that the latter came to look on WPB as equal rather than superior. It was impossible to be a protagonist and at the same time accepted as umpire.

MILITARY CHALLENGE TO WPB

Shortly after the creation of WPB, General Somervell, head of the Army's Services of Supply, prepared an organization chart for WPB which, it has been claimed, "would have placed complete control of WPB and of the economy under the Joint Chiefs of Staff." [42] Nelson rejected this general proposal, but he began, almost at once, to yield many of his powers to the military, piecemeal. He agreed to leave the power of procurement with the Services, although he intended to maintain policy-control. In a joint memorandum of March 12, 1942, Nelson and the Under-Secretary of War outlined to their staffs the relationships between the agencies and their respective responsibilities in regard to military supplies. A similar agreement was concluded between WPB and the Navy a few weeks later. The agreements, in effect, stated that the Services would continue to handle procurement, expediting, and follow-up on production, with WPB passing on over-all scheduling, general policy, and planning.

These agreements did not eliminate jurisdictional disputes because specific problems were to arise in connection with facilities, priorities, materials, and production. Relations with the Army and Navy Munitions Board were not clarified; and in the face of real problems the agreement was subject to a variety of interpretations even on the matters it covered.

The Army Services of Supply duplicated WPB activities to such an extent that conflict was inevitable. Nelson did not insist on WPB's supremacy. He agreed to a division of duties between the WPB regional offices and the SOS procurement offices on the principle that functions which were being performed satisfactorily should not be disturbed regardless of logical or organizational considerations. Production expediting and engineering for end-items were left to the procurement agencies, while WPB retained responsibility for the increased production of raw materials, semi-finished items, and certain components.

The WPB agreement with the Services did not cover relations with ANMB. After the President's WPB executive order, provid-

[42] *The United States at War*, p. 129.

ing that ANMB should report to the President through WPB, the ANMB redefined its own function as advocate of the demands of the military before the civilian agencies. It also was to coördinate Army and Navy facilities and materiel requirements and harmonize their munitions procurement plans. WPB then delegated administrative powers to ANMB. It was soon apparent that there was enormous overlapping and confusion between the functions of the two bodies.

On July 23 an Army-Navy-WPB agreement was signed which retained ANMB and its staff as the advocate of military requirements before WPB and provided for the assignment of representatives of the Services to WPB divisions. This effort at "coördination by infiltration" failed, just as Nelson's assignment of some of his key personnel to the Services failed to obtain greater unity. Nelson later told the Senate Defense Investigating Committee that he had turned over some of his best officials on production and purchases to the Army, Navy, and Maritime Commission in order to help them with their problems.[43]

There was one sphere in which ANMB gained so much power that WPB was threatened with becoming subsidiary to it. The ANMB "had gone to the President and received, independently of Nelson, a delegation of priority power that not only transcended the limits of the authority Nelson had vested in it, but that also threatened the supremacy of Nelson's own priority powers."[44] This priority directive gave ANMB authority to plan production and made it a liaison body, between WPB, which was supposed to make production plans, and the Joint Chiefs of Staff, which made the strategic plans.

A bitter struggle ensued which was to continue throughout the war. Since the March–April agreements gave the military clear authority over procurement, production-expediting, and follow-up, the logic of the situation led to further negotiations in which it appeared that Nelson might be ready to transfer all WPB production responsibility for military materiel to the War

[43] *N. Y. Times*, June 28, 1942. The head of WPB's Production and Purchases Division, William H. Harrison, was commissioned a Colonel to perform similar duties in the Army. Albert Browning, another high WPB official, went to the Army as a Colonel to head up the Purchases Division. This followed the commissioning of William S. Knudsen as Lieutenant General to be a Special Adviser to the Under-Secretary of War on production problems.

[44] *Industrial Mobilization for War*, pp. 221–222.

and Navy Departments. Before anything official was released, the newspapers indicated that the transfer was "in process." A furor was promptly raised in Congress and elsewhere about military dominance of the economy and Nelson denied he had any such intention or that his earlier agreements with the military could be so interpreted. However, the military was apparently intent upon another "concession" and a dispute arose which finally came to the President.

The Army and Navy came to regard Nelson and WPB as advocates of a comfortable civilian economy, which would resist to the end curtailments to expand military production.[45] As soon as WPB was tagged with the label of "civilian claimant," primarily as a result of the functions of one of its divisions, Civilian Supply, the stage was set for a battle in which the military agencies refused to recognize the higher authority and "national interest" status of WPB. To Nelson, on the other hand, the issue was always a matter of military control of the economy. Citing the President's admonition that the armed forces tend to acquire too much power during war, Nelson asserted it was his job to maintain "an equitable balance of power between the military and civil authorities." [46] But instead of clearly setting himself up as the arbiter, he placed himself organizationally in the position of advocate of the latter.[47]

As the daily disputes mounted, Nelson's position became precarious. The Army and Navy made frequent representations to the President indicating lack of confidence in him. In September 1942, they forced him to accept the appointment of Ferdinand Eberstadt, head of ANMB, to vice-chairman of WPB in charge of Programs and Schedules. However, even before Eberstadt's appointment became official, Nelson moved to undercut his authority. Two days earlier he made a surprise appointment of Charles E. Wilson, President of General Electric Company, as another vice-chairman and head of a new Production Executive

---

[45] On July 8, Nelson announced to the press that WPB would have the last word in determining how much of the limited supply of raw materials and finished products would be allocated to the armed forces and how much would be retained to maintain a "slim" but efficient civilian economy. (*N. Y. Times,* July 9, 1942.)

[46] *Arsenal of Democracy,* p. xvii.

[47] It was this situation which caused one of Nelson's former WPB executives to tell the author that Nelson had probably erred in resisting congressional moves to transfer the Office of Civilian Supply out of WPB.

Committee to consist of one representative each for the Army
Service Forces (successor to SOS), the Navy, Air Forces, and
Maritime Commission, with Wilson acting for the WPB chairman.[48] The military-WPB fight seemed destined to continue as
bitterly within WPB itself as it had previously on an inter-agency
basis.

Every time Nelson had to bring a production or procurement
conflict to the White House, he and the armed forces were placed
on an equal plane of authority, with the President as referee. The
fact that the President had ceased to regard WPB as the super-
agency was gradually established.[49] In mid-February Nelson
learned that Roosevelt, disturbed by WPB's inability to keep
peace in its own home as well as with the military, was prepared
to listen to a military demand for Nelson's removal. Nelson saved
himself by firing Eberstadt and promoting Wilson to executive
vice-chairman of WPB in complete charge of all programs including production scheduling.[50] It was no secret that Eberstadt's
dismissal did not come because of disrespect for his abilities but
rather derived from the fact that he was the symbol for the military within WPB, and such an assertion of authority was essential
if Nelson was to survive this crisis. After this incident, the *New
York Times* said: "It may give impetus to plans put forward by
some officials for establishment of a 'super' board . . ."[51]

[48] "Officials of the WPB who commented on the plan said that the broad
powers given Wilson meant the recapture by the WPB of full control of any
phases of the war production effort which may still remain in the hands of
the Armed Forces." (*N. Y. Times*, September 18, 1942.) It did not turn out
that way.

[49] The President was reported to have said the WPB, Army, and Navy
officials were supposed to agree, and when they did not, he would lock them
in a room and tell them they would get no food until they came out with
an agreement. (*N. Y. Times*, November 25, 1942.) If true, this would have
represented a unique experiment in administration.

[50] For Nelson's version, see *Arsenal of Democracy*, pp. 388–389; also see,
Bruce Catton, *The War Lords of Washington*, Harcourt, Brace, 1948, pp.
205–207.

[51] *N. Y. Times*, February 17, 1943. Nelson states that immediately following the Eberstadt incident he asked the President to call a meeting with the
Army officials to reassert the authority of WPB. The President refused. (*Arsenal of Democracy*, p. 389.) At the time of Nelson's appointment, Byrnes had
said to the President, "The man will last only as long as it is recognized that
he has your complete confidence." (James F. Byrnes, *Speaking Frankly*,
p. 16.)

CONFLICTS AMONG OTHER AGENCIES

A series of events seemed to conspire during late 1942 and early 1943 to upset public confidence, dramatize the duplicating and overlapping functions of the various war agencies, intensify the bitter publicly enacted disputes among the top layer of administrators, call particular attention to the absence of unified policy on the domestic front, and generally create an impression that things were falling apart.

On August 21, 1942, the President took notice of the undignified behavior of his various agency heads and sent a public letter to all, stating clearly that he would not tolerate such public disputes. There was only a temporary lull in the squabbling. In December, the public read the testimony taken in executive session before the Senate Banking and Currency Committee in which was aired a violent dispute between the Vice-President and the Secretary of Commerce, in their capacities as heads of the Board of Economic Warfare and RFC, respectively.[52]

In the spring of 1943 there came with rare intensity a flow of unseemly quarrels in fields over which Nelson did not have or was unable to retain control: Jeffers *versus* Patterson and Forrestal; Ickes *versus* Jeffers; Jeffers and Patterson *versus* Nelson; Jeffers *versus* Elmer Davis (chief of the Office of War Information); OPA Administrator Brown *versus* Ickes over petroleum rationing. These disputes usually concerned overlapping jurisdictions and competing demands for scarce resources. More quietly it had become clear that General Hershey was not accepting Paul McNutt's paper authority over Selective Service. Basically disturbing to Congress and the public was the sense that short of periodic ability to catch the ear of the President, already overtaxed with problems of military strategy, there was no one with authority or sufficient standing available to resolve these disputes.

Not only had the conflicts among agencies reached the stage of public scandal, but even more disconcerting, crack-ups within

---

[52] Secretary Jones complained about Wallace's meddling and indicated dissatisfaction with a presidential directive of the previous April which had eliminated his former power to prohibit RFC loans for foreign purchases the BEW regarded as strategically necessary. Wallace, on the other hand, complained of inordinate delays in getting RFC approval of BEW commodity-purchase projects. (*N. Y. Times*, December 17, 1942.)

agencies appeared. After Eberstadt was fired from WPB there followed some wholesale resignations. WPB underwent the discomfort of having one of its division heads, Joseph Weiner of Civilian Supply, testify before a congressional committee against his chief, Nelson. In late May, the press announced resignation of several key officials in OPA's Food Price Division and the reported withdrawal of more than a dozen others, and Administrator Brown had to deny publicly rumors of a "mass crack-up" in OPA. This and similar developments in Washington led to such press comments as the following:

The OPA flare-up was regarded by observers, moreover, as the first of a number of such developments, unless President Roosevelt or some one else with adequate authority steps in to clean up a condition spreading among the agencies dealing with some of the most vital phases of the civilian end of the war.

Intramural bickering and inter-bureau politics are moving toward a new high point in bitterness with energy that might be devoted to outdoing the Axis being turned by subordinate officials to undoing one another.[53]

The "Battle of Washington" was not merely a clash of strong personalities. Fundamental policy attitudes as well as specific programs were in sharp conflict and apparently nobody short of the President was in a position to resolve these differences or to enunciate government policy. The Army and Navy were strongly and publicly advocating the necessity for national service legislation, whereas the War Manpower Commission, primarily responsible for manpower, had had a change of heart and said it was unnecessary. The Selective Service System, nominally under WMC jurisdiction, supported national service despite WMC disapproval. And, more peculiarly, both WMC and Selective Service were issuing and supporting "work-or-fight" measures designed to enforce essential work upon certain persons in lieu of national service. A dispute in which government agencies took varying positions was raging in Congress in connection with proposals to grant statutory draft deferment status to fathers, a matter of deep emotional concern to the people. Disputes were frequent between government agencies concerned with production and those fighting inflation. Procurement agencies, together with WMC and WPB, did not hesitate to apply conspicuous pressure upon OPA

[53] *N. Y. Times*, May 25, 1943.

or the War Labor Board whenever they felt their tasks would be
eased by a price or wage increase.

On October 3, 1942, the President had taken a partial step toward resolution of difficulties in one explosive area. Acting quickly
after passage of the Emergency Price Control Act of October 2,
1942, he established an Office of Economic Stabilization with the
following broad powers:

> To formulate and develop a comprehensive national economic policy
> relating to the control of civilian purchasing power, prices, rents, wages,
> salaries, profits, rationing, subsidies, and all related matters—all for
> the purpose of preventing avoidable increases in the cost of living,
> coöperating in minimizing the unnecessary migration from one busi-
> ness, industry, or region to another, and facilitating the prosecution of
> the war. To give effect to this comprehensive national economic policy
> the Director shall have power to issue directives on policy to the Fed-
> eral departments and agencies concerned.[54]

As director, he appointed James F. Byrnes of the Supreme
Court who, as a symbol of his important position, set up office
in the White House. With this development it was clear that
Nelson was no longer top man on the home front. Although
Byrnes's authority was related to price controls, wage stabilization, rationing, and other aspects of economic stabilization, these
frequently impinged upon areas of WPB responsibility. When
they did, it became known that the decision of the Director of
Economic Stabilization was controlling.

CONGRESSIONAL DRIVE FOR CENTRALIZED AUTHORITY

It has already been indicated how congressional investigations
and criticism regarding lack of a strong centralized authority over
production and procurement in OPM and SPAB had contributed
to creation of WPB. The same pattern of criticism soon bom-
barded WPB.

Starting early in 1942 and continuing until establishment of
the Office of War Mobilization, the Tolan and Truman Committees, and several additional congressional committees, hammered
away continuously at Nelson to exercise the great authority vested
in him under the WPB executive order, or to have such authority
superseded. In March 1942, the Tolan Committee asserted flatly
that the country would not achieve President Roosevelt's high

[54] E.O. 9250, October 3, 1942.

armament production goals for 1942 or 1943 unless a single civilian-directed procurement agency for all Army, Navy, Maritime Commission, and Lend-Lease needs were established.[55] A more powerful committee, the House Military Affairs Committee, voiced its strong dissatisfaction in a report on WPB on June 23.

In September, Senator Truman, chairman of the Special Committee Investigating the Defense Program, stated on the floor of the Senate that war production had been mismanaged and that the confidence of the people in the war effort was being undermined. He declared that Nelson was finding it difficult to exercise his powers. In October, the Tolan Committee made its third highly critical report to the House, concluding: "The present dispersal of responsibility for production has been actively promoted by the War Production Board." [56]

In this report, the Committee first urged statutory creation of an Office of War Mobilization as supreme authority for directing the war economy. A week later, the chairman of the Committee introduced a bill in the House to set up such an office to be guided by "an economic general staff" to be known as the Committee on Requirements and Programs. A similar bill was introduced concurrently in the upper chamber by Senators Kilgore and Pepper. During the following month the chairmen of five special Senate and House groups investigating the conduct of the war on the domestic front joined in a drive to legislate an Office of War Mobilization.[57] All five were active supporters of the Administration, but risked a clash with the White House on this issue. Senator Pepper immediately scheduled open hearings and, on January 6, 1943, his subcommittee reported favorably on an Office of War Mobilization bill to the full Committee on Education and Labor.

In the spring of 1943 there began a struggle to cut from WPB a substantial proportion of its priorities and production responsibility, a move which marked descent of the agency to its low point in prestige. Hearings began in March on a bill offered by

[55] 77th Cong., 2nd Sess., House, Select Committee Investigating National Defense Migration, *Third Interim Report*, March 9, 1942.

[56] *Sixth Interim Report*, October 1942, p. 22.

[57] Senator Truman (Special Committee Investigating the National Defense Program), Senator Kilgore (Subcommittee on Technological Mobilization of the Military Affairs Committee), Senator Murray (Special Committee on Small Business), Senator Pepper (Subcommittee on Manpower of Committee on Education and Labor), and Representative Tolan.

Senator Maloney of Connecticut calling for an independent supply agency for civilian production.[58] On April 20 the Maloney bill
was approved by the Senate Committee, despite Nelson's strong
objections. Three days later, the President, at Nelson's request,
added three new members to the War Production Board in order
to strengthen its civilian supply representation, the heads of
WMC, ODT, and Petroleum Administration for War. With this
move, Nelson issued an order giving his Office of Civilian Requirements more sweeping authority. Despite this action and
opposition of the Truman Committee, the Senate adopted the
Maloney bill by a decisive vote on May 10. It died in the House,
but the incident revealed how great was Congress' loss of faith
in WPB as a central war agency.

On May 6 the Truman Committee, reporting on priority conflicts in the synthetic rubber, aviation gasoline, and destroyer
escort ship programs, stated that the basic fault lay in weaknesses
in control of the war effort, and too many independent "czars."
The report claimed the principal weakness was caused by dilution, on repeated occasions, of the original broad powers delegated to Nelson. "Today discussion of the over-all legal authority
of the WPB is mere pedantry. Although the authority may exist,
it has not been exercised." [59]

On May 13, 1943 the subcommittee on War Mobilization reported to the Senate Military Affairs Committee that immediate
action was "urgently necessary" for creation of a War Mobilization Board as an interim arrangement pending continued hearings on the Office of War Mobilization bill. The report stated:

> The Executive Order establishing the War Production Board clearly
> intended to set up a central agency fully empowered to mobilize the
> Nation's resources for war . . . It would appear, however, that most
> of these powers were delegated to the various agencies which now com-
> pete with one another in such a way as to engender conflicts inimical
> to maximum production.
>
> In no single phase of the war production program does centralized
> control exist at the present time.[60]

Meanwhile the President, partially prodded into a decision

[58] 78th Cong., 1st Sess., S. *885*, March 16, 1943.
[59] 78th Cong., 1st Sess., Senate, Special Committee Investigating the National Defense Program, *Report No. 10*, Pt. 9, pp. 4–5.
[60] 78th Cong., 1st Sess., Senate, Subcommittee on War Mobilization, *Report to the Committee on Military Affairs*, May 13, 1943.

by growing support for the inflexible and unwelcome Kilgore-Pepper-Tolan bills, after extended conversations with his OES director, James F. Byrnes, devised a plan of his own based upon the OES experience. Benjamin V. Cohen, OES general counsel, and Wayne Coy, Assistant Director of the Budget, coöperated in drawing up an executive order incorporating the decisions arrived at by Byrnes and the President. On May 27, the President issued the executive order announcing the birth of the Office of War Mobilization. In an accompanying statement, Roosevelt gave full recognition to the validity of congressional criticism and, despite some significant differences from the congressional proposals, the new order received uniform approbation in Congress.

Arrival of the Office of War Mobilization was the culminating step in an evolutionary process. It came neither suddenly nor arbitrarily, but in line with the march of events. It might have happened through legislation or it might have been ordered in some other form, but the unavoidable necessity for fulfilling the functions set for it had long been clear.

INADEQUATE EXPLANATIONS OF NEED FOR OWM

The basic causes which made creation of OWM a universally acknowledged necessity have been commonly ascribed to a variety of appealing but oversimplified factors. The press emphasized the clash of personalities in high office. Much has been written regarding the military struggle with civilians for domination of the war economy. Many students have pointed to general bad organization of government for conduct of war. There are degrees of truth in all these points, but they do not, individually or collectively, get at the basic problem which beset us.

PERSONALITIES

There were indeed personalities high in the administration who clashed in philosophy and temperament. The "old curmudgeon," Harold L. Ickes, and the volatile William Jeffers were admittedly not easy people to work with. Nor was it likely that an easy-going Donald Nelson[61] and the hard-driving Robert Patter-

[61] Nelson's personality has been the subject of much speculation. His WPB career has been a subject of eloquent controversy. On the one extreme he has been portrayed as incompetent and weak. (See, for example, H. L. Stimson and McGeorge Bundy, *On Active Service in Peace and War*, Harper, 1947, pp. 493–494.) On the other, he has been represented as a Galahad

son would work in ready harmony. But it should be obvious that
an enterprise as vast and variegated as government, particularly
in time of war, cannot be manned entirely by leaders equipped
to deal with each other in continuous harmony. The attempt to
achieve such an end might mean the costly rejection of many
men with drive, viewpoint, and courage. These men clashed because in the main they were able and vigorous, with important
responsibilities which could not be carried out without impinging
on the province of others. The disputes also reflected basic differences in philosophic attitude on questions of degree and timing
of civilian sacrifice or "all-out" war. Such differences were unavoidable and not far removed from normal divergencies of
opinion in government as well as within the nation as a whole.

A conflict of viewpoint in wartime was not only inescapable
but probably desirable. It is a questionable efficiency which
eliminates opportunity for vigorous presentation of different
viewpoints, for aggressive debate, and adequate public awareness of alternative courses. The ultimate difficulty did not lie in
the fact that certain of the means Jeffers regarded as necessary
to achieve the objectives of his program ran head-on into means
needed to achieve objectives of Ickes' programs, nor even that
both men, as well as Forrestal and Patterson, expressed their attitudes strongly, and sometimes publicly.[62] The real problem lay in

fighting against fearful odds to keep the economy from falling into military
hands. A dispassionate examination of the record indicates that he was a
man of great abilities and character and yet was probably not tempera-
mentally suited to the onerous job he undertook in WPB. He was mild-
mannered and intellectual, not given to quick decisions. He was not adept
at and did not welcome the "in-fighting" of the power struggles involved in
high administration for high stakes. The very qualities which contributed to
his great success in his pre-WPB positions were his undoing in that job. In
NDAC and SPAB, where others were the controlling powers in conflict, he,
as an affable, intelligent, and competent go-between proved a most useful
catalytic agent who quietly got things done. Pushed into the position of
supreme power himself, these qualities were no longer suited. One of his
friends and associates told the author, "He was too nice a guy for the job."
For an interesting and balanced appraisal of Nelson, see *Industrial Mobilization for War*, pp. 209–211.

[62] President Roosevelt apparently believed in the value of dispute. He has
been quoted as saying: "There is something to be said too for having a
little conflict between agencies. A little rivalry is stimulating, you know. It
keeps everybody going to prove he is a better fellow than the next man. It
keeps them honest too." (Frances Perkins, *The Roosevelt I Knew*, Viking,
1946, p. 360.)

the fact that, short of the President, who could not possibly attend to all these disputes personally, there was no place to go for any effective resolution or to determine what the controlling policy would be. There was no central channel to provide that, even if the problem deserved the President's personal attention, it would get to him on time, or that it would get to him in such a way as to help him make an intelligent, considered judgment.

MILITARY VERSUS CIVILIAN CONFLICTS

It is equally unsatisfactory to regard the issue merely as a struggle between civilian and military interests. True, the clash between the War and Navy Departments and the Maritime Commission, on the one hand, and such civilian agencies as WPB and WMC, on the other, went on in one form or another throughout the war. The military agencies had enormous responsibilities, constantly and heavily impinging upon or invading the civilian economy and cutting across the fields of civilian agencies. The military aggressively fought for its viewpoint, for its programs, and for as much authority and influence as it could get. Civilian agencies fought back. This type of struggle is not unique in government, in war or peace. It was lent a special coloring and quality by the immensity of the canvas covered by military interests, by their special status and advantageous position during war, and by the traditional American suspicion of the man in uniform. These factors affected the tactics, techniques, and balance of power. But the essential nature of the struggle was no different from the clashes among civilian agencies, contests between conscientious men responsible for different parts of an important task, whose responsibilities frequently appeared to be in conflict, and who were prejudiced sincerely and deeply for the interest they represented.[63]

There was nothing fundamentally wrong in the clash. It was probably useful. Had the civilian agencies not challenged the reasonableness of the military demands, we might have cut the civilian economy below the point of safety without particular military advantage; had the military failed to present its demands as forcefully as it knew how, inadequate military production could easily have resulted. There were few who understood fully

[63] For an interesting view on this problem by a party in interest, see Henry L. Stimson and McGeorge Bundy, *op. cit.*, pp. 491–495.

both sides of the picture; fewer still who were far enough removed from the heat of the struggle and from arduous personal responsibility in it to allow for totally unfettered thinking. The constant debate, even the passionate feelings on both sides, made their useful contributions to the ultimate balance.

Here again the basic difficulty did not lie in the fact that the system allowed for controversy, but that the victory would go to him who could overpower his opponent. Again it was the fact that the government lacked a place where, within reasonable time, a synthesis could emerge from the struggle, a normal and automatic funneling to the President himself, if necessary.

ORGANIZATION FOR WAR

The charge that our governmental structure for war was organizationally unsound also falls short of the main problem. True, the war organization was an amorphous, unwieldy, and baffling agglomeration of agencies, largely improvised as the developing situation seemed to dictate.

It could be maintained that this was largely unavoidable in a democracy which was drawn into war piecemeal and reluctantly. Circumstances led the President to reject all ready-made blueprints such as the Industrial Mobilization Plan. His clear reluctance to ask for new legislation forced early reliance on makeshift and improvised agencies based upon his existing powers and half-forgotton laws still conveniently on the books.

In any event, by the time war actually broke out and reorganization could be undertaken more forthrightly, we had been operating a defense program for more than 18 months, the war program was well under way, and there was great reluctance to start from scratch. There was a real question whether fundamental reorganization at that stage might not mean a dangerous delay in production. There was also real question whether some of the apparent malorganization was not inherent in the political imperatives of our kind of democracy.

The structure, developed by bits and pieces in 1940 and 1941, was destined to remain the basis for the war organization to the end. However, as we have seen, awareness of its inadequacies was general and periodic crises and frequent attacks from Congress resulted in many valiant undertakings to cure the ills, long before OWM came on the scene. The general nature of the major attempts and suggestions is worth examining.

APPRAISAL OF PRE-OWM ATTEMPTS
TO ACHIEVE COÖRDINATION

From the beginning, the ever-resounding demand for reform centered around the absence of coördination, centralized authority, and central policy-making—all facets of the same problem, the varying emphases simply reflecting different attitudes as to degree and nature of the necessary synthesis. The various methods of coördination tried or proposed can be conveniently arranged under several general headings.

COÖRDINATION BY AGREEMENT

This was the essence of the Supply Priorities and Allocations Board, as well as many of the Cabinet-form proposals of the time. Essentially it was an attempt to obtain policy and operating decisions and to coördinate activities by meetings of the heads of agencies. The value of having top officials meet and attempt to resolve their difficulties is not questioned. Also, as an advisory body such a device may be excellent. But as an instrument for decision-making, as the locus of authority, such a body is rarely adequate.

Men with top administrative responsibilities cannot get to-gether in the same room often enough or long enough for policy- and rule-making responsibilities; the job tends to be delegated to men who lack the status to make decisions stick. They rarely can strip themselves of primary concern for their own administrative responsibilities and gain the essential over-all perspective. Since power resides in the body as a whole, and decisions are collective, there arises a degree of irresponsibility stemming from lack of personal accountability. Instead of coördination, this device generally brings treaties, delay, and uncertainty.

COÖRDINATION BY INFILTRATION

In this category were several attempts to obtain coördination by transfer of particular officials from one agency to another, which were in dispute, in order to dilute the sources of conflict. The transfer of Ferdinand Eberstadt from the Army and Navy Munitions Board to WPB and Nelson's sending to the Army and Navy some of his top purchasing and production officials represented such gestures. One of two results appear to follow. Either the area of the fight is extended, from inter- to intra-agency, causing violent eruption within a particular organization, as in the Eberstadt case, or the transferred men become completely absorbed within their new agency, soon becoming additional opponents of the organization from which they were transferred, as was the case with the men who moved from WPB to the Army.

COÖRDINATION THROUGH LIAISON

The Office for Emergency Management was in effect the first of the war agencies, serving as a great legal convenience and holding company for most of the non-legislated war agencies. The head of the Office was to serve as Liaison Officer (that was his title) among the several agencies themselves and between the agencies and the President. However, the Liaison Officer had no authority and could not act, either in his own name or in that of the President.

There was some early anticipation that wise use of holding-company and liaison functions might evolve into central coördination of operations. That never happened. Top officials will not bring their troubles to a man without authority; nor do they want an intermediary to deal with the decision-maker; they want to present their own case. The Office for Emergency Management never was accepted as a centralizing force and even its liaison functions—whatever they were intended to be—never materialized. For a period it furnished housekeeping help, in such fields as fiscal control, personnel, and space, to the war agencies, but even this disappeared.

COÖRDINATION BY AMALGAMATION

Coördination by Amalgamation was a type of proposal which involved uniting all important operating agencies as subdivisions in one huge organization with a "boss" at the top, and had widespread backing in different form from groups holding diverse political views. The military and big businessmen espoused it in the Industrial Mobilization Plan. Labor and liberals had a similar device in the Kilgore-Pepper-Tolan bill.[64] The idea has the attraction of simplicity: if you have trouble coördinating two, five, or

[64] See Chapter 2, pp. 49–51, for fuller discussion.

ten agencies, just put them all into one bigger agency. But paper unification does not always achieve either unity or coördination. Carried to its ultimate extreme it returns the problem precisely where it found it. The new agency may eventually encompass most of the government; of necessity the bureaus within it then become as large and influential as present departments; essentially the man at the top of the hierarchy substitutes for the President,[65] with almost as little time and considerably less prestige. He ends up needing the same kind of coördinative assistance which led to the proposal in the first instance.

This is not to say that reorganization and judicious combinations of functions or agencies are not frequently necessary and helpful in reducing the size of the coördinating job. For instance, it might have been wise to place PAW and other "czar" agencies, which were responsible for particular commodities, within WPB. But when half or more of the government is combined within a single agency, as was proposed in the Kilgore-Pepper-Tolan bill, there is serious doubt of administrative feasibility, and even such a vast empire cannot encompass all departments with interrelated responsibilities. The need for the over-all coördinating job remains as real as before.

SECTIONAL COÖRDINATION

The Office of Economic Stabilization represented a bona fide attempt at real coördination, including the necessary instruments of adequate authority, prestige, clarity of purpose, and Presidential backing. The main limitation on its effectiveness was the fact that it was given only a sector of the job to handle. It was not accountable for governmental coördination as a whole but was only accountable for that section presumably related to economic stabilization.

Although OES was in many vital ways a successful mechanism, it was extremely difficult to set clear boundaries to the area of economic stabilization. It found that agencies with economic stabilization responsibilities impinged on agencies without such responsibilities, and the latter, in turn, had functions influencing

---

[65] It was suspected in some quarters that those who held the Industrial Mobilization Plan in high esteem did so partially because it would have meant "virtual abdication by the President." See, *United States at War*, pp. 23–24.

stabilization. It was clear that economic stabilization needed to be coördinated with many other problems of government. It was not accidental that eight months after OES was established, OWM came on the scene, with the OES director transferred to the OWM directorship, this time to do the entire coördinating job.

COÖRDINATION BY OPERATING AGENCY[66]

The War Production Board was granted in its first executive order authority and powers provocatively similar to those later assigned to OWM. The phrasing of the order, plus the initial failure to eliminate OPM, has led some people to speculate on the possibility that WPB was at first intended to be the central coördinating policy unit which OWM later became, with OPM serving as the operating arm for production. Whether this be true or not, in a short time WPB took over OPM and all its activities and tried to combine these vast duties with the policy-making and coördinating functions granted in the executive order. The operating duties brought the agency down to the same level as the agencies it was supposed to coördinate. It became itself one of the daily protagonists. As such it could not be accepted as ultimate adjudicator. The lower order of function soon dissipated the effectiveness and acceptance of the higher. Furthermore, such an agency could not be embellished with the symbols of prestige and authority necessary for achievement of the top coördinating job.

This is not to say that WPB was a failure. On the whole, it carried out its operating job as effectively as the circumstances would allow; further, it performed regularly essential lower level coördination of agencies. But as an attempt to achieve the necessary over-all synthesis it proved inadequate.

[66] The use of the term "operating" in this study may be questioned. It is true that the major tasks of WPB's requirements committees, the setting of priorities and allocations, were at their core coördinating functions in the sense that they involved bringing together large numbers of interested agencies. A purer distinction might be to recognize different levels of non-operating functions, ranging from the most detailed allocation of a particular raw material to the broadest policy issues. But, whatever terminology one prefers, the point is that the detailed tasks of lower level "coördination" required a huge staff, creating a tremendous internal management problem for WPB top personnel, leaving little energy for the broad issues and policy synthesis.

These categories of examples indicate that many earnest attempts were made to pull together the government war operations before OWM came into existence. They also demonstrate that whether or not the war organization was set up as well as it might have been, there would, in any event, have existed a need for over-all coördination. A breakdown of government functions into many agencies is unavoidable. The inescapable influence of one function upon another, the impossibility of drawing exact lines, the sheer interdependence of all phases of modern society, make it unavoidable that some degree of overlapping and conflict must remain in whatever form of organization. The war dramatized the ever-present need for coördination, and OWM finally resulted.

CHAPTER 2

OFFICE OF WAR MOBILIZATION

*T*he order creating OWM was sweeping and general.[1] The authority conferred on the new Office was vast. It was empowered:

(a) To develop programs and to establish policies for the maximum use of the nation's natural and industrial resources for military and civilian needs, for the effective use of the national manpower not in the armed forces, for the maintenance and stabilization of the civilian economy, and for the adjustment of such economy to war needs and conditions;

(b) To unify the activities of Federal agencies and departments engaged in or concerned with production, procurement, distribution or transportation of military or civilian supplies, materials, and products and to resolve and determine controversies between such agencies or departments, except those to be resolved by the Director of Economic Stabilization under Section 3, Title IV of Executive Order 9250 [agricultural prices]; and

(c) To issue such directives on policy or operations to the Federal agencies and departments as may be necessary to carry out the programs developed, the policies established, and the decisions made under this Order. It shall be the duty of all such agencies and Departments to execute these directives, and to make to the Office of War Mobilization such progress reports as may be required.

The order appeared to comprehend virtually all home-front functions of the executive branch and was generally so accepted. It appeared to omit only foreign, diplomatic, and strategic military considerations.

Two months later OWM's jurisdiction was extended to the foreign economic field.[2] It was made coördinator of government activities relating to "foreign supply, foreign procurement, and other foreign economic affairs, in conformity with the foreign policy of the United States, as defined by the Secretary of State." The sheer impracticability of a clean split between domestic and international affairs made this inevitable. Increasing conflict had

---

[1] E.O. 9347, May 27, 1943.
[2] E.O. 9361, July 15, 1943.

occurred among agencies concerned with various aspects of domestic and foreign responsibilities, including the State Department, RFC and its subsidiaries, the Board of Economic Warfare, the Department of Agriculture, WPB and the Treasury, climaxed by the notorious Wallace-Jones dispute over RFC financing of certain foreign economic operations.

The omission of military strategy and international political relations from OWM's purview was deplored by a small minority which had hoped for a merging of the entire scope of the war effort on the theory that balanced programing could be assured only by fusing all military, production, and political considerations.

A larger group was disappointed because the new order did not include any reassembling of war agencies or general reorganization of the executive branch. The new agency was superimposed on the existing structure. But wide latitude was granted OWM to exercise its powers and duties "through such officials and such agencies and in such manner" as the director might determine, presumably permitting him to undertake such reorganizations as he thought necessary.

ADVANTAGES OF THE EXECUTIVE ORDER
OVER PROPOSED LEGISLATION

The most ready explanation of the particular context of the executive order is that it represented a reasonable compromise of all the demands and varying recommendations on the type of machinery needed to coördinate the home front. More likely, however, is an interpretation based on the President's conception of his executive office and personal accountability to him. The harassing experiences of NDAC, OPM, SPAB, and WPB led to the clear all-inclusiveness of the War Mobilizer's jurisdiction. The relative success of the OES experiment contributed to a determination that an extension of that type of authority would be workable. The President had discovered that real integration would have to come out of his own office and that ultimate top-side coordination could not be partial or selective.

Wayne Coy, one of the participants in the conferences which led to final formulation of Executive Order 9347, told the author that the President's clear intent was to create a "chief of staff" for the entire domestic front, inclusive of everything but military strategy.[3] The broad phrasing of the order also suggests the "chief of staff" concept more than an agency, in any conventional sense. The composition of the War Mobilization Committee[4] suggests that the way was to be left open for the War Mobilizer to employ such a body as a facsimile of a War Cabinet, if he chose.

The great objection to the proposed legislation for an Office of War Mobilization, then pending in Congress, was its inflexibility and its unwieldy administrative structure. The constantly shifting exigencies of war had already indicated the urgent need for adaptability in policy, structure, and administration. An agency established by Congress could not have the complete elasticity required, while one established by executive order could be remodeled, expanded, curtailed, or abolished whenever the President saw fit.

The Tolan-Kilgore-Pepper bill [5] set up a giant administrative body which would have encompassed all or parts of fourteen existing agencies. It was to be subdivided into four offices—the Office of Production Supply, the Office of Manpower Supply, the Office of Scientific and Technical Mobilization, and the Office of Economic Stabilization. The new body was to absorb, in entirety, WPB, WMC, OES, OPA, PAW, the Smaller War Plants Corporation, and the Selective Service System. In addition, certain subdivisions of permanent agencies—War, Navy, and the Treasury—as well as parts of the Maritime Commission, Lend-Lease, the Federal Loan Agency, and the Department of Commerce were to be included.

Nevertheless, the proposed agency would not have encompassed all government offices concerned with war activities. Vital war agencies, such as ODT, WFA, and the Committee on Congested Production Areas were omitted.[6] The bill would also have

---

[3] Personal interview, August 12, 1946. As might be expected regarding such an event, there is some disagreement about the exact circumstances accompanying the drafting of the executive order. I have based my interpretations largely on discussions with Mr. Coy and Harold D. Smith and communications from Justice Byrnes and Benjamin V. Cohen.

[4] See pp. 56–57.

[5] 78th Cong., 1st Sess., *H.R. 2285*, March 23, 1943.

[6] Since virtually every arm of government, including old-line agencies, was engaged to a lesser or greater degree in war work, the strict logic of the proposed structure would have required the absorption of virtually all executive offices and functions in order to encompass fully all war activities. However, directive power over all omitted agencies was incorporated in the bill.

established certain new offices requiring additional personnel, particularly the Office of Scientific and Technical Mobilization.

Even those who were convinced of the necessity of further integration of the war effort nevertheless felt that so gigantic an agency would be too cumbersome to achieve its ends. Furthermore, the greatest need was for coördination of policy rather than administrative unification. The sponsors of the bill placed greater weight on the latter, while the executive order was primarily concerned with the former. Unhampered by operational responsibility, and armed with sufficient authority, OWM would be able to do the policy job and make its decisions stick. More important, an agency free of day-to-day administrative decisions and squabbles could keep the respect of other agencies and maintain the impartiality of a quasi-judicial body.

A clear example of the greater flexibility of the executive order is the case of materiel procurement. A chief aim of the congressional proposal was the transfer of materiel procurement from military to civilian control. The bill required that its proposed agency assume responsibility for all letting of contracts and procurement. The appropriate subdivisions of the War, Navy, and Treasury Departments, the Maritime Commission, and Lend-Lease were to be shifted promptly to the new agency. Under terms of the executive order, on the other hand, while the director of OWM had full authority to effect such a transfer of procurement functions, he was not committed to any particular change nor to any fixed program of transfers. OWM could make complete or partial changes in the procurement picture, either immediately or gradually as the situation dictated. Such adaptability seemed more desirable in view of the war situation in mid-1943.

The ability of an over-all policy agency to implement the powers granted it, either by Congress or an executive order, depends chiefly on the status it wins within the government. The conditions of the President's order gave OWM a more elevated position than it would have enjoyed under the proposed legislation. The OWM Director was in effect Assistant President and was clearly more powerful than Cabinet members, a situation in keeping with Bernard Baruch's advice that the chief of war production should be above the Cabinet level in order to perform his job successfully. The Tolan-Kilgore-Pepper bill failed to meet this requirement.

On balance, the executive order appears to have been more workable and better suited to existing conditions than the congressional proposal. The latter contributed greatly, however, in forcing or expediting executive action.

THE DIRECTOR OF OWM

The lack of precise detail as to the nature and scope of OWM's activities lent special significance to the views and characteristics of its director. His concept of the job was bound to influence the structure and activities of OWM to a greater extent than would be the case in agencies with more clearly defined powers, with operating rather than policy responsibilities, and with larger staffs.

An early OWM staff memorandum declared: "It follows from the character of the Office that its decisions must be those of the Director . . ." The importance of the director was also emphasized in a Budget Bureau memorandum:

The OWM is not at all comparable with an ordinary department in which generous delegation to subordinates must be the rule . . .

When department and agency heads request a decision from the OWM, they expect and should have a firm decision by the Director. Quite apart from the treatment which their position should command, they have a right to demand that decisions of the OWM should really be the considered action of the Director on which they can operate rather than the decision of a subordinate which may be reconsidered if and when the issue should happen to come to the attention of the Director.

Questions that the Director might be willing to delegate to his staff for settlement are not important enough for decision by the OWM as it now seems to be conceived. Questions that the Director feels he should not be burdened with personally should not burden his staff either.[7]

The selection of James F. Byrnes as the first of the four directors of OWM and OWMR was almost inevitable and completely uncontested. It was a choice generally popular with Congress, the officialdom, and the public.

Justice Byrnes was a veteran public servant with the rare ex-

[7] V. O. Key, "The OWM Staff Question," Intra-Office Memorandum, Bureau of the Budget, August 16, 1943. (Transmitted to OWM.)

perience of having served in all three branches of the Federal government. He had been a member of Congress from South Carolina for almost a quarter of a century during which time he gained the respect and confidence of both parties. He was widely regarded as conservative in his views, yet he was a loyal and trusted follower of President Roosevelt and had acted as floor leader in the Senate for much of the most bitterly contested New Deal legislation. He was often assigned the task of winning over the doubtful votes, especially those of his Southern colleagues.[8] He was known in the legislative halls as a master strategist.

The administration's high approbation of Byrnes was given concrete evidence when the President appointed him Associate Justice of the Supreme Court in 1941.[9] The following year he relinquished the luster and security of the Supreme Court to head the newly created Office of Economic Stabilization. Although the OES directorship concerned economic stabilization only, the Justice's prestige, the drama surrounding his appointment, and the announcement that his office would be in the White House gave a wider significance to the appointment. By making a broad interpretation of his assigned functions and exhibiting no reluctance to issue directives to other agencies, Byrnes enhanced his own status and soon was regarded as second only to the President on the home front.[10] By his frequent exhibition of confidence in Byrnes, the President helped established public and governmental understanding and recognition of his position. Byrnes made the first public announcement of certain executive orders,

[8] His affability, calm disposition, and ability at compromise made him an extremely popular member of Congress. To most of the legislators he was known as "Jimmie," an appellation which persisted even after he acquired the distinguished title of "Justice."

[9] Byrnes has since revealed that even while serving on the bench he was an intimate adviser of the President and worked closely with him on domestic front issues. (*Speaking Frankly*, pp. 13–17.)

[10] Harry Hopkins was undoubtedly a more intimate personal adviser to the President and his assignments were of the highest order of direct representation, but Hopkins held no formal post in the administrative pyramid. Furthermore, he was engaged largely in international political and military strategy. His biographer points out that because of Hopkins' lack of legal position, "Roosevelt could delegate all sorts of authority to him, but any Cabinet member who wanted to ignore this could do so, on firm legal grounds, and most of them did." (Robert E. Sherwood, *Roosevelt and Hopkins*, Harper, 1948, p. 212.) Sherwood probably exaggerates the legal factors as opposed to the institutional.

delivered radio addresses on questions of broad governmental policy, and personally handled for the President special tasks obviously not within the formal compass of his job.[11]

When the nature of Byrnes's responsibilities and actions is considered, it seems remarkable that he retained his popularity throughout his directorship of OES. The stabilization act of October 2, 1942, which served as the direct occasion for Byrnes's appointment, had been almost literally forced through a highly reluctant Congress. The famous "Hold-the-Line Order" of April 1943, while one of the most noteworthy domestic accomplishments of the war, was not designed to make the affected interests happy. Byrnes was responsible for prescribing the regulations for the President's $25,000 salary limitation order, a restriction so unpopular that it was finally removed by congressional action. It was Byrnes who instructed the WLB to stop all wage increases not strictly within the limitations of the "Little Steel Formula." So unpopular was this order that it threatened to wreck WLB, causing Byrnes to revise the order. Other officials administering such highly charged programs, Leon Henderson of OPA, for example, were bombarded by criticism which finally destroyed their political usefulness, but Byrnes weathered the storms handsomely.

The explanation for this success may lie, partially at least, in the fact that he accepted the OES position with the understanding that he could follow his deep inclination to avoid actual operations.[12] He left all actual enforcement, regulation, and red tape to other agencies. The burden of public criticism therefore fell on others. The personal qualities which had aided Byrnes's rise in politics were also of inestimable value to him. His skill at compromise, coupled with ability to act incisively and with authority when necessary, and a shrewd awareness of sources of power in government served him well.

[11] The President is reported to have told Byrnes, "All these new agencies we have had to create mean an increasing number of jurisdictional conflicts which come to me for decision. I want you to settle these conflicts for me; . . . I'll let it be known that your decision is my decision. The Director of Economic Stabilization is an important job but it will be less important than the other duties I want you to perform for me by direct delegation." (*Speaking Frankly,* p. 18.)

[12] In announcing his appointment, the President described the job as calling "primarily for judicial consideration . . . administrative action will be carried out by existing agencies."

When, after eight months of OES, Roosevelt designated Byrnes OWM director, there was no criticism. He was already commonly referred to as "Assistant President," despite the fact that the President himself disliked the title. The new office was in fact a logical extension of his powerful role in OES. In selecting Byrnes, the President indicated the preëminent position the new Office of War Mobilization was to have.

For his part, Byrnes was markedly successful in establishing the authority of OWM. He made it clear that he regarded himself as the President's deputy on the home front and that his decisions carried full presidential authority. Byrnes recognized the importance of the symbols of prestige. He instructed his staff not to go to other agencies but to have them bring their problems to OWM and to hold their meetings in OWM offices which were deliberately located in the White House. The aura of the presidential office was extended to OWM.

OWM ORGANIZATION

An early Budget Bureau analysis said of the OWM director, "As the President's agent he should see that things are done rather than build up a huge organization to do them." [13] Byrnes followed this principle strictly, as a result of personal predilection, previous experience—especially with OES—and his conception of the OWM job.

As had been true at OES, there was virtually no internal organization to buttress the director. The handful of staff members were in effect his personal assistants. After a year of operation, OWM had a regular staff of only ten paid persons of all ranks. For special jobs Byrnes enlisted the services of outside experts, borrowed personnel from and assigned tasks to other agencies, especially the Budget Bureau. The OWM permanent professional staff consisted of four men: Benjamin V. Cohen, legal adviser, brought from OES; one assistant for press relations, Walter Brown; Donald Russell, a former law partner and friend from South Carolina whose function appeared to be chiefly "to protect the boss and relieve him of details"; and Fred Searls, Jr., a businessman who had served as an unpaid official of WPB and the

[13] V. O. Key, "Possible Lines of Development of the Office of War Mobilization," Memorandum to the Director of the Budget, June 24, 1943. (Transmitted by Mr. Smith to the Director of OWM.)

War Shipping Administration.[14] When specialists were required, as in the case of the OWM representatives on the procurement review boards, discussed in Chapter 4, Byrnes brought in experts, either on a part-time or full-time basis and usually for a short period of time.

A unique arrangement was worked out with Elder Statesman Bernard M. Baruch. Mr. Baruch, adviser to President Roosevelt and World War I Chief of the War Industries Board, agreed to act as special adviser and consultant to OWM. In the summer of 1943 Baruch, his assistant John Hancock, and a few staff members were added to OWM as a special unit to consider plans for the postwar adjustment of the economy. The unit was disbanded early in 1944 after its famous report, *War and Post-War Adjustment Policies,* was delivered. Byrnes carefully modified the customary administrative arrangements in order to fit Baruch into the organization and at the same time protect the latter's prestige. So that his position should not appear to be that of a subordinate, he was granted freedom with regard to the subjects he studied, the presentation and publication of reports, press relations, and general independence of action.[15]

The functions of the OWM staff differed from those of other agencies. Instead of acting, as other staffs did, on behalf of the head of the agency, the OWM staff was instructed not to constitute an isolating "layer between the director and the heads of agencies. It is the job of the staff to facilitate the relations of the director with agency heads by bringing promptly to the attention of the director questions requiring his consideration, and to serve agency heads by expediting matters requiring action by the director." [16]

The small staff maintained by OWM was both a safeguard and a barrier. On the one hand, it prevented OWM from engaging in administrative activities and operations and from undertak-

[14] Byrnes has described him as "a quiet, unassuming man, with extraordinary knowledge of industrial processes. Throughout the war, he ably filled a number of responsible positions, refusing salary and reimbursement for expenses and avoiding publicity." (*Speaking Frankly,* p. 46.)

[15] Attention might be called to "some of the unhappier consequences of having a free-wheeling genius in the house," as one able observer put it to the author. However, on balance, Byrnes found the price a cheap one.

[16] Memorandum for the Staff, "General Plan for the Operation of the Office," July 27, 1943.

ing or interfering with the normal functions of other agencies. No amount of persuasion or appeal could ensnare the Office into details or low-level meetings because there was no one to handle the work. On the other hand, the staff was also inadequate to perform the type of central planning function which many people considered OWM's most important duty. However, Byrnes felt that most planning should be conducted at agency levels and that it was his job primarily to coördinate such plans.

WAR MOBILIZATION COMMITTEE

As was customary in many of the war agencies, the heads of several other agencies were established in OWM as a consultative body. OWM's War Mobilization Committee included the Secretaries of War and Navy, the chairmen of the Munitions Assignment Board and the War Production Board, and the Director of Economic Stabilization, with the Director of OWM as chairman. The latter was authorized to call in heads of additional agencies when the Committee considered matters especially affecting them.

This device to coördinate activities of the several executive agencies did not infringe on Byrnes's final authority. The latter needed only to "advise and consult" with the War Mobilization Committee. Its actual status depended entirely on him. He could treat it as a top policy council or merely as a discussion body.

According to Donald Russell, assistant to Byrnes, the Committee met often in the early stages, but less frequently as time went on. Byrnes regarded it chiefly as a sounding board to test decisions, to review attitudes and opinions of the leading administrators, and to relieve suspicions. Decisions were the responsibility of the President or Byrnes.

President Roosevelt presided personally over many of the meetings, lending even greater apparent significance to the group than the executive order suggested. The chairman confined the discussion to matters of basic policy set forth in a specific agenda, usually circulated in advance. The agenda generally dealt with current concrete controversies rather than general long-range problems. Techniques of arriving at a decision varied. Sometimes the President or Byrnes would try to get the body to agree upon a conclusion at the meeting. Frequently, the decision would not be announced to the group until after the meeting, by letter or phone call.

Both the President and Byrnes were careful to prevent the meetings from degenerating into a court of appeal by one agency against another. It was a strict rule that only the highest officials of agencies could attend; if the designated member of the Committee was unable to come, he had to inform the secretary in advance and could substitute no one but an approved official of his agency. Technical advisers were invited only after special consideration.

The War Mobilization Committee, as such, was not essential to OWM, because the director inevitably would have consulted the heads of other agencies, either singly or in groups. Its existence, however, occasionally facilitated Byrnes's work since he was able to use decisions arrived at with the Committee's advice as precedents. On occasion, he could use the existence of the Committee as a convenient excuse to avoid setting up *ad hoc* committees advocated by agency heads to deal with issues of special interest to them.[17]

The legislation which established OWMR did not provide for such a committee and its formal existence terminated with OWM. However, the OWMR directors could and did call frequent meetings of heads of agencies on policy issues, thus serving approximately the same purpose.

SUBSIDIARY AGENCIES

OWM was made a holding company for certain subsidiaries. In November 1943, a Joint Contract Termination Board was established in OWM. It operated as an inter-agency committee, including all which had responsibility for contract termination. No additional staff was required. The Office of Contract Settlement was created by legislation in mid-1944 and succeeded JCTB. The Office was later appended to OWMR.

The Surplus War Property Administration, created on February 19, 1944, by Executive Order 9425, was placed under the gen-

[17] For instance, in October 1943, the Department of State requested establishment of an inter-agency committee within OWM to determine policies in the procurement field, particularly mineral supplies, when it appeared expedient to reduce purchases at home or abroad or both. Byrnes replied that new machinery was unnecessary and the problems could be brought before the War Mobilization Committee augmented by representatives of other appropriate agencies. (Letter, James F. Byrnes to E. R. Stettinius, Jr., October 16, 1943.)

eral direction of OWM. Although William Clayton, the administrator, atttended OWM meetings, his staff remained distinct
from OWM. As a result of the Baruch-Hancock reconversion recommendations, the Retraining and Reëmployment Administration was established by Executive Order 9427 on February 24,
1944. It was responsible to OWM, but actually was not a part of
the OWM organization either.

While the relations of these subsidiary agencies with OWM
were not much more direct than those of WPB, for example, the
precedent had been set whereby specialized agencies were attached to OWM and this was continued later in OWMR. Making
the agency a holding company for sub-policy groups was a mistake. As soon as the opportunity arose, OWMR shook off as many
of these agencies as it could. It was inconsistent with the underlying theory of OWM's functions and role in the government.

CONCEPT OF THE JOB

An early staff memorandum written by Byrnes's assistant, Donald Russell, presents a clear statement of OWM's functions as the
Office understood them:

> The Office of War Mobilization acts for the President . . . The job
> of the Office is not to perform the functions of the established depart-
> ments and agencies but to see that these functions are well performed
> by those charged with responsibility for their performance. The other
> primary task of the Office is to assure coördination of separate pro-
> grams, by securing policy integration, resolving conflicts and rendering
> responsible authoritative and firm decisions on controversies.[18]

As the description of staff organization suggests, the OWM
director scrupulously avoided involvement in administrative details and operating responsibilities. In a statement before the Senate Military Affairs Committee, Byrnes warned that a staff which
goes into administrative work "becomes a competitor of the other
agencies and the troubles commence . . . I have had many very
important persons try to urge me during the last year to embark
into the administrative field, but my life would be even unhappier had I consented to go along with them." [19]

[18] Memorandum, "General Plan for the Operation of the Office," July 27,
1943.
[19] 78th Cong., 2nd Sess., Senate, Committee on Military Affairs, *Mobilization and Demobilization Problems, Hearings on S. 1730 and S. 1823*, Pt.
VII, p. 295.

This policy saved him from a setback at the very outset. Whenever a new agency appears, particularly one with broad powers, the older departments become restive and insecure until the lines of authority are clearly drawn. The situation was intensified in wartime because the top-executives in many agencies had no permanent attachment to government service and would remain in Washington only as long as their prestige and freedom were protected. OWM was therefore greeted with uneasiness in some areas. There had been talk that Donald Nelson, Charles E. Wilson, and other high WPB officials would resign. This mood died down after Byrnes assuaged them by assurances that he had no intention of taking over their jobs. But he also rejected WPB's suggestion for a statement delineating the duties and areas of the two agencies.

Many occasions arose when WPB authority might easily have eroded by permitting matters within its sphere to move up to OWM. This the Office was careful to avoid. As far as possible things were done in the name of the administratively responsible agency. Attempts to by-pass appropriate agencies were discouraged. A typical instance appears in a dispute between WPB and the military agencies. A suggestion had been made that the scheduling of production of military supplies be filtered through OWM. John Hancock, Baruch's assistant, wrote Nelson that he thought nothing would be gained through such a procedure and that the armed services should continue to report directly to WPB regarding revisions in programs. "I think there is ample machinery for having the right procedure set up with concurrence of the WPB and the Services, and I do not believe that Byrnes' organization should take jurisdiction—at least until it has been shown that the Services and WPB cannot agree." [20]

The fact that OWM avoided operations has been suggested as one reason for its acceptance by the military as neither WPB nor its predecessors were accepted. There was no question that the War Department accepted OWM as final judge. Under-Secretary Patterson allowed nobody outside his own office to negotiate directly with Byrnes. On supply matters, the War Department did not attempt to go over his head, even when highly dissatisfied with an OWM decision. In fact it tended to consult

[20] Memorandum, October 14, 1943.

Byrnes rather than run to the President, even on matters outside OWM jurisdiction.[21]

Careful as he was to maintain OWM's authority, Byrnes also meticulously side-stepped avoidable intrusion on the jurisdiction of other agencies. If a Congressman, for example, called his office with regard to a question which was the sole responsibility of an executive agency, Byrnes generally referred the questioner directly to that agency. He would not even act as intermediary.

Nor would he act as a higher appeals board in such cases. For instance, in 1943 Senator Wheeler and Congressman Mansfield proposed to Prentiss Brown, the OPA Administrator, that supplemental rations be supplied for miners at Butte, Montana; Brown refused on the ground that it would create an impossible administrative problem. When the two Congressmen took the issue to Byrnes he referred them to Brown as final authority on rationing.

Byrnes's formal relations with Congress showed the same tact and feeling for status and jurisdiction. When a congressional committee, holding hearings on the west coast, invited OWM to be represented, Byrnes declined on the ground that the executive branch should not participate in legislative matters except to provide specific information. However, he did use his friendship and prestige with members of Congress for extensive informal influencing of legislative activities.

There is no doubt that Byrnes's steadfast devotion to the principles that OWM must not administer anything, must not interfere with normal operations of existing agencies, and must protect their prestige and status, was a pillar of strength for the new agency.

ADJUDICATION

It was one of Byrnes's major accomplishments that public disputes among government officials were kept to a minimum. He performed the role of arbitrator or adjudicator with rare skill and effectiveness. In ironing out differences, he had to be certain that no other high-level official either by-passed him or went over his head directly to the President.

[21] Interview with John H. Ohly, Special Assistant to the Secretary of War, April 22, 1946. An exception was the Montgomery-Ward strike case, involving government seizure, which the War Department took before the Cabinet because it was regarded as a military matter involving the use of troops.

Conversely, Byrnes rejected the tendency for increasing numbers of minor disputes, not of "presidential level," to flow up to the top—an unfortunate corollary of successful arbitration. Frequently he found that complaints or proposals from one agency regarding another could be resolved without any real intervention on his part. His technique in such cases was to send copies of the original complaint or proposal to all interested agencies with a request for comments. He would then send the comments back to the original agency. This exchange might go on for some time, during which Byrnes generally refrained from comment. In a large number of cases the issue thus seemed to resolve itself.

When OWM stepped into a major conflict, Byrnes would bring together the interested parties and attempt to work out an acceptable compromise. Sometimes such disputes would result in a new program proposed by OWM. For example, in August 1943, immediately before Byrnes announced his West Coast Manpower Program, WMC had planned to set up committees, headed and controlled by WMC, to establish priorities in the allocation of manpower. WPB wanted at least equal authority with WMC on such committees; WMC did not approve WPB's recommendation; neither had power to enforce its will on the other. Byrnes's plan was framed to be acceptable to both agencies without loss of status to either.[22]

When firm intervention was necessary, however, he did not hesitate. In one somewhat minor but typical example, involving public relations, the OWI director wrote Byrnes that he was unable to secure from the armed services the type of pictures he thought he needed to do his job. He felt they were holding from public information the more gruesome aspects of war, confining releases to successes. The War Mobilizer wrote the War and Navy Departments pointing out that he had previously been obliged to enforce relaxation of previous restrictions by the Services on material given OWI. He emphasized that lack of military candor was making the problem of the domestic economy difficult to handle and he urged immediate action by the Services to end the basis of OWI complaints.[23]

In order to maintain OWM's position as a final court, Byrnes

[22] For fuller description, see Chapter 5, pp. 143–153.
[23] Letter, James F. Byrnes to John J. McCloy, September 2, 1943.

did not permit his staff to take part in organized inter-agency committees. He made it clear that OWM could not be an observer or a voting member on such bodies. When Ickes invited OWM to be represented on PAW's Petroleum Board, Byrnes replied that it would be inadvisable.[24] By remaining aloof, OWM would not be committed to a position at an early stage and would not be handicapped if later called on to make the final decision.

SUPERVISION OF AGENCIES

Despite its judicial approach, OWM did not always wait for disputes to be reported before taking action. When Byrnes considered a matter to be basic to the war effort, he did not hesitate to make pointed inquiries of agencies or to institute critical reviews of their programs.

A crucial task for OWM was review of Army and Navy supply activities. It was clear that OWM's status would depend on an early demonstration that a civilian agency could take active supervision over these supply functions. The attitude of officials in civilian agencies was expressed to Byrnes by a member of his own staff who had previously held high posts in the War Shipping Administration and WPB:

> The Executive Order, creating the War Production Board, gave authority to its chairman to control and adjust military procurement, and see that it maintained a proper balance with respect to civilian needs. This authority was allowed to atrophy through timidity and disuse. The President's Executive Order of May 27, creating the Office of War Mobilization, has given to you a similar authority. If Mr. Nelson had used his Order, there would have been no necessity for yours. The people in uniform have successfully reduced his authority. I am very much afraid that, within the next 30 days, they will accomplish the same end with respect to yours.[25]

Before he was in office a month Byrnes wrote to all procurement agencies that he desired a critical review of their activities, but it was clear that the real targets were the military procurement agencies.[26] The letter from Byrnes to Secretary Knox of the Navy was typical of those which went to all:

[24] Letter, September 14, 1943.

[25] Memorandum, Fred Searls, Jr. to James F. Byrnes, September 14, 1943.

[26] This was one of the earliest occasions for WPB recognition of the advantages of OWM's presence. WPB had lost most of its disputes with the military, despite its nominal authority in the procurement field. Now OWM, a civilian agency, would pass final judgment. The historians of WPB con-

One of the duties imposed on the Office of War Mobilization by the President's Executive Order of May 27th is that of correlation of the programs and war effort of the several agencies of the Government that are directly or indirectly engaged in the total effort . . .

Initially objectives were to produce as much of everything as possible because our needs were so urgent. We were not too concerned at the time as to accurate balance . . . We have now developed production facilities and inventories which have eased the situation, and gained experience on rates of attrition and life of equipment. All these things point to the desirability of making an objective review of requirements, giving special consideration to current strategic concepts, transportation possibilities, inventories, rates of use and attrition, and production potentialities.

It is my feeling that a review of this character should be made through a process and by personnel different from that which was used in developing the current procurement and requirement objectives . . .

I have already discussed with the War Department the advisability of a unit at the General Staff level, which would be charged with the continuous review and coördination of its several procurement programs . . . I should like to see the Navy adopt a similar procedure and should like to have a representative of my office become a member of the group set up to make this review . . . It should . . . assure that the supply programs, which you report to me as a result of its action, have received fresh consideration, and that there have been deleted from them all items which are not, under present conditions, regarded as urgently necessary.

I plan, of course, to make parallel requests of other organizations and claimant agencies to the end that there may be submitted within a few weeks to the attention of the War Mobilization Committee an integrated picture of what is being done and what it is intended to do to meet the requirements of our military forces and our allies, and to properly maintain a civilian economy.[27]

Procurement review boards were established in the Army, Navy, Maritime Commission, and in Lend-Lease, with Byrnes's personal representative on each. Although this did not initially represent the over-all integration and analysis of total requirements so frequently urged, the procedure, nevertheless, had successful results. Not only did it produce cutbacks of considerable size in several of the programs, particularly the Army, but it

cluded, "The varied activities of the Office of War Mobilization, coördinating in character, contributed to the process of smoothing out relationships between WPB and other agencies . . ." (*Industrial Mobilization for War*, pp. 556–557.)

[27] Letter, June 24, 1943.

also established beyond question the propriety and authority of OWM sponsored review. It ended the assumption of the military agencies that they need look only to the Joint Chiefs of Staff for ultimate procurement decisions.

Although the military agencies proved less difficult to handle than had been expected, Byrnes had to assert his authority over the War Department at the outset. As a result of the establishment of a procurement review board for the Army, the OWM found it needed some testimony concerning military matters. The Army originally refused to show these papers to outside civilians, but after Byrnes indicated that he would carry the matter to the President, it gave in.[28]

Several examples of the manner in which Byrnes impressed OWM authority on other agencies indicate his approach. When an OPA official gave a statement to the press which suggested that OPA did not agree with an OWM decision, Byrnes wrote a sharp letter to Chester Bowles, OPA administrator, asking for the resignation of the official who had publicly criticized the decision of the OWM director. Byrnes said that if Bowles did not fire the guilty official, the issue would be brought to the President immediately.[29]

PLANNING

When OWM was created, the Sub-Committee on War Mobilization of the Senate Committee on Military Affairs voiced its hope that OWM would put into effect "a vigorous policy of programing, scheduling, and actively directing the war agencies in the performance of their mutually dependent programs." Recalling that earlier reorganization of the war effort did not establish an over-all war program, the Sub-Committee warned that "if the Office of War Mobilization follows in the weakness of its predecessors and confines itself to the adjudication of personal and agency disputes, it cannot but fail . . ."[30]

In general the agency did not follow this senatorial advice. Byrnes, with his distrust of all staffs, was particularly averse to a regular planning staff. Over-all and centralized planning by an

[28] Letter, James F. Byrnes to Henry L. Stimson, October 9, 1943.
[29] Letter, September 21, 1944.
[30] 78th Cong., 1st Sess., Senate, Sub-Committee on War Mobilization, *Report to Committee on Military Affairs*, June 22, 1943.

agency such as OWM did not appeal to him, although he saw no objection to planning by other agencies. Byrnes had established his fame on the basis of his talent for reconciling divergent attitudes, and had always met problems when they arose. He considered good solutions of actual problems the most practical type of planning.[31]

In some cases the planning role was forced on OWM. As early as the fall of 1943 the need to plan for demobilization and readjustment of the economy became an issue. The War Mobilization Committee devoted several meetings to consideration of a broad program for war veterans. The need for OWM action in this field was emphasized when the general problems of contract termination and disposition of surplus government property came up. Several agencies held heated debate with regard to the power of the Comptroller General to review terms of contract settlements and adoption of a uniform contract termination policy. WPB believed that it should take responsibility for devising uniform policy and practice. The War Department made a different set of proposals. The issue was so broad and important that the President and Byrnes agreed OWM should establish a special unit to deal with postwar adjustment problems.[32]

The background of the Baruch unit, outstanding example of OWM's broad planning, indicates the extent to which planning grew out of OWM's arbitration function. The unit became, however, an important force in OWM's development toward a broader view of its duties. OWM became the leader in government planning for reconversion. As a result of the Baruch-Hancock report and the President's actions on it, OWM–OWMR was assigned basic policy-making, and coördinating responsibilities in the whole reconversion field. However, such undertakings did not reflect any calculated over-all design. Byrnes, the mediator and arbitrator, was also the sensitive master politician and responded

[31] While Byrnes was certainly not a planner in the broader sense, there is some support for the claim of some observers that the pains he took to reiterate before congressional committees his disinterest in planning was in part a "political line." He was aware of the unpopularity of the term on the Hill. He told Congress planning was unnecessary on the very issue on which he carried out his largest planning enterprise—reconversion. (78th Cong., 2nd Sess., Senate, Committee on Military Affairs, *Mobilization and Demobilization Problems, Hearings on S. 1730 and S. 1823*, Pt. VII.)

[32] See Chapter 6, pp. 175–178.

quickly to political stimuli; the circumstances of late 1944 and early 1945 pushed him into more affirmative programing.

RELATIONS WITH OTHER COÖRDINATING AGENCIES

OWM's relations with other coördinating agencies were more complex than was the chain of command to clearly subordinate agencies. When OWM was created there were already in existence several important agencies including the Budget Bureau, OES, and the Joint Chiefs of Staff whose chief purpose was to coördinate the activities of other agencies or to establish policies in certain areas.

BUREAU OF THE BUDGET

From 1939 onward, when the Bureau of the Budget was transferred to the Executive Office of the President, there developed a progressive expansion in the conception of the Executive Office of the President itself and of the Bureau's role therein.

Harold D. Smith, Director of the Budget, was an early and effective exponent of the Budget Bureau as the logical policy-coördinating arm of the President's staff as well as the center of management control. He headed a school of thought which held the view that budgetary control, administrative management, and policy could not be logically or effectively separated. Smith was an able executive and developed the Bureau into one of the most competent and well-rounded staffs of public administrators ever assembled in a government agency. He enjoyed an excellent personal relationship with President Roosevelt. With the President's support, the prestige and the power of the Bureau expanded rapidly from 1939 to 1942 and it became, in effect, the personal technical staff of the President as well as an important policy adviser.

The coming of war had varied effects upon the Budget Bureau. In the early days, it was deeply involved in the rapidly increasing administrative problems of the proliferating agencies. This activity declined after 1942. With the creation of new "top-level" coordinating agencies, a new tempo of governmental action and less orderliness in procedures and relationships, the Bureau's hand became less conspicuous, particularly in matters of policy negotiation. With the wartime influx of industrial executives, serving the government at the personal invitation of the President, and unacquainted with the ways of government, there was a growing tendency to disregard the Bureau and to act independently except for direct approval or disapproval of the President. The Bureau was either not equipped for or not regarded as adequate to the job of top-level coördination or policy-making in the rapidly expanding war effort. Smith refused to accept these developments even as an emergency situation and continued to feel strongly and fight for the position of the Budget Bureau as the President's main policy arm.[33]

Creation of OWM was a blow to Smith's concept of good governmental organization. He referred to it as an "abortion." [34] He felt it was an unnecessary agency duplicating many of the Bureau's functions, without the Bureau's facilities for carrying them out. This was because Smith regarded OWM as just another top-level agency. However, this did not jibe with Byrnes's conception. The latter did not conceive of OWM as "another agency" but rather as a delegation of authority over the domestic front by the President to him: in effect, that he, Byrnes, was "Assistant President." Thus he saw no particular problems of overlapping jurisdiction between himself and Smith. Byrnes assumed that Smith would

[33] The role of the Bureau during this period is something of a disputed point. It is worth calling attention to the observations of two former Bureau officials who read an earlier draft of this chapter. Don K. Price wrote, "I would say that its job multiplied in importance while the general range of problems increased by geometric progression. After all, the BB was transferred to the Executive Office only shortly before the outbreak of War in Europe and as late as 1944 and 1945 the President delegated to it certain types of authority really staggering in nature. There is no doubt, however, that relative to what its director wanted to make of it, the Bureau did not become as much of a policy staff as it might have. I think your summary of the relations between the Bureau and the OWM is a very good and a very fair one."

V. O. Key said, "In negotiating administrative organizational arrangements, my recollection is that the role didn't really taper off until about the fall of 1942. In a sense it tapered off because the major part of the job of arranging administrative mechanisms was completed; later there was a little juggling here and there; but the problem in general changed to one of day-to-day operation; further there was some change in personnel in the Bureau and in organization; Gladieux who carried the main burden of organizational planning got lost in an intra-Bureau shuffle."

[34] Personal interview with Harold Smith, August 21, 1946. On several other occasions he indicated there was room in the Executive Office for another type of "presidential arm" in addition to the Bureau, but it is clear that OWM was not what he had in mind. (For example, see Robert E. Sherwood, *op. cit.*, pp. 210–211.)

have the same relation to him as Smith had to the President. Byrnes was simply doing the President's job on the home front. Smith, on the other hand, did not accept this interpretation and was seeking a definition of areas of responsibility between OWM and the Bureau. The two points of view were in obvious conflict and considerable tension existed between the two men, although there was never much doubt as to who had the upper hand.

The clashes are vividly reflected in some of their early correspondence. Smith frequently complained of Byrnes's alleged intrusions into areas which he regarded as the jurisdiction of the Budget Bureau. Typically, he said, "What I am concerned about is, in short, the growing number of jurisdictional problems which, if not settled, will remain to plague you and me and the operating agencies." [35] However, the problems were never settled and did not appear to plague Byrnes, at least, for the simple reason that he did not agree that there could be room for jurisdictional disputes between "the President" and part of his staff.

Byrnes did not try to injure the prestige or status of the Budget Bureau. He used the Bureau as one of his aides in the same way the President might.[36] Relations between OWM and the Bureau staff were always cordial, despite the fact that no clear definition of relationship was ever agreed upon. Not only did OWM use the services of the Bureau by making requests for special investigations, studies, and routine information, but Byrnes frequently borrowed personnel for special projects.[37]

OWM files are full of examples indicating Byrnes's deference to the recognized functions of the Budget Bureau. For instance,

[35] Letter, Harold D. Smith to James F. Byrnes, November 8, 1943.

[36] This approach was in full accord with the recommendations made by Dr. V. O. Key of the Bureau staff in his original memorandum covering the proposed OWM setup: ". . . The Bureau functions as a management arm of the President. If Mr. Byrnes is acting in the line of authority for the President, the Bureau should occupy the same relation to him as it does to the President . . . The facilities of the Bureau ought to be at the disposal of the OWM, or perhaps, to put it in a better way, he ought to consider the Bureau as a part of his immediate staff resources . . ." (*Op. cit.*, June 24, 1943.)

[37] Budget Bureau personnel were, for instance, borrowed to assist OWM representatives on the procurement review boards; OWM asked the Bureau to report on efficiency of administration and operations of the West Coast Manpower Program.

on July 8, 1943, 23 Senators asked him to set up within OWM a Central Scientific and Technical body with broad powers. Byrnes referred their letter to the Budget director who disagreed with the proposal and Byrnes followed Smith's advice. On July 16, 1943, the assistant director of the Budget wrote Byrnes, attaching a copy of a letter which he had sent to Donald Nelson regarding activities in connection with metals and minerals research. "This results from an analysis of the present methods of dealing with the subject made after receipt of the letter from Secretary Ickes to you [Byrnes] on June 11. Your office referred the matter to the Bureau of the Budget. In this letter, Secretary Ickes proposed a transfer of WPB's Metals and Minerals Research Staff to the Bureau of Mines." [38] The Budget Bureau did not approve of Ickes' proposal and it was never adopted.

These examples of OWM deference to the Budget Bureau in regard to problems of administrative organization are typical and also may throw light on the conflict between Byrnes and Smith. It is perhaps significant that both the Senators and the Cabinet member addressed their original requests to Byrnes, rather than to Smith. It is not likely that Ickes lacked knowledge as to the Budget Bureau's responsibility for administrative management; his writing to OWM more probably reflects his understanding of where the ultimate power lay and the common tendency of highly placed officials to deal only with the final sources of authority. It is equally understandable that Senators would address themselves to the highest echelon in the White House rather than to the Budget director. Also, on occasion, issues presented by high government officers would lead to more direct activity by members of Byrnes's staff, since political considerations did not always make it possible to satisfy Congressmen or Cabinet officers with a decision of the Bureau. This sometimes led to incidents which Smith interpreted as intrusions by Byrnes's office upon his jurisdiction.

The Budget Bureau had for some time been the agency which reviewed the opinions and attitudes of Federal agencies on proposed new legislation and indicated whether they were in accord with the President's program. Although Byrnes continued to re-

[38] Letter, Wayne Coy to James F. Byrnes, July 16, 1943.

spect that responsibility of the Bureau,[39] it was inevitable that as head policy man for the home front the Congress would look to him for the attitude of the Executive Branch and that his office would frequently have to deal with the agencies which might be affected by proposed legislation. Here again there arose occasions to support Smith's feeling that overlapping or duplicating activity was taking place, if one accepted Smith's basic premises regarding OWM.

As the relationship between the two agencies evolved, the Bureau of the Budget was gradually pushed further aside in the field of policy coördination and formulation. The trend was clearly away from that which Smith had nurtured from 1939 on; the Bureau came more and more to be regarded as the administrative management arm of the Presidency while OWM–OWMR became the policy arm.[40]

OFFICE OF ECONOMIC STABILIZATION

While the problem of economic stabilization was primarily related to activities of OPA and WLB, it was obvious that the jurisdiction of the OES director cut across many of the basic functions of WPB, WMC, PAW, ODT, and other agencies. Partially because of his personal prestige and the spread of his authority in OES, Byrnes, while still director of OES was already considered the highest arbiter over home-front issues.

When OWM was created, it was correctly understood to be an extension of Byrnes's authority to include everything on the home front, an extension which flowed logically and easily from the OES experience and from the fact that boundaries of the OES jurisdiction had been getting progressively more vague and widespread as the exigencies of war kept forcing a broader interpretation of that authority. Strict logic and organizational precision might have indicated that with the creation of OWM, OES could

[39] For instance, on June 22, 1943 Byrnes wrote John W. Scott, Federal Power Commissioner, "I beg to acknowledge your letter of June 10 with reference to HR–2754. I think it best that the Commission send the comments on the Bill to the Bureau of the Budget so that the views of the various agencies concerned may be cleared in the usual manner."

[40] It was always clear that budgeting, administration, and policy could not be neatly compartmentalized. As an incident to its basic work the Bureau was always involved in policy considerations. OWM, on the other hand, could not completely disengage itself from the Bureau's province. It was a question of primary focus and specialization.

be eliminated or at least combined with it, since its functions were encompassed within the latter's authority. It is possible that had OWM preceded OES in time, no such organization as OES would have been created.

However, OES continued to operate. When Byrnes was appointed OWM director, Fred M. Vinson was appointed director of OES. His background and talents were remarkably similar to those of his predecessor. He too had served in both legislative and judicial branches of the Federal government before entering the executive. He had served as Congressman from Kentucky for 13 years and held the influential post of chairman of the Tax Subcommittee of the House Ways and Means Committee, before Roosevelt appointed him to the Circuit Court of Appeals for the District of Columbia in 1938. He was called directly from the Federal judiciary to serve as director of OES.

Since the authority of OWM was clearly supreme there was in a sense no conflict of jurisdiction between the two agencies. The question was really whether a sub-coördinating agency was needed. Apparently both Byrnes and Vinson felt it was not. After the OWMR legislation passed, Byrnes wrote the President:

Some days ago Fred Vinson suggested to me that the Office of Economic Stabilization should be placed under the Office of War Mobilization and Reconversion. From the attached Law, you will see that the Congress placed under this Office the Office of Contract Settlement, Surplus War Property Administration and the Retraining and Reëmployment Administration.

Vinson suggests, and I agree, that OES should in the same manner be placed under the Mobilization Office. The enclosed order represents our views. You will note that it provides that the Stabilization Director shall, in addition to the duties heretofore performed by him, exercise such other functions as shall be prescribed by the Mobilization Director.

In urging this action Vinson states that while he and I have never had a difference, that the conflict in the duties of the two offices is such that but for the close personal relationship existing between us, conflicts would be unavoidable. He thinks that while the situation is good, as it is at the present time, OES should be placed on the same footing with the other offices named in the Act. At the same time I could authorize him to participate in some of the work of this Office which he thinks would be interesting to him.[41]

The President did not act upon the advice of Messrs. Byrnes and Vinson. Roosevelt apparently felt that since the two offices

[41] Memorandum, November 29, 1944.

were getting along quite well, as Byrnes had indicated, he ought to leave well enough alone. Many people, including some former OES officers, also felt there were distinct advantages to a system of "spreading the heat." They argued that instead of having OWMR handle directly the numerous difficult problems with which OES had to deal and which generally involved assuaging potent pressure groups, there were advantages in a filtering process which allowed for the "safety-valve" effect of a decision by Vinson. If so great a crisis developed that an appeal came to OWMR over the OES decision, it strengthened the government's hand to have an independent decision from Byrnes. The combined prestige of the two men in independent offices was most difficult to override by any dissident groups. Nevertheless, these advantages were saving graces in a somewhat illogical administrative pattern, largely the accident of chronology.

When Vinson left OES to become Federal Loan Administrator, a man already identified with OWMR, Will Davis of the OWMR Advisory Board and former chairman of the National War Labor Board, was chosen to head up the Office of Economic Stabilization. Vinson shortly thereafter became director of OWMR, so that once again the OWMR director was an ex-director of OES.

When, after the war, Davis left OES, the President placed OES within OWMR and wrote a public letter to Davis in which he indicated that Davis had recommended such a step:

. . . I have also accepted the view which you repeatedly expressed to me in our several conferences that with the war over reconversion and stabilization became essentially one problem.[42]

With the war at an end, relations between the agencies were not always harmonious. Some later disputes on economic policy led to another separation until finally in August 1946, the offices were merged and John Steelman was made director of both stabilization and reconversion.

To the excellent personal relationship of the directors of both offices must go credit for the remarkable absence of conflict between OES and OWM—OWMR before 1946.

[42] Letter, September 19, 1945. It appears, however, that Davis more probably had in mind an actual merging of the two offices rather than the establishment of OES as a separate unit within OWMR.

JOINT CHIEFS OF STAFF

When OWM was established, some of its original staff members believed that the director should be represented at the top level of the Joint Chiefs of Staff which not only passed on all military procurement objectives but held prime responsibility for over-all military strategy. According to Fred Searls, Jr., the creation of OWM was in some measure related to the President's vague dissatisfaction with the Joint Chiefs of Staff. He gave as evidence the President's denial of a request by the Joint Chiefs for an executive order legalizing its functions and authority, the President's request for improved "logistic" control of the determinations of the Joint Chiefs, and "his nearly contemporaneous and entirely unsolicited instruction to you [Byrnes] to review the shipbuilding program and the shore and advanced base program of the Navy." [43]

Byrnes could not vigorously insist on a civilian voice in the Joint Chiefs' meetings. He was hampered by the fact that the Services, particularly the Navy, resisted civilian participation in military secrets. Establishment of the procurement review boards and creation within JCS of the Joint Production Survey Committee with representation from OWM were a compromise between full integration of procurement and production planning with military strategy and the earlier situation where no civilian agency coördination with military planning existed.[44]

From the point of view of members of Byrnes's staff who were anxious to see close supervision of the procurement policies of the Services, OWM relations with the Joint Chiefs were not always satisfactory. Searls, for example, regarded the Joint Chiefs as a rival to OWM in certain respects and as a military obstacle to a clear line of authority between the civilian agency, OWM, and the civilian heads of the Army and Navy. The handling of rela-

[43] Memorandum, Fred Searls, Jr. to James F. Byrnes, February 24, 1945. Searls maintained that one of the weaknesses of JCS was its reliance upon relatively junior officers for drawing up strategic plans which were merely initialed by senior officers. He said junior officers were "often subject to the bias and 'party line' of the service to which they belonged and not necessarily of sufficient maturity and experience to exercise the functions and wield the actual authority, which the Nation never conferred upon them or knew they ever had."

[44] For fuller detail see Chapter 4, pp. 117–125.

tions with the Joint Chiefs of Staff was the foremost challenge of the OWM job—it was the general area in which WPB had met its strongest rebuffs. Byrnes was, however, able to establish his authority over JCS on matters of supply despite difficult situations which continued to arise throughout the war.

LIAISON WITH CONGRESS

The directors of OWM–OWMR—especially Byrnes and Vinson —were sometimes asked to fill in the essential liaison functions between President and Congress. To illustrate, when the administration was carrying on its fight in 1943 against likely passage of the Ruml plan, involving a one-year tax moratorium, Byrnes integrated the government's opposition and represented the executive branch in day-to-day negotiations with Congress. In part, this probably reflected the President's recognition of the Secretary of the Treasury's lack of popularity on the Hill. It also indicated that in matters of highest urgency the administration saw the advantage of sending to Congress a man recognized as the President's spokesman and able to speak for all parts of the executive branch.

A situation of this kind would, however, naturally upset a Cabinet officer when the issue was clearly within his province, and it would not be conducive to helping his long-range relationships with Congress. The record indicates that both Byrnes and Vinson recognized the delicacy of the situation and stepped in only at the President's specific request.

On the other hand, departments sometimes asked the directors to use their influence to intercede for them with Congress, on departmental affairs.[45] The directors generally did not feel this was their proper function and tended to avoid such action.

At a much later date, President Truman decided to set up, through OWMR, formal machinery for coördinating relationships of the executive departments with Congress to advance the administration's legislative program sent to Congress on September 6, 1945. He wrote to Director Snyder:

In order to coördinate the whole program I want the Office of War Mobilization and Reconversion, in coöperation with the Bureau of the

[45] For example, in a memorandum to Byrnes, June 17, 1943, the Secretary of Labor said, "As I told you on the telephone, the cut in our requested appropriation is very serious in some particulars and I ask your help in securing restoration of these funds in the Senate . . ."

Budget, to watch the course of the various proposals, to resolve differences which may arise where several agencies are interested in the legislation, and in general to render all possible assistance to the agencies charged with specific responsibility for various parts of the program.

I have asked the various departments and agencies to report to me on the first and fifteenth of each month showing current developments and problems on legislation. I have also asked that copies of these reports be sent to you in order that you may coördinate the whole administration program on legislation.[46]

The device was not successful and did not endure. This was primarily due, of course, to the fact that congressional sentiment was opposed to the specific program, but it was also clear that OWMR was not designed for that type of political work and was a poor instrument for it. Such success as had been achieved in the war days was due to the general momentum of the war program and to Byrnes's and Vinson's skillful personal relations with Congress as former popular members of that brotherhood. Experience indicates that this important aspect of the President's job requires a special kind of political assistance and cannot be effectively regularized by an institutional staff arm designed for other purposes.

The OWM period came to a formal end in October 1944 when the President signed the bill creating the Office of War Mobilization and Reconversion. Although the provisions of the statute and the scope of the OWMR gave some ground for impression that a new agency was making its appearance, the carry-over of the top personnel of OWM made the transition easy and unspectacular. It was a new agency largely in name. As new directors came on the scene and the character of the period changed, more decided revisions in the concept and area of OWMR's activities emerged.

[46] Letter, October 18, 1945.

CHAPTER 3

OFFICE OF WAR MOBILIZATION
AND RECONVERSION

*E*arly in 1944, Congress began to consider plans for an agency to handle the difficult problems of reconversion and demobilization. As military victory seemed assured, problems of the transition to peace began to gain ascendancy. The hasty, unplanned demobilization and reconversion after World War I was recalled by congressmen who hoped to avoid a repetition of the errors of the earlier period. Contract termination and the disposition of surplus property were the first subjects to gain congressional attention, but gradually the entire range of problems, from human demobilization to relaxation of wartime controls, came under consideration.

There was another reason for early congressional interest in reconversion. During the mobilization period the legislature had surrendered many powers to the executive. Now that the danger point had passed, Congress was restive, eager to reassert its own authority. It was determined that reconversion be directed by legislation and not by executive order. Justice Byrnes, a former Senator, understood this sentiment. Appearing before a special Senate committee in November 1943, shortly after he had set up the Baruch postwar planning unit, he stated his objectives modestly. He said that the President had asked him, as Director of War Mobilization, to work out uniform policies for the executive departments with regard to termination of war contracts and disposition of surplus property. Senator Vandenberg immediately asked whether Byrnes was indicating that an executive order would soon be forthcoming. Byrnes assured him he knew of no such order and, in conciliatory fashion, said he was anxious that Congress share the job with him and that he foresaw the need for legislation on some reconversion issues.

Later evidence indicates that the legislation which converted

OWM into OWMR was not entirely welcome to the President. According to testimony of those close to the situation, both Roosevelt and Byrnes considered the legislative device inferior to the executive order approach even at this stage of the war, but, sensitive to the temper of Congress, they coöperated freely, thus influencing the final act more than they might have otherwise.[1]

OWM's Baruch-Hancock Report, which appeared in February 1944, was warmly received by Congress. Stressing the need for congressional leadership in planning postwar readjustments, the Report helped to subdue suspicions regarding intentions of the executive branch. The Baruch-Hancock analysis of the chief reconversion issues—settlement of war contracts, disposition of surplus property, relaxation of wartime controls, curtailment of war production, resumption of civilian production, and the human side of demobilization—became the focus of congressional planning.[2]

Meanwhile, Congress had independently undertaken serious study of reconversion through Special Committees on Post-War Economic Policy and Planning, in both houses. These Committees, chaired by Senator George and Representative Colmer, together with the Senate Committee on Military Affairs, and the Senate Special Committee Investigating the National Defense Program, were primarily responsible for the legislative developments which led to establishiment of the Office of War Mobilization and Reconversion on October 3, 1944.

So intent was Congress on treating reconversion policy as a unit that it might have passed a single comprehensive law to cover all reconversion matters, had not political necessity dictated separate enactment of the contract settlement and surplus property disposal bills. In spite of splitting-off those two subjects, the

[1] This view was confirmed in personal interviews with Wayne Coy, former Administrative Assistant to the President (August 12, 1946), James Doyle, long-time associate of Byrnes (July 22, 1946), and others.

[2] Congress was also impressed by professional and lay predictions of heavy transitional unemployment. Many legislative proposals and much congressional debate were devoted to the alleviation of anticipated unemployment. Despite OWM advocacy of liberalized unemployment compensation benefits, no such measure was passed, although Title IV of the OWMR Act permitted advances to States from the Federal Fund to meet unemployment compensation obligations.

Act which established OWMR was an omnibus law, and, as might be expected, was enacted only after months of discussion, wrangling, and amendment. The final Act[3] was a compromise consisting of portions of the numerous bills which had been discussed by the Senate[4] and almost the whole of the third report of the Colmer Committee.[5]

FUNCTIONS OF THE NEW AGENCY

The Colmer Committee had concluded, in its fourth report, that central policy guidance was required for liquidation of war production, demobilization, and reconversion. The new legislation embodied this objective and generally followed the pattern set by the OWM executive order. It was deeply influenced by the OWM experience. The final version of the Act rejected the idea that OWMR should be an operating agency as well as the suggestion that an Office of Demobilization be set up side by side with the existing Office of War Mobilization. It was evident throughout that Congress intended complete continuity between OWM and OWMR.

The law granted the director the same type of sweeping powers. The Act, in fact, probably represents the broadest delegation of authority ever granted by Congress to an executive agency. In addition to the director's powers to coördinate the nation's war mobilization, the law provided that subject to the President's direction he should:

(1) formulate or have formulated reconversion plans;
(2) issue orders and regulations to executive agencies regarding reconversion plans (the agencies were specifically ordered to carry out such directives);
(3) recommend to Congress appropriate reconversion legislation;
(4) develop procedures to inform executive agencies of proposed demobilization and reconversion plans and settle controversies between executive agencies in the development and administration of such plans;

[3] 78th Cong., 2nd Sess., *PL 458*, October 3, 1944.
[4] The chief measures considered by the Senate were S. 1730, the Murray-George Bill; S. 1823 and S. 1893, the Kilgore Bills; S. 2051, the George Bill; and S. 2061, the Murray-Kilgore Bill. (78th Cong., 2nd Sess.) S. 2051 and S. 2061 were merged to some extent and, together with the House proposals, developed into *PL 458*.
[5] 78th Cong., 2nd Sess., House, Special Committee on Post-War Economic Policy and Planning, *Third Report*.

(5) determine which war agencies should be simplified, consolidated or eliminated and which should be transferred from an executive order status to a statutory basis;[6]

(6) determine the need for relaxation or removal of emergency war controls;

(7) institute a specific study, for submission to the President and Congress, of the present functions of the various executive agencies concerned with manpower and develop a program for reorganizing and consolidating such agencies to the fullest extent practicable;

(8) consult and coöperate with State and local governments, industry, labor, agriculture and other groups concerning reconversion problems and methods of achieving the objectives of the Act;

(9) submit quarterly reports to the President and the Congress summarizing and appraising the activities of the various executive agencies in the field of demobilization and post war adjustment;

(10) with regard to contract termination:

    (a) determine whether any prime contract for war production, scheduled for termination, should be continued either to benefit the government or avoid substantial physical injury to a plant or property;

    (b) establish policies to be followed by the contracting agencies in selecting individual contracts or classes of contracts for curtailment, nonrenewal, or termination; and

    (c) establish policies providing for consultation between the executive agencies and war contractors.

In spite of the fact that the 1944 law placed several subsidiary agencies—the Retraining and Reëmployment Administration, the Surplus Property Board, and the Office of Contract Settlement—within OWMR, they were treated almost as independent bodies. In making this arrangement, Congress was establishing no precedent, for OWM's status as exclusively a policy-making, super-coördinating body had already been marred by giving it responsibility for two of these agencies.

The extent of their participation in OWMR affairs was generally limited to attendance by their directors, General Hines, Mr. Clayton, and Mr. Hinckley, at OWMR staff meetings. However, the arrangement proved awkward and OWMR took the initiative in planning their transfer, in two cases successfully. RRA went to the Labor Department by executive order in September

[6] Assignment of this task to OWMR was an unwise duplication of functions of the Budget Bureau. The same was true of item (7) in this list. Difficulties were generally avoided, however, by OWMR's recognition of the more appropriate jurisdiction of the Bureau.

1945. The surplus property functions were similarly transferred in January 1946 to RFC's War Assets Corporation and later to War Assets Administration. The Office of Contract Settlement remained a part of OWMR, but the course of the agency was so smooth and efficient that no difficulties were encountered and OCS was independent in all but form.

A series of executive orders during the next two years added to OWMR functions, usually through special assignments. Among these was Executive Order 9568 of June 8, 1945 which brought OWMR directly into the scientific field by giving the director power to review classified scientific information which had been developed by or for the government, to make recommendations to the Secretaries of War and Navy for its release and to take measures to effect publication of the information. Later these powers were extended to enemy scientific and industrial information.[7]

The following year OWMR responsibility in this field was broadened when the President designated its director chairman of his Scientific Research Board. He was directed to report on the Federal research program, and to make suggestions for improving its administration and coördination with non-Federal research development and training activities.[8]

The range and character of OWMR functions placed it in a unique and leading position. Virtually no issue of consequence was regarded as outside its purview. Like its predecessor, OWM, it was in effect, despite some awkwardness in the legislative mandate, the central coördinating arm of the executive branch, physically and symbolically located in the White House.

OWMR ORGANIZATION

The internal organization of OWMR differed from that of OWM in three important respects. The legislation did not include the War Mobilization Committee, it established an Advisory

[7] By a delegation of authority from OWMR, the Inter-Departmental Publications Board, established in the Commerce Department, and its operating arm, the Office of Declassification and Technical Services, were made responsible for collecting and disseminating technical and scientific information accumulated during the War by United States scientists and former enemy nations.

[8] A five-volume report was published a year later: The President's Scientific Research Board, *Science and Public Policy,* Government Printing Office, 1947.

Board composed of non-government personnel, and the new functions of OWMR required expansion of the tiny staff and a more formal pattern of organization.

The professional staff soon began to grow although OWMR continued to perform its functions largely through the facilities and personnel of other agencies. One month after OWMR was created the total staff numbered sixteen. In June 1945 there were eighty. Peak strength was reached in May 1946 when the Office proper had 146 employees. By December 1946 it was down to 106.

As the agency expanded a new type of personnel was recruited. Instead of relying exclusively on top-level personal assistants to the director, the Office began to hire additional staff for these assistants, thus developing an administrative hierarchy. It meant the addition of technicians—economists and statisticians, at first, later, lawyers and information specialists. Although versatility remained a prime characteristic, nevertheless, as staff increased, a greater degree of specialization appeared.

In the opinion of some staff members as well as outside observers, OWMR was always too small for its job and was particularly weak in its lack of statistical-analytical personnel. It was also charged that poor organization within the Office led to excessive attendance at meetings, lack of sufficient specialization and overlapping of activity. However, more prevalent is the view that the special status and prestige of such an agency is dependent partially upon a small and relatively unspecialized staff. When personnel is enlarged there is a tendency—from which OWMR did not entirely escape—to reach into issues of insufficient significance for the attention of the director. This in itself has some tendency to dilute the status of an "over-all" agency. In addition such developments result in staff members making decisions in the name of the agency and thus, in effect, placing themselves in a higher status than heads of other agencies. Shortly after the end of the war, some resentment by executive agencies resulted from this type of activity by a few staff members.

THE DIRECTORS AND CHANGING TIMES

The Office of War Mobilization and Reconversion had four directors during its brief two-year span of life. Byrnes, despite his publicly expressed intention to depart when the legislation was passed, was persuaded by the President to remain. Although he resigned one month before V–E Day, he may be regarded as director through the two-front war period. Fred M. Vinson, who succeeded him on April 2, 1945, remained until shortly before the Japanese surrender. His regime encompassed all of the one-front war period. The third director, John W. Snyder, served almost a full year, through the major transition period of industrial reconversion. John R. Steelman was appointed director in June 1946 and remained until December, when the agency was, in effect, terminated.

BYRNES STAYS ON

During his directorship, Byrnes maintained the same relationship to the President as he had under OWM and continued to be known generally as "Assistant President." There was no break in continuity between OWM and OWMR and most patterns of operations and relationships, set under OWM, were continued under the new legislation.

No real expansion occurred until the middle of December 1944 when the Battle of the Bulge dramatized the continuing need for war production. Byrnes then asked the War Department for assignment of Major General Lucius D. Clay, previously director of materiel of the Army Service Forces, to organize the enlarged office and spearhead the new production drive. Administrative responsibility for the entire staff was lodged in General Clay whose presence in the agency caused some circles to suspect the development of a "pro-military" bias. Byrnes, however, regarded Clay as an extraordinarily able administrator and there is little evidence that his presence caused OWMR to favor the military.[9]

With General Clay came the first organization chart in OWM–OWMR history and the first tendency to regard the agency as an organization rather than Byrnes's personal office. In keeping with its expanded functions, several new key positions were created. In addition to his over-all supervisory functions, Clay was also deputy director for war programs, the central position under

[9] Byrnes told the President "I . . . obtained his assignment to my office, because, after dealing with officials of all the departments, I had found no man more capable than Clay and no army officer who had as clear an understanding of the point of view of the civilian." (*Speaking Frankly*, p. 47.)

Byrnes. Another deputy director, John B. Hutson, was in charge of agricultural programs, primarily for reorienting farm production to peacetime conditions.[10] Byrnes's old law partner and OWM assistant, Donald Russell, was recalled from the Army in France, and Benjamin Cohen continued in the key position of general counsel.

The chief divisions under Clay were Manpower Liaison and Coördination headed by William Haber, former assistant executive director of WMC; Information and Reports, headed by Joseph A. Livingston who edited the quarterly reports which added much to OWMR prestige; Production Liaison and Coördination, under Fred Searls, Jr., who continued from OWM; and Planning, under Thomas C. Blaisdell, who came from WPB's Planning Committee. The staff remained small and most division chiefs had only one or two assistants. General Clay was the only official with authority to make decisions in Byrnes's name. In general, Byrnes wanted agency heads to know that decisions rendered by his office were his own, and were to be accepted as final and authoritative.

As long as the war in Europe continued, OWMR devoted its major efforts to war production and the final victory drive, the chief area of concern during this period being manpower shortages (discussed in Chapter 5). However, as later chapters describe, it was not remiss in its concern with reconversion and trimming the over-expansive plans of the military.

Dramatic swings in the tides of war caused considerable confusion and some sharp policy reversals. Successful invasion of the continent in the spring of 1944 and the rapid military progress which followed lead to a modest program of reconversion in August 1944 after some of the bitterest inter-agency feuds of the war (See Chapter 6). The stretching of supply lines and alleged materiel shortages, which followed, and finally the setbacks in the Battle of the Bulge, put a temporary end to reconversion steps. A series of special measures for fuel and manpower conservation—involving a ban on horse-racing, the "brown out" program, and restrictions on conventions—was sponsored by OWMR. But, throughout, with the outcome of the war only a question of

[10] Mr. Hutson's personal status as former Under-Secretary of Agriculture probably accounts for the special position given to agricultural programs, as distinguished from manpower liaison and coördination, for example, which was set up as a division under Deputy Director Clay.

time, OWMR was deeply involved in planning for contract cut-backs and decontrol measures after V–E Day, and anticipating special new difficulties which V–E Day was expected to aggravate rather than reduce, such as railroad transportation, shipping, economic stabilization, food distribution, foreign economic operations, and housing.

Adjudication and coördination continued to be the primary administrative approaches, but, as in the later days of OWM, the accelerated crises which arose with prolongation of the war forced more aggressive participation in early stages of inter-agency work and more direct formulation of policies. In the brief period between December 1944 and April 1945, when OWMR was under the leadership of Byrnes and Clay, the agency became more aggressive and took the initiative in a larger number of issues, beginning a new trend which was later to lead it into somewhat lower-level activity.

However, avoidance of operations and the normal difficulties and inter-relationships among agencies remained a prime characteristic of the Office. The tiny top-level staff gave assurance that none but the most crucial problems would occupy OWMR time. Byrnes continued to feel, despite some criticism, that the more general types of long-range planning belonged in the individual agencies, and thus the Planning Division of OWMR played a very minor role under Byrnes. Thomas Blaisdell, the division's chief, resigned after a short period.

VINSON'S BRIEF REGIME

When victory in Europe appeared certain, Byrnes was at last permitted to resign from government office, effective April 2, 1945. The choice of Judge Fred M. Vinson as his successor was almost inevitable.

Vinson, who had moved from OES to head the Federal Loan Agency only a few weeks earlier,[11] had had the same long years of legislative and judicial experience as his predecessor. He was highly regarded for his political shrewdness, courage, and effectiveness. As Economic Stabilizer, Vinson achieved great prestige for his willingness to stand firm against pressure and influence,

[11] Vinson's remarkable sweep from head of OES to Federal Loan Administrator, to head of OWMR, to Secretary of the Treasury, to Chief Justice of the Supreme Court was all accomplished in little more than one year.

as he did in the railway wage case.[12] His designation to OWMR was the last major appointment made by President Roosevelt, two weeks before his death.

During his brief directorship, Vinson displayed, in general, the same judicial approach as had Byrnes. He too regarded himself primarily, but not exclusively, as a judge settling conflicts between contending parties, but under him OWMR began to move ahead of the agencies in planning, and to establish closer relationships to the operations of individual agencies. As an operator he proved to be remarkably effective. He too exhibited the effects of a previous background in legislative and judicial work rather than in the executive branch. His excellent relations with Congress were, as in the case of Byrnes, a great boon to the agency.

A tendency which had begun with Clay's arrival reached some fruition in the Vinson period. Instead of a "one-man show," the organization developed in the more orthodox agency fashion. Vinson revealed more interest in staff organization than his predecessor and was more willing to rely upon and delegate authority to his deputies.

The growing importance of reconversion was reflected in internal reorganization and appearance of new faces. Vinson brought with him from OES, Edward Prichard, Jr., with the title of general counsel of OWMR. However, Prichard was really a close personal over-all assistant to Vinson and played a paramount policy-making role. At Prichard's suggestion, Robert R. Nathan, former chairman of WPB's Planning Committee, was brought in as deputy director for Reconversion, filling a post which up to that time had been vacant. Donald Russell became deputy director for War Programs and John B. Hutson remained deputy director for Agriculture.

The division of functions between Russell and Nathan was based on the idea that war-connected matters, such as military procurement, production, transportation, foreign operations, demobilization planning and cutback procedures should remain under Russell while economic stabilization, employment, surplus

[12] Jonathan Daniels tells a story about Vinson. Frank Graham, then President of the University of North Carolina and member of the War Labor Board, asked Vinson for "the secret of your rugged immobility." " 'You know,' he said, 'where I come from it was dangerous to be afraid.' " (Jonathan Daniels, *Frontier on the Potomac*, Macmillan, 1946, p. 156.)

disposition, and elimination of production controls should be under Nathan's direction. Inevitably, with the decline of the war, the latter's functions and staff became increasingly important and were dominant by the time John Snyder became director.

Under Nathan's leadership, the Office for Reconversion attracted a group of young men with a New Deal slant and greater faith in general planning than had been visible in the agency before. Vinson gave this office relatively free rein and through its planning for reconversion after V–J Day and frequent inter-agency meetings, it exercised considerable influence. It was a period during which staff freedom resulted in extraordinary independent initiative. This had its virtues and its difficulties. It was a period of humming activity and leadership. But sensitivity about administrative prerogatives resulted in some agency resentment about rulings apparently made by personnel below Vinson, leaving room for the suspicion they had not received the director's personal attention.

Despite the fact that Vinson remained at OWMR only three months, he influenced greatly the direction of the agency's work. The brief period covered a vital span—from V–E Day to just before V–J Day. The largest issues facing him involved the extent to which wartime controls could be abandoned before V–J Day, the extent of curtailment of military procurement for a one-front war, and preparation for full-scale reconversion after V–J Day. Some sharp differences on the first issue appeared within the administration. WPB favored more rapid decontrol than did OWMR and pressure for such action was rapidly gaining momentum. But, for the most part these matters remained in the study stage during the Vinson period and the real heat was directed toward his successors.

The approaching end of the war called for a more aggressive review of military production programs and enabled recommendations of cut-backs with greater confidence. More vigorous protection and expansion of the civilian economy was feasible and desirable. The end of one phase of the war also meant that more attention had to be devoted to section 202 of the Reconversion Act of 1944 which concerned certification by OWMR of war contracts no longer essential to conduct of the war but which should be continued because their performance benefited the government or avoided substantial physical injury to a plant or property.

Problems of economic stabilization became more difficult with increasing inflationary pressures complicated by fear of the alleged deflationary influence of the end of the war. Fear of widespread unemployment was reflected in a public request by President Truman that OWMR undertake a study of unemployment compensation in terms of its adequacy to meet the predicted crisis.

These knotty reconversion problems led OWMR to initiate much wider use of inter-agency committees, which it chaired, and more direct follow-up and staff work to insure that policies were carried out. Conflicts between agencies did not subside and on one occasion the President was obliged to make a public request that Vinson adjudicate a nasty impasse between the War Food Administration and OPA.

Despite aggressive and affirmative actions on many fronts, Vinson ended his stay without substantial attacks from any quarter.[13] He left OWMR with his reputation for wisdom, balance, and forthrightness unsullied. His appointment to the Cabinet, as Secretary of the Treasury, in July 1945 was highly acclaimed.

JOHN SNYDER CARRIES ON

President Truman's appointment of John W. Snyder as OWMR director in July 1945 came less than a month before the end of the war and heralded a new period—peace and decontrol.

Snyder's appointment was regarded in some ways as a break from the previous tradition of directors except in the vital element of closeness to and complete confidence of the President. His background and personality were different from those of his predecessors, although, like Vinson, he came to the job from the directorship of the Federal Loan Agency. He was a relative newcomer to Washington, lacking Byrnes's and Vinson's long political experience and intimacy with Congress. Although he was not new to Government service, he had served mainly in St. Louis and had not achieved national prominence until shortly before coming to OWMR.

---

[13] Coming after V-E Day, some of Vinson's activities involving the lifting of restrictions rather than their imposition—such as the curfew, the brownout, and the ban on horse-racing—were inevitably popular.

Snyder regarded himself primarily as a businessman. A close friend of President Truman, dating back to World War I days, he had been a banker in Missouri and Arkansas and for some years had held responsible positions with the RFC loan agency in St. Louis. He became executive vice-president and director of the Defense Plant Corporation in 1940. In this position he was reported to have differed with his superior, Jesse Jones, on the speed with which war plants were being built in 1940–41. According to reports, Jones was anxious to finance new construction conservatively and "soundly," while Snyder, convinced that war was imminent, favored building them at any cost.[14] Nevertheless, Snyder's banking background opened him to immediate suspicion from New Dealers and others to whom he represented a conservative trend and a break with the Roosevelt tradition.

Snyder was a modest and retiring director of OWMR, avoiding exercise of authority over other agencies. He shied away from the issuance of directives, formal or informal. He tried to avoid publicity. Rather than head of a powerful agency, he appeared primarily as a personal adviser to and representative of the President. While this improved his standing in some circles it hurt him with those who felt that more affirmative action was called for. Some members of his own staff shared this view and it led to considerable gossiping in the "columns" about White House intrigue involving OWMR.

Snyder undertook no immediate staff reorganization, but rapid shifts in personnel occurred as the war ended and many persons returned to their peacetime pursuits. Two former deputies, Russell and Hutson, left with Vinson. Snyder brought one of his former associates, Hans Klagsbrunn, to OWMR from RFC to act as deputy director and second in command. The other deputies were Robert Nathan for Reconversion, Anthony Hyde for Information and Reports, and Lieutenant General L. H. Campbell, former Chief of Ordnance in the Army, for Production. The last-named was appointed in September 1945 with the task of clearing the factories and plants for peacetime production. A relatively large military staff came and departed with General Campbell, whose job did not present any special difficulties, and who left within a few months. Nathan also resigned at the end of the year, so that

[14] *Newsweek,* April 30, 1945, p. 46.

two chief offices were vacant. Thereafter, top staff members continued to resign faster than they were replaced, leaving the Office with a smaller staff when John Steelman took over in mid-1946.

There were differences of opinion between Snyder and some of his top staff due in part to the fact that they were largely inherited rather than his own appointees, and in part reflecting the growing division throughout the government concerning the rate at which decontrol should be undertaken. The schism in the organization, which came to be known outside the agency, marred its effectiveness. In general, many of the professional staff, led by Nathan, subscribed to less rapid relaxation of government controls than the director. These philosophic differences, while serious, would not have been sufficient to cause the deep lacerations which occurred had they not been accompanied by some basic suspicions involving competence and loyalty to the director.

Shortly after he took office, Snyder issued a special report to the President, prepared by the staff, which forecast a transitional deflationary period, involving considerable unemployment, and predicated policy recommendations on these forecasts.[15] Snyder had a predisposition against this point of view in the first instance, and when the predictions turned out to be invalid and injurious to the agency, he built up a resistance to all staff studies and recommendations. On top of that, there occurred some leaks to the press on intra-office matters, which were highly embarrassing, and Snyder shared the general suspicion that staff members were responsible, despite their denial.[16] An atmosphere of distrust developed which kept the staff from knowing what the director was planning or doing on many vital matters. By the end of 1945 Director Snyder and Deputy Nathan had a much more distant personal relationship than their official posts required. A close observer said that OWMR was having more trouble coördinating itself than in coördinating the rest of the government.

Nathan's departure helped clear the atmosphere, and a reorganization of the Office took place in January 1946. Seven staff

[15] John W. Snyder, *From War to Peace: A Challenge,* Government Printing Office, August 15, 1945.
[16] One notable instance occurred during October 1945 when a confidential study of the staff indicated that industry should be able to grant considerable wage increases without increasing prices. The press had the story almost immediately and very sharp criticism followed.

divisions were created, all to operate directly under the deputy director. The seven divisions were Foreign Operations and Surplus Property, Stabilization Controls, Manpower and Veterans Affairs, Fiscal Policy and Program Analysis, Science, Construction, and Agriculture. The director's office included the general counsel with a staff of lawyers, an economic adviser, and a sizable information staff. The increasing use of legal and information personnel differentiated Snyder's staff from that of his predecessors.

Under the general counsel, a Section 202 Review Committee was assigned to review war production contracts which were subject to termination. The Reconversion Working Committee continued the work started under Nathan. In addition, the Office of the Housing Expediter, under Wilson W. Wyatt, was established in OWMR prior to being set up as an independent body.

Both the temper of the staff and the attitude of the director pointed toward increasing organization of, and participation in, inter-agency committees which operated at two levels—among agency heads and among the working staff members. There was also less aloofness from the day-to-day activities of other agencies. The former strategy of acting as adjudicator was augmented by more generalized participation in formulating policies and working with other agencies before the "final decision" stage. A disposition against issuing of instructions to other agencies and avoiding as many issues as possible contributed to a recession in OWMR's earlier over-all central role. In part, Snyder appeared to desire this change. This, plus his lack of the kind of personal prestige enjoyed by Byrnes and Vinson, reduced the agency's status.

In many ways Snyder's job proved tougher than that of his predecessors. The unity within the government—the single drive to "win the war"—was over, and normal cleavages, interest groups, and divergent economic philosophies began to reassert themselves.

The long list of OWMR actions during Snyder's term indicates the nature of post V–J Day problems: economic decontrol, demobilization of troops, recruitment of railroad workers, stimulation of coal production and transportation, cancellation of war contracts, and development of administrative machinery for control of atomic energy. Through OWMR leadership on inter-agency committees, swift action was taken on many of these problems. On the coal shortage, for example, OWMR, in concert with Solid Fuels Administration, the War Department, WPB, and WMC, drew up a seven-point program to make manpower available to the coal mines, reduce absenteeism, increase food rations for miners, supply mining equipment, and provide coal cars.

When V–J Day came, the Office promptly announced its reconversion policy in its report, *From War to Peace: A Challenge,* and an Inter-Agency Reconversion Working Committee was established. The government's policy concerning wartime controls during the transition was formulated by OWMR. It stated that controls would be continued only to assure war production as long as needed, to facilitate the flow of materials into civilian production, to give small business equal chance to compete for civilian markets, and to protect the economy of the nation against inflation. This policy proved easier to formulate than to administer.

Pressure for removal of controls on industry grew by leaps and bounds. Even within the government there was considerable disagreement over the rate and timing. Snyder was frequently attacked as "pro-business," particularly in connection with construction and housing problems and price control. In general, he was considered to favor more rapid decontrol than had Vinson, for which he was simultaneously denounced and praised in different quarters. In any event, it was a period in which the tide of public opinion was forcing the administration to abandon effective controls much more rapidly than it thought wise.

A dramatic episode illustrates some of the general confusion. An issue arose as to whether Order L–41, the wartime regulation controlling construction materials, should be dropped. In July 1945, Snyder appointed Hugh L. Potter of Texas, a past president of the National Association of Real Estate Boards, as Construction Coördinator in OWMR. On September 1, Potter recommended removal of L–41. After several inter-agency meetings, Snyder announced that L–41 would be repealed effective October 15.[17] Almost immediately a hue and cry arose and the action was condemned as a disastrous blow to housing. Later events indicated that a mistake had indeed been made, and, at the request of

---

[17] Simultaneously, Snyder announced a six-point program to speed expansion of the construction industry.

OWMR, the Civilian Production Administration (successor to WPB after November 1945) issued Priorities Regulation 33 in December to bring scarce materials back under control, in effect a return to the principle of the abandoned L-41.

Potter's motives were publicly questioned in congressional hearings[18] and Snyder was sharply criticized for supporting him in dropping L-41. Yet, at the time, there had been considerable agreement, even among liberals, regarding the desirability of dropping the order. Will Davis, then Director of Economic Stabilization, put in writing his sentiment in favor of dropping it.[19] The Housing Administrator, John Blandford, favored keeping it in relaxed form for three additional months. Snyder's professional staff, led by Nathan, went along with the proposal because they felt that deflationary forces would soon be operative and that the demand for housing as well as materials would be less than it actually turned out to be. WPB Chairman Krug clearly favored the termination. Only OPA Administrator Chester Bowles strongly opposed the move. Had Snyder come to his decision by counting heads among the top interested government officials and his own staff he would have concluded to drop the order as he did.

The incident reveals the difficulty of accurately anticipating economic developments, of weighing contrary economic philosophies, and of deciding what governmental action is most likely to accelerate production, and meet other needs. It was a period in which severe criticism could not be avoided.

The housing problem remained a key issue and OWMR assumed leadership in organizing the emergency housing program. In his report to the President on December 8, 1945, the OWMR director recommended appointment of a special Housing Expediter with "responsibility for coördinating and expediting the housing program, and for recommending new steps that may be needed." Four days later, the President appointed a Housing Expediter within OWMR. CPA Priorities Regulation 33 was issued, on OWMR instructions, and a few days after that the OWMR director gave stern instructions to the War and Navy Departments

[18] 79th Cong., 2nd Sess., House, Committee on Banking and Currency, *Hearings on H.R. 4761,* December 1945—January 1946.
[19] Memorandum, Will H. Davis to John W. Snyder, September 17, 1945.

to suspend all construction not immediately essential in order to check the drain on supplies.

On January 26, 1946, the President issued Executive Order 9686, giving the Expediter broad authority to develop the emergency housing program, and, at the same time, the OWMR director delegated to him "all functions, powers, authority or duties vested in me by the War Mobilization and Reconversion Act of 1944" which were necessary to carry out his program, including "power to issue orders, regulations, or directives to other executive agencies." [20] The Patman Housing Act reaffirmed this transfer by statute a few months later. This directive and the legislation set a poor and unworkable administrative pattern. It was not clear whether OWMR was empowered to coördinate the Housing Expediter, who was no longer within OWMR.[21] Reconversion policies, affecting the economy in its entirety, could not be sliced into independent sections. Furthermore, it soon became clear that despite paper authority other agencies would not accept as binding, orders from an agency they considered to be on an equal plane. NHA's disputes with other agencies, such as CPA and RFC, always bounced up to OWMR for resolution.

Another decontrol problem involving inter-agency disagreement concerned wages. Between September 1945 and February 1946, OES was a subsidiary unit of OWMR and Snyder was deeply involved in the drafting of Executive Order 9651 of October 30, 1945 which clarified the government's policy of raising wages wherever possible without endangering stabilization controls. OWMR was also responsible for approving wage increases authorized by the War Labor Board in cases where maladjustments or inequities were interfering with effective transition to a peacetime economy.

OWMR's jurisdiction over wages and prices was short-lived, however. In early 1946 a major steel strike occurred. The steel companies insisted that the wage increase demanded by the union could not be granted without a price increase which appeared to "break the line" of price policy. Snyder favored a more generous

[20] OWMR Directive, January 26, 1946.
[21] The legislative debate indicates that Representative Patman clearly intended to make the Expediter a completely free agent, outside the jurisdiction of the OWMR.

price increase than Price Administrator Bowles. Although Snyder's view prevailed, the President made a public gesture which appeared to rebuke OWMR. OES was split off from OWMR and returned to its former independent status with Bowles designated director. This administrative change injured OWMR's prestige.

The Office was active in curtailing war production and in planning the liquidation and merger of war agencies. In August 1945, the President created the "SSR Committee" made up of John Snyder, chairman, Harold Smith, Director of the Budget, and Samuel Rosenman, "for the purpose of making recommendations to me, from time to time, on the proper disposition of the various war agencies." [22] Despite Snyder's chairmanship and the OWMR legislation conferring this function on the director, Snyder accepted the Budget Bureau's leading role in administrative organization and a good working relationship resulted.

Inter-agency committees, created and usually chaired by OWMR, flourished during late 1945. One was the Policy Committee on Rubber, headed by William L. Batt, formerly a vice-chairman of WPB. This Committee's objective was to develop a coördinated United States policy for an adequate supply of rubber, both natural and synthetic. Active committees were also set up to expedite shipment of wheat and coal to liberated areas. The Federal Inter-Agency Committee on Manpower Shortages made arrangements to permit key personnel required for reconversion activities to be released from the armed forces.

An Inter-Agency Committee on Veterans' Affairs, headed by OWMR and composed of ten high-ranking government officials, was named in April 1946 to expedite veterans' education, employment, training and rehabilitation. It undertook review of the problems presented by the extension of educational benefits under the "G.I. Bill of Rights" and a program of action by Federal agencies to make sure that the maximum number of veterans seeking higher education would be able to enter schools and colleges. OWMR prepared a comprehensive report on the veteran and higher education.[23] Effective action by various agencies followed and increased college facilities in many places.

---

[22] Letter, the President to John W. Snyder, August 21, 1945.
[23] John W. Snyder, *The Veteran and Higher Education,* A Report to the President, Government Printing Office, May 20, 1946.

It seemed for a brief period that OWMR might come to an end with Snyder's appointment as Secretary of the Treasury on June 6, 1946. When the appointment was announced, the President told the press that no new director would be appointed. The President's statement seemed to indicate that OWMR would be permitted to lapse and that only a few functions would be shifted to Chester Bowles, the director of OES. The OWMR Advisory Board was disturbed by the possibility that OWMR might go out of existence. Many agency heads and the press also opposed its end.[24] As a result of these representations, the President reconsidered and soon asked his special assistant, John R. Steelman, to assume the directorship. Dr. Steelman became OWMR director about ten days after the announcement of Snyder's shift to the Treasury.

The difficulties of a period of great national readjustment, general restiveness, outbursts of passions pent up during almost four years of war, and the resurgence of conflicting objectives were not conducive to easy maintenance of the kind of prestige which the agency had built up during the war years. With the apparent readiness of the President to give up the agency, whether intentional or accidental, an additional blow was struck at its status. When John Steelman took over in the summer of 1946, the agency's standing was relatively low.

FINAL DAYS UNDER STEELMAN

Dr. Steelman was groomed for the position of OWMR director through his work as special assistant to President Truman. A former professor of sociology at Alabama College, Steelman joined the United States Conciliation Service of the Department of Labor in 1934 and rose to become its director three years later, a post he held until 1944 when he resigned to establish a public relations firm in New York City. He was summoned back to Washington to become Truman's adviser in 1945. Steelman's previous work before coming to OWMR was largely confined to labor problems, but he was close to the President, on good terms with Congress and the press, and experienced in governmental affairs.

Although weakened by the President's first suggestion that the agency should lapse—this was somewhat counteracted by the ensuing good publicity—and by the gradual departure of key

²⁴ *N. Y. Times,* June 15, 1946.

staff members, OWMR's early days under Steelman were surprisingly vital. Steelman started out with vigor and apparent conviction that the agency could and should be the core of the executive branch.

He promptly undertook reorganization of the staff. Interest in organizational structure had waned during the previous year and the staff had become largely an array of individuals all reporting to the "boss." Steelman established three deputy directors, under whom the organization was to operate: Harold Stein, deputy director for Production, J. Donald Kingsley, deputy director for Employment, Veterans' Affairs, and Fiscal Policy—about twenty economists served under them—and Anthony Hyde, deputy director for Information, who had a fair-sized staff. A small legal office completed the professional personnel.

Whereas Snyder had let his effectiveness derive from the common knowledge of his friendship with the President, Steelman reverted to the Byrnes-Vinson approach which combined the role of Presidential confidant with active independent use of the Office and its great powers. On the other hand, Steelman's relationship to the President was relatively recent and, in the eyes of Washington officialdom, which measures such things carefully, still a little uncertain.

When he took over, there was still great public confusion regarding the speed and extent to which controls should be lifted and "normalcy" restored. The administration reflected the prevailing uncertainty and in general was in a state of retreat on this and other issues.

When the Price Control Extension Act was signed in July 1946, OWMR undertook a vigorous campaign to restore and maintain controls which had virtually lapsed during the bitter congressional debate. This role was emphasized by Steelman's appointment as stabilization director on July 25, 1946 and the virtual merging of OWMR and OES. Steelman restored many subsidies which had been suspended by expiration of the old price control law. But the congressional struggle during the summer had damaged the status of price controls beyond repair and as the preëlection decontrol pressure mounted, the administration was forced to yield. The President's price decontrol decision on November 9, immediately after election day, automatically ended most subsidy operations and stabilization measures.

Directives, issued mainly in his capacity as OES director, were widely used in the first months to coördinate the government's economic program. As part of the anti-inflation drive, Steelman ordered curtailment of Federal construction in order to keep within the President's budget. OWMR Directive 128 declared a moratorium on new contract awards between August 6 and October 1 during which time a review of all projects was undertaken in order to weed out the least essential ones.[25]

An imminent shutdown in shoe production, due to an almost complete stoppage of hide and leather distribution after price control was reimposed, produced a prompt reaction from OWMR. Bringing CPA and the Department of Justice into a concerted program to stop the withholding of hides from the market, Steelman in a strongly worded statement berated "hoarders who seek to extort excessive profits from the public by withholding production from the market." [26] He threatened the use of the administration's powers under the Second War Powers Act, and criminal and anti-trust laws. However, these powers were never used. A month later, Steelman announced a program to step up imports and hold exports of leather to a minimum. In a preëlection decontrol move at the end of October, however, he ordered the removal of price controls from hides, skins, and leather "in the best interests of production and supply to consumers."

These and similar activities in other crises revealed a wide use of press releases to obtain favorable public response and coöperation. They indicate Steelman's unenviable position in presiding over the expiration of the government's price control program. Time had been when an OWMR press announcement or mere "request" was generally as effective as a legal order in securing compliance, but such days were over for OWMR, as they were for the administration generally.

In settling the famous shipping strike in the fall of 1946, Steel-

[25] On October 19, Steelman announced that 14 agencies had been authorized to proceed with construction programs, representing a cut-back of $300,000,000 in the put-in-place values originally planned.
[26] *OWMR Press Release*, August 6, 1946.

man made a basic amendment to wage stabilization regulations which permitted wage increases to be given more freely than heretofore.[27] Although the decision was probably inevitable, embarrassment and loss of prestige were inflicted upon the Wage Stabilization Board (successor to WLB) which was placed in the position of having been publicly rebuked through a quick shift in government policy. The end of wage stabilization was in sight.

OWMR was extremely active in regard to education and veterans' affairs during this period. In July 1946 the President appointed a Commission on Higher Education, composed of prominent educators and public figures, to examine the social role of higher education. The Commission operated through Steelman's office, first as director of OWMR and later as Assistant to the President, and issued five reports on higher education policy.[28] The Inter-Agency Committee on Youth Employment and Education, organized by OWMR in April 1945, made its first report to Steelman in October 1946. The Committee outlined a broad long-range program to meet the educational and employment needs of young people. OWMR undertook to effectuate those recommendations which were the responsibility of the Federal government. Veterans' education was assisted by OWMR which arranged top priorities on classroom and laboratory equipment held by the War Assets Administration for colleges and universities participating in the veterans' education program. Considerable Army and Navy facilities and equipment were also secured.

The veterans' housing program continued to be of great concern to OWMR despite the apparent transfer of all its authority in this field to the Housing Expediter, whose authority was not respected by other agencies, particularly CPA. John Small, CPA Administrator, was known to favor an early dissolution of his office and relaxation of government controls including those essential to the housing program. Acrimonious debates between representatives of the two agencies were frequent and Small finally threatened to surrender all his powers relating to construction

[27] The amendment authorized governmental agencies, engaged in activities in which private business was also engaged, to pay the same wage rates as those paid by a substantial portion of that industry. (*OWMR Press Release,* September 12, 1946.)

[28] President's Commission on Higher Education, *Higher Education for American Democracy,* 5 vols., Government Printing Office, December 1947.

materials to NHA. OWMR stepped into the dispute and rendered a verdict which reinforced NHA. It was announced that CPA would not be terminated on December 31, 1946, as rumored, which in effect would have ended materials control.

Increasing participation of the Federal Government in scientific research and Congress' failure to pass the OWMR-sponsored National Science Foundation bill led to issuance of Executive Order 9791 which established a Presidential Research Board with Steelman as chairman. Other interested agency heads were specified to serve on the Board which was designed "to insure that Federal scientific research will promote the most effective allocation of research resources between the universities, the research foundations, industry and the Federal Government." [29]

In general the agency was involved in as broad a sweep of activities during this period as ever before, perhaps far too many. It had carried further the tendency, begun at the end of the war, to intrude on inter-agency affairs of too low a level and too commonplace a character to maintain its high position. It also suffered greatly from the administration's generally uncertain and shifting policies which contributed to an appearance of OWMR weakness. With such developments it was inevitable that the director would often appear uncertain whether he was at a higher level than department heads. This led to indecisiveness in relations with the agencies. Steelman was the first OWMR director to tolerate a flouting of his orders by a subordinate agency. One such incident occurred late in 1946 when an order to the CPA Administrator to channel materials so as to assure production of not less than 7000 freight cars a month was disregarded. No enforcing action was taken.

The coal strike, late in 1946, rendered another blow to OWMR status. It was a critical issue. Steelman, best known as a labor relations expert, was conspicuously omitted from White House operations on the case. The press was rampant with rumors that the OWMR director's role in the White House was in decline.[30]

With the almost complete tapering-off of war-connected activities and growing public impatience with agencies identified with

---

[29] *OWMR Press Release*, October 17, 1946.
[30] Later events proved that the rumors regarding Steelman were quite wrong, but they did affect the agency status at the time.

wartime controls, the administration decided to move quickly toward liquidation of all war agencies. The Bureau of the Budget, assigned to work out the organizational changes, easily decided that OPA and CPA should be absorbed in a new liquidation agency. But an issue arose over what should be done with OWMR. Obviously, the title of "War Mobilization and Reconversion" was obsolete. But most persons in the Bureau and elsewhere in the government agreed that the basic purpose of the agency was not and could not become obsolete, although difference of opinion existed as to where, in long-range terms, its functions should be located.

Long sessions were held among the Bureau, OWMR, and other agencies, and many plans written and considered. The most popular proposal would have moved the OWMR functions and staff into the Executive Office of the President to continue its over-all coördination job but probably without directive powers of its own. This was consistent with the final recommendation of the Colmer Committee for "continuation of a Presidential agency to act as a sort of over-all general staff to coördinate the formulation and execution of policy." [31]

However, the decisive Republican victory at the polls hung as a cloud over the deliberations. Fear was expressed that the new Congress would never approve a budget for an expanded executive office and that such a move might be interpreted as an attempt to maintain war controls or to increase the powers of the President. The new Congress was committed to a program of slashing the executive to the bone. The advocates of caution prevailed, and the idea of shifting the agency was reluctantly abandoned, in the final instance at Steelman's own recommendation although he had previously informed his deputies that he was convinced of the necessity for continuing a White House coördinating staff, such as OWMR, but smaller.

On December 12, 1946, OWMR, as such, was relegated, with other agencies to be liquidated, to the Office of Temporary Controls.[32] However, Truman announced that he was appointing Steelman Assistant to the President "to continue to aid me in

<hr />

[31] 79th Cong., 2nd Sess., House, Special Committee on Post-War Economic Policy and Planning, *Eleventh Report,* December 12, 1946, p. 5.

[32] E.O. 9809, December 17, 1946.

coördinating federal agency programs and policies." [33] The statement also noted that Steelman would be "assisted by a small staff," which caused some temporary hope that the central coördinating concept might be carried out after all and this small staff might serve as nucleus for future development. J. Donald Kingsley, an OWMR deputy, joined Steelman, with the title "Program Coördinator," reflecting awareness of the problem, but no further indications appeared of development of a regular coördinating unit.[34]

The OWMR power to issue directives reverted to the President himself, presumably still to be handled by Steelman, but now in the President's name, until its legal expiration. Also to Steelman went the coördination work of the President's Scientific Research Board and the Commission on Higher Education.

It was understood that OWMR, under the Office of Temporary Controls, would spend its remaining days winding up its affairs, which still included certain responsibilities such as the wartime subsidy program. Although its statutory life did not end until June 30, 1947, for all practical purposes OWMR can be considered to have expired as of December 12, 1946.

THE ADVISORY BOARD

Increasing use of non-government personnel in an advisory or consultative capacity within the wartime government led Jonathan Daniels, wartime administrative assistant to President Roosevelt, to write "the government has asked the chiefs of the pressure groups to sit on so many governmental committees that many of them now have more governmental work to do than most government officials." [35]

As the government assumed increasing control of the economy, its decisions came to bear ever more heavily on the daily lives of business, agriculture, and labor. It became more difficult to base decisions entirely on the knowledge and experience of public servants alone. Similarly, the concern of the interest groups about government actions led them to clamor for representation. Most war agencies made extensive use of advisory bodies, and their power in some of the agencies was considerable.

[33] *White House Press Release,* December 12, 1946.
[34] Kingsley left the job within a few months and the title was forgotten.
[35] *Frontier on the Potomac,* p. 147.

When OWM was established in 1943 there was some articulate resentment in labor circles that no advisory committee, with labor representation, had been established, as was the case in other agencies. So great was the pressure that President Roosevelt took the opportunity at a press conference to explain that he did not believe such an advisory board was required.

However, the congressional discussion which preceded the OWMR Act brought an advisory board into prominence. The Murray-George Bill, S. 1730, provided for an advisory board of industry, agriculture, and labor, but left to the discretion of the OWMR director whether the members should be used individually or as a committee. The final Act, however, based on recommendations of the Colmer Committee, called for a board of 12 to be appointed by the President with the consent of the Senate. Three of the members were to be drawn from a business background, three from labor, and three from agriculture, as well as three from the general public, but all were to represent the general public and the public interest. Just how this Utopian objective was to be achieved was not made clear. The chairman was to be designated by the President from among the three public members.

The President's appointees to the Advisory Board were mainly official representatives of the major interest groups. For business, there were Eric A. Johnston, President, United States Chamber of Commerce; George H. Mead, formerly employer representative on the National War Labor Board; and Nathaniel Dyke, Jr., of the Smaller War Plants Corporation. Labor's members were President William Green of the American Federation of Labor, President Philip Murray of the Congress of Industrial Organizations, and President T. C. Cashen of the Switchmen's Union of North America. The representatives of agriculture were Edward A. O'Neal, President, American Farm Bureau Federation; James G. Patton, President, National Farmers Union; and Albert S. Goss, President, National Grange. The public members were O. Max Gardner, former Governor of North Carolina, William H. Davis, chairman of the National War Labor Board, and Mrs. Anna M. Rosenberg, regional director of the War Manpower Commission. Mr. Gardner was appointed chairman.

The membership of the Advisory Board underwent only two

changes. Will Davis resigned in September 1945 at the same time that he gave up directorship of OES. Chester Davis, prominent as a member of the Board of Governors of the Federal Reserve System and War Food Administrator, was appointed to fill Davis' place, but resigned in July 1946 and was not replaced. George Taylor, formerly WLB chairman, became chairman of the OWMR Advisory Board in July 1946, replacing Gardner who was appointed Under-Secretary of the Treasury.

The Advisory Board was empowered to make recommendations to the director concerning legislation, policies, and procedures, which advice he was free to accept or reject. However, during Byrnes's administration the board was kept in the background and played no role in policy development. It struggled to obtain influence and recognition,[36] but found Byrnes consistently elusive.[37] His great personal prestige and the urgency of war created conditions whereby he apparently felt no need to cultivate these influential groups. In fact, his associates suggest that he would have opposed establishment of an Advisory Board had he not planned to resign from office soon after OWMR was created.[38]

Byrnes felt strongly that security considerations prevented a frank discussion with the Board of many of the most significant problems facing OWMR. Dealing as he was daily in "top secret" matters with the Joint Chiefs of Staff, through whom he had information not accessible even to very high public officials, Byrnes did not feel free to engage in discussion with private citizens regarding decisions closely related to such data.

[36] In testimony before the Senate Military Affairs Committee, O. Max Gardner, then chairman, indicated the Board's concept of its job and implied that it was not performing in that fashion. Gardner told Senator Kilgore that the Board felt it should advise the OWMR director before decisions were made rather than afterward. (79th Cong., 1st Sess., Senate, Committee on Military Affairs, *Hearings, The Mobilization of Civilian Manpower*, p. 259.)

[37] The former secretary of the Board, William Davlin, told the writer that he found such a schism between OWMR and the Board that he soon had to make a decision as to which he was working for. He had to be either the Board's man or OWMR's man. He chose the former.

[38] This view is substantiated by Byrnes's reaction to the first proposal for an advisory board in the Murray-George Bill. He told the Senate Military Affairs Committee that he thought it wise to leave to the discretion of the director whether the advisory group should meet as a committee at all, and favored consultation of each member of the group on his own specialty only. (78th Cong., 2nd Sess., Committee on Military Affairs, *Hearings*, Pt. 7, July 12, 1944, pp. 259–260.)

OWMR staff members claim that Byrnes also felt that Board members lacked a broad over-all viewpoint. They were prominent and able people, but generally with primary obligations in other quarters. Byrnes was not encouraged by the fact that Board members sometimes used their meetings to champion what he considered sectarian causes. Mr. Murray of the CIO, for example, having failed to win a WLB revision of the Little Steel Formula, used the Advisory Board to reopen the issue. Similarly, Mr. Goss of National Grange, having failed to secure increased prices for agricultural products from the OPA, brought the issue to the OWMR Advisory Board. These cases were not exceptional, since that was the way all the "interest" members had to operate.[39]

The situation was aggravated by the fact that Byrnes's deputy director, Clay, shared the director's distrust and, since Byrnes was at the Yalta Conference for a month early in the Board's career, Clay was responsible for developing OWMR relations with the Board. Originally Clay did not even permit the Board to draw up its own agenda. The Board doubted the propriety of a military man exercising great influence over reconversion problems, which they regarded as a civilian job. They felt that a man of high military rank could not have proper understanding of civilian problems such as unemployment, economic stabilization, or housing. Clay soon became the target of Board criticism. The issue between Clay and members of the Board was on the verge of an unpleasant crisis when Byrnes announced that Clay was resigning in April 1945 to become Deputy Military Governor of Germany.

There was some apparent improvement in the Board's position during Vinson's short term of office. Vinson attended its meetings more regularly. The OWMR staff participated more in Board sessions and projects, and the general work of the agency was discussed more freely. The Board began to meet with officials of the armed services and civilian agencies. During this period the Advisory Board formulated and issued two major statements of objective and principles: the first dealt with objectives for the postwar economy of the nation; the second set forth a series of

[39] Jonathan Daniels cited the Board as a prime example of "statesmen of perennial petition in person." (*Frontier on the Potomac*, p. 149.) However, advocates of "functional representation" in government argue that this is not necessarily a criticism, since the public interest is to be found only in the clash and resolution of particular interests.

reconversion principles calculated to facilitate a smooth transition to a prosperous postwar economy. However, despite the varied subjects discussed at Board meetings, such as revision of the Federal tax structure, allocation of food reserves and output, and disposal of surplus property, there was still little evidence that the Board was permitted to review in advance or influence policies.

With the end of the war, Director Snyder showed more respect for the influence of Board members and steps were taken to improve its status.[40] Board resolutions and statements received great publicity. The OWMR quarterly reports gave more space and generous praise to the work of the Board, which in turn showed more initiative in making proposals. Many more respectful gestures were made in the Board's direction. For example, within a week after Wilson Wyatt, the Housing Expediter, arrived in Washington, the Board met with him.

Increased attempts were made to use the group to help gain public acceptance of policy decisions, as in the case of OPA continuation, but without conspicuous success. In internal governmental affairs, its support was sometimes successfully employed to develop new programs, as in the case of OWMR's establishment of a high-level coördinating committee among government agencies to further veterans' interests.

The Board became more aggressive in the range of subjects it regarded as its province and made more requests of the staff for studies and information. Its agenda now included revision of the economic stabilization program, labor-management relations, industrial bottlenecks, needs of liberated areas, foreign commitments, disposal of surpluses, housing and proposals for full employment legislation.[41] Passage of formal resolutions became more common. Among those made public were resolutions on the world food crisis and the United States' financial agreement with Great Britain.

[40] In his first regular report, Snyder paid generous tribute to the Board. Speaking of its meetings, he said: "These sessions have been particularly useful to us; they have afforded my staff and me an intimate and frank reaction of the general public, labor, industry, and agriculture to government policies." (John W. Snyder, *Three Keys to Reconversion*, OWMR, Fourth Report, Government Printing Office, October 1, 1945, p. 45.)
[41] OWMR, Fourth and Sixth Reports, October 1, 1945 and April 1, 1946.

A most significant phase of the Board's development began when President Truman consulted with it before issuing Executive Order 9651 of October 30, 1945, which redefined the government's position on the wage-price question. Shortly thereafter it became the Board's habit to consult with the President regularly after their meetings.

The trend of apparent increase in Board stature continued under Steelman. The last of the directors was the first to attend its meetings faithfully. He rendered more apparent deference to the Board than any of his predecessors. More issues were discussed, more press attention was given to the Board, and the quarterly reports expressed increasing praise and gratitude for its assistance. The Board had increasing success in calling to public attention problems in which it was particularly interested, such as the study of guaranteed annual wage plans.[42] Its support for controversial directives was sought more frequently.

In keeping with the accents of the period, the Board devoted a great deal of time to economic stabilization. In his last quarterly report, Steelman quoted extensively from a Board recommendation to the President that drastic cuts be made in government expenditures and a balanced budget be achieved during the current fiscal year. The Board reviewed and endorsed a staff proposal that all Federal construction not absolutely essential should be postponed to future years and that expenditures of the armed forces should be examined to determine where drastic reductions could be made. At one of its more impressive meetings, the Board heard the heads of Federal agencies report on their portions of the Federal budget and a staff analysis of the total. The Board reported its reactions to the President.

The Board continued to meet with the President after each of its sessions throughout the Steelman regime. In its last days it took on the appearance of a presidential advisory board as much

[42] The study was undertaken during Byrnes's term. WLB had requested a commission to study the subject and the President suggested the Advisory Board as a suitable group. (*OWMR Press Release*, March 30, 1945.) Somewhat later the research staff was assembled under Murray W. Latimer who reported directly to the Board. The results were published in: Advisory Board, OWMR, *Guaranteed Wages*, Report to the President, Government Printing Office, January 1947.

as an OWMR board.[43] These meetings with the President resulted in considerable more attention and respect from the press, which portrayed the group as valuable to Truman "as a bouncing board." [44]

However, despite the general recognition and dignity finally achieved by the Board, it appears from the minutes of Board meetings and from the testimony of staff members, who regularly attended meetings and were responsible for continuous relations with it, that in this last period, as before, important policies were not really cleared with it in advance; nor did it carry much weight in actual policy decisions.

When it became clear that OWMR was to be abandoned in December 1946, there was some hope that an arrangement might be made to continue the Board as a presidential advisory body. The President is represented as having expressed an interest in such a plan.[45] However, the Board's prestige was not sufficient to prolong its life, and the executive order of December 12 transferred it along with the rest of OWMR to the Office of Temporary Controls, the equivalent of termination.

The Board's failure to reach the full measure of influence and significance which the advocates of such a body had envisaged in drawing up the legislation was in part due to its own inadequacies. Its members were inevitably too busy with other projects and full time highly responsible jobs to devote the time required to make it an effective agency. Attendance at meetings was irregular and frequently poor. Inadequate staffing heightened the problem. The representation of such diverse interests made it extremely difficult to obtain agreement on significant policies and led to some tendency to avoid taking positions as a body. Discussions tended to be discursive and real issues frequently failed to come to a head.

[43] Speaking of the Board's meetings with the President, Steelman reported, "This enables the Board to receive from the President information and special requests for counsel or comment on particular questions, and makes it possible for the Board to bring directly to the President the observations, conclusions and recommendations of its members." (OWMR, Seventh Report, July 1, 1946, p. 68.)

[44] *Business Week*, September 14, 1946, pp. 5–7.

[45] Interview with Edward Felker, Executive Secretary to the Advisory Board, December 17, 1946.

Creation of the Advisory Board reflected the growing tendency during the war of what has been aptly called, "enlisting the participation of the regulated in the process of regulation." [46] By the time the OWMR legislation was drawn, almost all the larger agencies, WPB, WMC, and OPA, had developed patterns of advisory committees comprised of private citizens. Their role in specific regulatory agencies was most helpful in bringing highly specialized knowledge into easy accessibility of the agency as well as in "selling" programs. The proper utilization of such a committee at the White House level for broad over-all public policy had more complicated and difficult aspects. Care had to be exercised to avoid a natural tendency on the part of the Advisory Board to usurp the policy-making function of government itself. There was considerable question regarding how much advance discussion could be entrusted to private citizens without risking "leaks" to the press, which might serve some private interests, or stimulate advance pressures which might jeopardize programs.

In the main, OWMR seems to have avoided many of the pitfalls possible in the use of advisory committees, and it found its Board an aid in many respects—development of mutual understanding between government and its citizens, help in gauging public response to policies, and creation of support for government activities by discussion with, and presentation of, detailed information to prominent public leaders. Whether or not such a Board could have been of more positive value in the development of policy, had it been given a real chance, cannot be finally answered from the OWMR experience.

[46] Lincoln Gordon, "Government Controls in War and Peace," *Bulletin of The Business Historical Society, Inc.*, vol. XX, No. 2, April 1946, p. 50.

CHAPTER *4*

ALLOCATION OF RESOURCES

*A*mericans learned early in the war that this was not a land of "unlimited resources." There was not enough to satisfy fully and smoothly the simultaneously increasing demands of a hungry war-making machine and of a thriving civilian economy.[1] Primarily because of this competition for limited resources, there developed bitter administrative and policy conflicts over such matters as military requirements and procurement, allocation of scarce materials and determination of priorities.[2] These would have been staggering problems under the best of organization and management. They loomed even larger under the diffusion of responsibility and agency autonomy which long prevailed.

It is not proposed to examine here either the technical aspects of these problems or the merits of the particular disputes, but rather to explain the role played and the administrative methods employed by OWM–OWMR in the resolution of the turbulent issues involved.

SOME MAJOR PROBLEMS

CONTROL OVER MILITARY PROCUREMENT

Logical organization and administrative niceties indicated the advisability of a unified procurement program under central direction. To such proposals the military voiced vigorous and successful opposition, resisting every attempt to channel their procurement through civilian agencies. As a result there was always urgent need for coördinating devices and reviewing machinery.

The implications of control over procurement were extensive. "Procurement" is more than purchasing. It includes responsibility for inspection and delivery. Procurement agencies had to follow details of manufacturing and assume responsibility for correction

---

[1] The national income more than doubled between 1940 and 1944.
[2] The great manpower and reconversion conflicts, which had the same basic roots, are discussed in Chapters 5 and 6, respectively.

of bottlenecks. If inadequate manpower or materials appeared to threaten a particular contract, the Army felt justified in taking action. If transportation facilities delayed delivery, it moved in on the railroad, trucking, and shipping business. Since shortages were universal, the military inevitably was in the middle of the business of almost all other government agencies.

The problem was complicated by the fact that businessmen turned to the buyer, the man who held the purse strings, when fulfillment of a contract was at issue. In event of a strike threatening production, an employer would be likely to call on the War or Navy Department before the War Labor Board. Furthermore, the peculiar prestige and power implicit in the uniform during war often meant that the military was in a position to get more done than the civilian agency technically responsible. The agencies themselves recognized this and would frequently call upon the military for assistance. For one reason or another the military establishments were thus involved in every facet of the home-front war program. Much of this was inevitable but it made avoidance of conflict difficult.

After appointment of the NDAC in 1940, the Procurement Division of the Treasury was legally authorized to make purchases for all government agencies except Army and Navy. The Commission recognized the importance of the procurement function and recommended to the President creation of a Coördinator of National Defense Purchases to advise on "most effective methods of purchase."

Donald Nelson, the President's appointee to the post, and his staff did much to modernize the procurement practices of the armed services,[3] but they remained subject to sharp criticism. It was charged that contracts were concentrated in a relatively few large corporations, that small business was being neglected, that the cost-plus-fee system was abused, that contracts were badly distributed geographically leaving pools of unemployment in some places while causing labor shortages in others, and that long delays in delivery reflected bad procurement.

Two weeks before Pearl Harbor, the Tolan Committee urged

[3] Negotiated contracts replaced the cumbersome competitive bid system; staggered timing and parceling out of larger contracts became a widespread practice.

that "a single civilian board of the Federal Government be charged with full responsibility for procurement and for planning war production and for the production of essential civilian needs." [4] This point of view was also shared by the Truman Committee and the proposal to transfer all procurement work to a single non-military agency, contained in the Pepper-Kilgore-Tolan bills, had wide support in Washington.

There was some indication that the President intended to end this criticism by centralizing war production authority in one man. When Nelson became WPB chief he was in a strong position to reorganize procurement. He shared the opinion that control over procurement by the military was the greatest single handicap of WPB's predecessor agencies. [5] He also knew that a majority of the congressional committees studying the war program sought a single civilian agency for all procurement and that "most of the outspoken critics of our war production between Pearl Harbor and the formation of WPB had urged the setting up of some form of Ministry of Supply, with full legal power to award all contracts." Yet Nelson decided against such a course. [6]

The executive order establishing WPB gave it power over procurement policies, plans, procedures, and methods, but not over the actual procurement process. Nelson explained that such a change at that time would have delayed the war program six to eight weeks. He repeated Bernard Baruch's warning that it would be unwise to allow contracts to be let by anyone not in uniform, and emphasized the inescapable tie between contracting and inspection. [7] He pointed out that the transfer of military procurement to a civilian agency might lead to a legal tangle requiring

[4] 77th Cong., 1st Sess., House, Select Committee Investigating National Defense Migration, *Second Interim Report*, December 19, 1941, p. 19.

[5] *Arsenal of Democracy*, p. 198.

[6] To the Truman Committee, Nelson said, "I have gone even to the point of being over-zealous in seeing that the contract powers were kept within the Army and Navy . . . As a matter of fact we enhanced that authority." (77th Cong., 1st Sess., Senate, Special Committee Investigating the National Defense Program, *Hearings on Senate Resolution 71*, p. 5089.)

[7] "Part of the job of buying anything is the job of taking a look at the finished product and determining whether or not it is up to standard. How would a civilian Director of Procurement have done this, in the matter of fighter planes, radar equipment, tanks, depth bombs, and the thousands upon thousands of strictly military items . . . ?" (*Arsenal of Democracy*, p. 199.)

legislation. In addition to these negative reasons, Nelson "felt absolutely certain" that WPB could work out buying policies with the Army and Navy that would answer much of the criticism.

In this he was not successful and WPB was widely criticized and accused of abdicating to the military. Denying this, Nelson emphasized his policy powers but many critics felt that WPB was, in fact, not setting policy. This controversy was one of the main factors leading to legislative proposals to centralize all procurement activities within one large civilian agency.

MILITARY REQUIREMENTS AND FEASIBILITY

The question of how much the military should be allowed to purchase and at what delivery rate was also of fundamental significance. It represented another source of conflict and reflected lack of integration of military strategy and procurement.

In the field of requirements, the disagreement between military and civilian authorities was quite different during the defense period and during the war. In the defense period the military was criticized as too conservative in its demands.[8] Actually, resistance came from several additional sources—the Federal Loan Administrator, who denied for a long time the necessary expansion funds; industry, like steel, which feared overexpansion; and many "business-as-usual" forces within the civilian war agencies.

The picture changed completely near the end of 1941, after which the military was steadily accused of making unreasonable demands. Toward the middle of that year came the strategic decision to aid Russia and the Army and Navy proposal to treble over-all production. Three days before Pearl Harbor a report by OPM and SPAB concluded that "the entire program to date must be doubled and achieved by September 30, 1943, if the Victory Program objectives are to be fully attained."[9] Clearly such a program was feasible only in terms of a full wartime economy.

[8] Speaking of 1941, the history of OPM states: "In forecasting over-all requirements, the Services reflected their long peacetime experience with limited appropriations by gearing their requirements to minimum levels. Consequently, through the whole range of raw materials, stated requirements were not adequate for a shooting war, and OPM exerted steady pressure to get them raised . . . Knudsen, Nelson, Hillman and Biggers pressed for doubling and trebling of military goals for particular weapons." (*Industrial Mobilization for War*, p. 119.)

[9] *Ibid.*, p. 140.

The question of feasibility led to debate and controversy. What proportion of the national product could be devoted to war production? At what point is the practical limit to be found? WPB's answers to these questions differed sharply from the total requirements stated by the President, the Army, Navy, and Maritime Commission. The President, fearful that the most determined effort was not being made, remained adamant and put more pressure on WPB to raise its sights for munitions than did the military itself.[10]

The contest over total annual production objectives involved more than the question of total availability of specific limited materials for particular end-products. Since there had not been established an agreed level at which the civilian economy was to be maintained, every expansion of military requirements forced the civilian requirements issue to the fore. At least until 1943, WPB made no real attempt to define the minimum level of civilian activities. WPB's Office of Civilian Supply acknowledged that during 1942, at least, it followed a residual theory in stating the needs of the civilian economy.[11] As military procurement objectives expanded, the civilian supply agencies made more vigorous demands. When the two types of demands began to impinge, the two sets of claimants insisted upon reviewing each other's demands.[12]

[10] This was confirmed by the former chairman of the WPB Planning Committee in a personal interview. In most instances it appears that Roosevelt set the broad war production objectives. Most of the time, WPB considered his objectives too high for attainment, but its actual quarrel was with the Army and Navy, both of which relied on the President's general program to justify their own requirements. Thus, the President's call for 60,000 tanks led General Somervell to recast everything in the Army supply program in order to be consistent with the utilization of 60,000 tanks. To WPB this was not implicit in the President's plan.

[11] Drumond Jones, *The Role of the Office of Civilian Requirements in the OPM and WPB*, Civilian Production Administration (Special Study No. 20), 1946, p. 75.

[12] Federal machinery for determining requirements included the Joint Chiefs of Staff, who drew up the basic military demands, the ANMB, Army, Navy, Maritime Commission, Lend-Lease, and WPB. Within WPB these requirements, together with those of other claimant agencies, such as PAW, Office of the Rubber Director, and WPB's own Office of Civilian Requirements, were assembled for determination of feasibility. WPB was, in theory, empowered to make decisions on reductions if its Planning Committee indicated the necessity for such a step. Because of its composition, however, tne Board itself could rarely agree on such matters, and it never claimed au-

SCHEDULING

The controversy involved more than the size of the annual program. Effectuation of that program, through monthly scheduling and follow-through on production of particular items, was equally important. Scheduled production of components frequently got out of joint with their need in end-items. At the end of eight months of 1942, production of munitions was less than half the amount forecast for the full year and the tempo of production increase was conspicuously slowing down.[13]

To deal with this problem—to maintain a constant check and control of programs and schedules—WPB set up in September 1942 its Production Executive Committee. Through PEC, Nelson hoped to recapture some of the authority he had delegated to the Services.

When late in 1942 production failed to meet expectations, WPB was critical of the Services, citing faulty scheduling and inadequate control over productive processes. It also accused the military of grossly misleading forecasts, charging that these were used for bargaining purposes as each claimant agency sought to protect itself by piling up critical materials, machine tools, and other resources.

In November, Charles Wilson, head of PEC, proposed review of the entire scheduling procedure of the procurement agencies to assure that monthly forecasts for 1943 be realistic and in line with production objectives set by the Joint Chiefs of Staff. He proposed to set up a PEC subcommittee on scheduling. Each procurement agency should establish a scheduling unit whose heads would in turn constitute the subcommittee. The latter would establish criteria for scheduling on the part of procurement agencies, review schedules for reasonableness and consistency, integrate them for feasibility, and insure proper balance. The Services took vigorous exception to the plan.

The President finally stepped in and required the Secretaries of War and Navy to reach an agreement with Nelson. This provided that PEC should determine whether or not the scheduled

---

thority to determine the order of strategic necessity. Accordingly, basic issues would generally be referred back to the JCS, who were supposed to make decisions based upon strategy, and report back to WPB.

[18] *Industrial Mobilization for War*, p. 507.

war production was within the productive capacity of the nation, except that any downward revisions of a military program had to be approved by the Joint Chiefs.[14]

Formal approval from the War Department was secured after assurances were given that the Army's responsibility for establishing and adjusting end-item schedules would not be compromised so long as these were within the limits of feasibility determined by the PEC chairman. However, WPB never obtained real control. The conflict was inherent in the split of responsibilities, which left the Services accountable for procurement and all the responsibilities flowing therefrom. The situation was also the inevitable outcome of the lack of a unifying point for synthesizing strategy, production, procurement planning, and operations.

PRIORITIES AND ALLOCATION OF MATERIALS

Closely related to controls over end-product and component scheduling was the issue of priorities and allocation of materials. The problem had plagued both NDAC and OPM. Shortly after creation of OPM, consideration was given to the possibility of centralizing priority functions in an OPM Priorities Board and eliminating the Army and Navy Munitions Board which had been setting and granting priorities for military procurement. This was not accomplished, however, and during 1941 ANMB retained authority to grant priorities for military items.

In addition to ANMB's preference rating orders, the enforcement of priorities was attempted through an allocation system, introduced early in 1941, for very scarce materials, starting with aluminum; through conservation orders, which restricted the uses to which a given material might be put; through limitation orders on the manufacture of civilian products; and through inventory control, designed to curb overbuying or hoarding of scarce materials. By the middle of 1941 this complex system was breaking down through the sheer volume of paper work. "Priorities inflation" took place and the rating system became generally ineffective. The sum total of priorities being held was far in excess of available resources. This led to a general movement away from the prevailing system of priorities to one of specific allocations. When WPB was established in January 1942, the President's

[14] WPB General Administrative Order 2–71, December 9, 1942.

order gave it all authority over priorities and allocations and presumably took care of any conflict with ANMB by providing that the latter would report to the President through the chairman of WPB. WPB, however, authorized ANMB to carry on its priorities function "under policies and procedures approved by the Chairman of the WPB." [15]

The existing duplication and confusion increased and by June 1942 reached the attention of the President. No forthright conclusion was provided, however. In the President's view, ANMB appeared to be coördinated under WPB. However, the close working relationship of ANMB with the Joint Chiefs of Staff, which controlled strategic priorities, created a situation in which concurrence of ANMB was almost mandatory in assignment of priorities and allocations of raw materials. This was interpreted to provide for its concurrence on all ratings.

With the collapse of the priority system, an alternative method of allocations was imperative. ANMB proposed substitution of a material allocations plan under which the Services would obtain a broad allotment of materials from WPB's Requirements Committee, based upon strategic directives of the Joint Chiefs, which the Services would in turn allot to producers in accordance with production schedules. Recognizing the inevitability of this approach, WPB strengthened its control of production schedules which would have to be the basis of any real control over distribution of materials. PEC instituted the "Controlled Materials Plan" to allocate materials to end-product manufacturers which they in turn could pass down the line to suppliers. This system of vertical allocation meant WPB's turning over blocks of materials to the Services for them in turn to distribute to industrial plants working on war contracts.

Despite fears that this vertical allocation system might mean the end of all WPB control, the CMP system prevailed.[16] It was generally agreed that the plan provided WPB its first mechanism by which claimant agencies were compelled to keep programs and schedules at a level compatible with the supply of scarce materials allotted to them. Introduction of CMP and the increasing authority of WPB over production scheduling, primarily

[15] WPB General Administrative Order 2–23, March 16, 1942.
[16] *Industrial Mobilization for War*, p. 484.

through the more effective functioning of PEC, did not, however, bring to an end the controversy over priorities and allocation.

MAIN COÖRDINATING DEVICES DEVELOPED BY OWM—OWMR

OWM–OWMR did not undertake any revisions of the basic machinery for procurement, allocation, and production controls which had been developed by mid-1943. Whether that machinery needed overhauling will long be argued but, in any event, most observers agree that it was too late in the game for that kind of change. The important point is that it did provide authoritative coördination for that machinery, a center of direction, and ended the deadly impasses caused by the previous lack of such authority.

Arrival of OWM did not end the controversies with the military. Many of the major problems involved in examining and reviewing stated requirements of the military which plagued WPB moved up to OWM. OWM was, however, in a better position organizationally and politically, to deal with the military, and aggressively developed some devices to cope with the problem.[17]

While on the surface this implied taking over many of WPB's fights on behalf of the civilian economy, much of the strength and effectiveness of the OWM approach lay in the fact that during the entire war it managed to maintain the position of impartial arbiter,[18] the position WPB had been unable to maintain.

PROCUREMENT REVIEW BOARDS

The arrival of OWM did not alter administrative responsibility for procurement. Apparently neither the President nor Byrnes seriously considered the possibility of transferring procurement to a civilian agency. As its first step, OWM promptly undertook to determine whether there was reasonable coördination among

[17] It may be added that OWM–OWMR also had the advantage of the time factor. The prospects of victory had enormously improved by 1943, thus strengthening the civilian agency position *vis-à-vis* the military. It has also been claimed that some part of the earlier difficulty may have been caused by the fact that until 1942, at least, no military strategy had actually been settled. We were setting up a shelf of as much military equipment as we could in contemplation of future campaigns, the plan for which could not be determined until the allies took the offensive. (*The United States at War*, p. 131.)

[18] The presence of an Army officer, General Lucius Clay, in OWMR for a few months in the winter of 1944–45 as deputy director, was the source of considerable suspicion of OWMR bias toward the military. The record does not support this suspicion.

the various procurement arms and reasonable balance within particular procurement objectives.[19]

Within a month after taking office, Byrnes wrote the heads of all procurement agencies pointing out that the duties imposed on OWM by the President involved a "careful scrutiny" of the war programs of all agencies. He said the situation called for "an objective review of requirements, giving special consideration to current strategic concepts, transportation possibilities, inventories, rates of use and attrition, and production potentialities," and called for establishment within each agency of a procurement review board to include civilian as well as military personnel, none of whom had direct responsibilities for the functions being reviewed. The review board was to be at the top level of the agency, headed by a senior officer, and to include a representative of OWM.[20]

The Army showed some initial shock, but after one exchange of letters entered into the project with full coöperation. The Maritime Commission and Lend-Lease complied without question. The Navy maneuvered and resisted sufficiently to require Byrnes to obtain presidential backing for his request.

The Secretary of the Navy appointed his board, July 7. It included two retired admirals, two private citizens, a civilian employee as executive secretary, and two lieutenant-commanders as secretaries. Byrnes informed Knox that he was designating as his representative, William Francis Gibbs, a well-known manufacturer of naval items. To assist Gibbs, Byrnes borrowed L. R. Boulware, an official of WPB.

The Navy review (as contrasted with the Army) promptly opened an issue which had long plagued civilians dealing with the military. The Navy claimed that Gibbs could not have certain information which the Navy considered too highly secret for any civilian. An exchange of correspondence between Byrnes and Knox, in which the OWM director called upon his full authority and threatened to bring the matter to the President, resulted in at least a temporary breakdown of the restriction. For several

---

[19] A staff memorandum of the period suggests that another purpose may have been OWM's judgment that an early assertion of authority was required to establish its position. See Chapter 2, p. 62.

[20] Letter, June 24, 1943. Portions of this letter are cited in Chapter 2, p. 63.

months more the Navy was difficult about "secrecy" but, before the review was over, the highly significant principle was successfully established that the military could not bar relevant information needed for the functioning of top civilian authority, regardless of its "secret" nature.

Before investigating internal aspects of the Navy program, Gibbs and Byrnes faced the problem of correlation of these programs with those of other agencies engaged in similar procurement. In August, from reports submitted by the agencies involved, a tabulated summary was prepared of barge, tugboat, and towboat construction programs of the Maritime Commission, the ODT, Army, and Navy. The summary information resulted in an identically phrased letter from Byrnes to the heads of the four agencies:

> I am advised that this is the first time an effort has been made to present in one tabulation the total programs for tug and barge construction of the various government agencies . . . It would seem at least possible that this trebling of the barge and tug boat population of our harbors and intercoastal waters may, to an extent, arise from failure on the part of some of the procurement agencies to take cognizance of some of the contribution to the total being made by other agencies. I am, therefore, requesting that each of the agencies send one or more of the procurement officers responsible for its tug and barge program to a meeting . . . August 26.[21]

The meeting resulted in small adjustments downward, particularly on the part of the Army.

On August 25, Gibbs reported to Byrnes that the Navy Procurement Review Board deliberations were completed. The OWM representative had no direct part in preparation of the final report but participated in discussions and interpreted Byrnes's wishes to the Board. Some specific economies were suggested, such as deletions in the blimp program, construction for the Army by the Navy of small vessels to eliminate duplication, and adjustment of lend-lease procurement in conformity with available ocean transport.

A few days later, Gibbs submitted a more thorough and critical analysis of the Board's final report, which contained some sharp and significant statements. As to ships, he said:

[21] Letters, August 18, 1943.

there was fairly open admission in the Navy that many of these vessels, particularly patrol craft and mine sweepers, were not required, but that there had been no definite action, so far, in cancelling any of the vessels or slowing down programs . . . It would seem proper for you to acquire convincing proof as to why the patrol craft and mine sweeper programs should not be cut drastically at once.

Aircraft . . . The Committee . . . believes too many aircraft are now being provided for the carriers and for the other bases on which aircraft will be located. The Secretary gives no indication, in forwarding you the report, that he is doing anything about the recommendations of the Committee that the estimation of attrition, spares and the inventory of combatant planes required back of the carriers or the front be revised downward. He also gives no indication that the trainer program has been cut, whereas it is frequently admitted by the Navy that there had been too many trainers, but trainer contracts are not being cancelled because the latter are made by the Army . . .[22]

The report had similar comments on such items as bases, ordnance, lend-lease, and manpower.

However, progress in revising the Navy's program and in securing a more coöperative attitude was a slow and difficult task. This was in part due to the fact that the civilian Secretary appeared to lack final control over military officials and in turn this was in part explained by the special status the Navy felt it had with President Roosevelt because of his interest in and knowledge of the technical aspects of naval affairs and his former position as Assistant Secretary of the Navy in the Wilson administration.[23]

Byrnes sent the President a memorandum regarding the discouraging aspects of the Navy review, in contrast to the War Department where the Chief of Staff had taken the Board into his confidence to the extent necessary to enable it to understand the objectives of Army procurement and where the new supply program was several billion dollars lower than the one published six months earlier, with a good deal accomplished in elimination of waste.[24] He told the President that no real appraisal could be

[22] Report, William Francis Gibbs and L. R. Boulware to James F. Byrnes, August 29, 1943 (dittoed).

[23] It was often stated by insiders in Washington that Roosevelt and Admiral King ran the Navy and King felt he needed to recognize no other authority.

[24] Byrnes's representative on the Army Review Board reported at its conclusion, "The Board has with unvarying politeness invited my joining in its work and has asked my opinions and suggestions. While the Report is the Board's Report, no point I have raised has passed without consideration nor

said to have been made by the Navy Review Board because of recurrent unwillingness to discuss future strategy with civilians.[25]

Here Byrnes was bluntly facing up to a key issue of top coördination in the war. How could OWM or any other agency be expected to carry out its production and scheduling responsibilities without knowing their relationships to military strategy?

The Navy did not accept Byrnes's conclusions. There was an attempt to justify portions of the program by direct communication to the President who promptly forwarded the memorandum to Byrnes.

The case for greater integration was strengthened by a staff report submitted to Byrnes dealing with simultaneous reviews being carried on in the procurement agencies, all of which illustrated confusion caused by lack of clear understanding as to which agency was responsible for a particular program.[26] For example, the Maritime Commission shipbuilding program included construction of 100 frigates which it had agreed to build for the Navy. However, the Maritime Commission Review Board regarded this item beyond its cognizance because it was not a Maritime Commission item. The report of the Navy Review Board made no reference to such vessels either.

The record, as to Navy reviews, grows vague here but apparently Byrnes achieved more by way of Naval recognition of his right to examine their affairs than in concrete changes in program. Also the process of critical examination and questioning had a lively effect within the Navy itself where some soul-searching appears to have occurred. As a result of a proposal from the Under-Secretary of the Navy that the entire naval building program be reëxamined, and Byrnes's own reports, OWM was able within a month to transmit to Knox a presidential request for a complete review of the shipbuilding programs of the Army, Navy, and Maritime Commission.

Such OWM "pressure" was apparently not without effect. After two months, Under-Secretary Forrestal reported to Byrnes that substantial dollar savings had been achieved, "through deliberate

---

has any question gone unanswered." (Letter, Frederick Pope to James F. Byrnes, August 31, 1943.)
[25] Memorandum, August 31, 1943.
[26] Memorandum, Fred Searls, Jr. to James F. Byrnes, September 4, 1943.

cutbacks brought about as a result of a reappraisal and revaluation of its authorized procurement programs." [27]

The amount of savings resulting from the Army review does not appear in OWM records but it is estimated at about $8,000,-000,000 by staff personnel familiar with the study.[28] Proportionate savings were accomplished in other programs. The review boards were able to eliminate some wasteful practices, undue advance procurement, and overlapping contracts for identical items among the Navy, Army, and Maritime Commission, due to lack of clarity as to where responsibility resided.

More important, the procurement agencies were forced to undertake critical review of their own operations. They became aware that they could and probably would be subjected to periodic examination from a higher authority. For the first time, the military had to consider their requirements in relation to the total situation. Emphasis was placed on the interrelationship of the various procurement programs of different agencies and the necessity for joint review. Perhaps most important, it dramatized the necessity for considering production and military strategy jointly.

JOINT PRODUCTION SURVEY COMMITTEE

As a direct result of these reviews, and at Byrnes's request, in September 1943 the President announced establishment, within the Joint Chiefs of Staff, of the Joint Production Survey Committee to advise the Joint Chiefs on changes in the procurement programs of the Services in the light of war developments, production progress, and changing military strategy.

The Committee is also to provide machinery for full coördination of the military and civilian branches of our government by establishing close working relationship between the Joint Chiefs of Staff and the Office of War Mobilization.

[27] Letter, November 24, 1943. Forrestal stated that the total value of deliberate cutbacks since July 1, 1943 amounted to $2,855,670,000 of which it was estimated that $722,299,000 would accrue for the fiscal year 1944; $1,794,931,000 for the fiscal year 1945; and $338,440,000 for 1946. The Under-Secretary emphasized that these represented clear savings, not to be compensated for by increases elsewhere.

[28] Memoranda in OWMR files; interview with Fred Searls, Jr., November 17, 1946. In a memorandum to Justice Byrnes, dated November 15, 1943, the Under-Secretary of War estimated the total cutbacks of the Army in the previous eight months to be $7 billions.

The Committee will work closely and constantly with representatives of the Office of War Mobilization, advise the Chiefs of Staff with regard to problems raised by that Office which involve the military production programs, and coöperate with that Office in the endeavor to promote economies in the use of material and manpower in the over-all production program.[29]

The JPSC was Byrnes's device for bringing military strategy into the unifying pattern emerging from OWM synthesis of production, procurement, and political factors. It was not an ideal arrangement, since it consisted entirely of military personnel and was accountable only to the Joint Chiefs. But it brought about a greater amalgamation than had been previously achieved and appeared to be the most that could be done at that stage of the war.

Fred Searls, OWM representative, was not a member of the Committee and did not vote, but he attended meetings and participated in all deliberations including discussion of strategic plans. His presence proved significant. He represented a powerful agency with vigor and courage. He later described his role in the Committee as that of a prosecuting attorney.

The Joint Chiefs could, of course, override any recommendation or decision of the Committee but by then Byrnes knew all the issues involved. He was in a position to know whether he wished to pursue the matter or let it rest with the Joint Chiefs. He personally attended many meetings of the Joint Chiefs themselves. He had no vote but his voice carried sufficient influence to force joint consideration of strategy and production. It was a reasonable facsimile of a Supreme War Council, although any party in it could appeal to the President.

Byrnes was not a man to invite a dispute if a situation could be handled in any other fashion. He did not bring his problems before the Joint Chiefs continually. His position in the White House gave him another avenue. There, he would confer frequently with Admiral Leahy, the President's military Chief of Staff who was also presiding officer of the Joint Chiefs. Problems would frequently be resolved personally by the President's top civilian and military aides.

Although the Joint Chiefs recognized in Byrnes a man who stood firm as the top authority on supply, the going was not always smooth. Irreconcilable difficulties were brought to the

[29] *White House Press Release*, September 24, 1943.

President, generally by the Navy. But with such procedure there can be no quarrel. The important thing was that the issue as finally formulated would present the totality of production, strategic and political considerations.

Byrnes asked the JPSC to follow up the many operating deficiencies revealed in reports of the various procurement review boards. An example of such follow-up by OWM, together with JPSC, is found in a letter the director addressed to the Committee in October 1943 regarding "alleged enormous waste of military supplies in the vicinity of army posts and landing fields" in North Africa.

Mr. Pope's [OWM representative on the Army Procurement Review Board] belief is that the waste of military material and construction in Africa is sufficiently serious so that, if continued and repeated in other theatres, it will become a severe drain on successful prosecution of the war . . . [As to] the criticism in the report of the McCoy Board [the Army Procurement Review Board] which you are asked to investigate and correct, I wish to informally suggest, before investigation is handled in any other way, that you send Mr. Pope, with an army officer of suitable rank as a colleague, to spend a few weeks in North Africa to report to your committee upon conditions, and, if corrections are needed, what steps should be taken.[30]

Again, the following month, he wrote JPSC as follows:

in view of the labor shortage and other difficulties which have operated to steadily reduce the contemplated production of airplanes . . . I cannot remain entirely satisfied that the ultimate accuracy has yet been achieved in respect to the balance in production of components and planes . . .

In a general way I must, of course, look to you for implementation or disapproval of the recommendations of the Procurement Review Boards of the Army and the Navy . . .[31]

In the fall of 1944, the Joint Chiefs reported to Byrnes that the studies he had requested through the JPSC had resulted in large reductions in the Army Air Forces program.

Since the Joint Production Survey Committee received your request to maintain a continuing review of the Army Air Forces program there have been reductions in the Army Air Forces working schedules of over 23,000 aircraft in addition to the recent cutback of 12,453 aircraft.[32]

[30] Letter, James F. Byrnes to Joint Production Survey Committee, October 23, 1943.
[31] Letter, November 10, 1943.
[32] Letter, Admiral William D. Leahy to Byrnes, September 8, 1944.

The letter described in detail the reasons for the cuts, their relationship to revised employment schedules of the Forces, and major developments in the program of maintaining balance among production of aircraft, personnel, component and spare parts, high octane gasoline, and training.

On January 1, 1944, General McNarney, Deputy Chief of Staff, issued a directive through the Joint Chiefs to give final implementation to recommendations of the Army and Navy Procurement Review Boards. Throughout the year, Byrnes kept in close touch with the Joint Chiefs to see that schedules were consistent with needs and previous recommendations. Replies received from the military to Byrnes's frequent inquiries always revealed concern for his approbation and recognition of his authority to request detailed analyses.

EFFECTIVENESS OF OWM–OWMR

A recital of OWM–OWMR participation in the resolution of top disputes would involve a several volume review of war issues. It will suffice here to select a few incidents which reflect the approach and the degree of top-side coördination. These incidents are selected because they throw light on the Office's relationship to the President, its dealings with another coördinating agency— the Bureau of the Budget—its relation to military authority, and the Office's dealings with the Joint Chiefs of Staff.

CONTROLLING MILITARY DEMANDS

Early in January 1945, Admiral King requested the Secretary of the Navy to secure the President's approval for an additional combat vessel construction program of 84 ships totaling 644,000 tons. Forrestal transmitted the recommendation to the President, by-passing OWMR, and was informed the next day by the President's Naval Aide that, "The President did not have time to study your recommendation but said that you could inform the Budget that he favored the construction and authorizes you to take it up with the Budget." [33]

The Director of the Budget was apparently appalled by the proposal and wrote a firm note to the President recommending that it be disapproved, on the grounds of its being unnecessary. Smith also mentioned that there were indications that the pro-

[33] Memorandum, January 9, 1945.

gram had its origin with the chairman of the House Naval Affairs Committee.[34] The President's reply rejected Smith's view and said, "I am inclined to support the proposal of the Secretary of the Navy."

This appeared to be a somewhat weaker endorsement than the approval which had been earlier communicated through his Naval Aide, but coming from the President it would normally be regarded as sufficient to close the issue.

However, the matter had reached the ear of the OWMR office and on February 24, Fred Searls wrote Byrnes a blistering but highly analytical condemnation of the Navy proposal. After reviewing the large programs approved for the Navy in previous years, over some OWM objection, he said:

Now in January 1945, however, because the Navy has suffered, chiefly by air attacks, a small part of the losses in ships, anticipation of which could alone have served to justify the ratio of allied to axis combat ships thus stubbornly maintained in 1943 to be required for future operations, the Navy comes forward with a new requirement of 84 additional combat ships, in large part not even contemplated during the review period above discussed . . .[35]

After the Director of the Budget had also brought the problem directly to him, Byrnes decided to move in on the issue in earnest. In view of the position already taken by the President it was a courageous thing to do. He went to the President, fortified by detailed information from his representative on the JPSC and other sources, and persuaded Roosevelt to allow him, Byrnes, to look into the matter further and to withhold final decision until then. He promptly wrote the Secretary of the Navy stating that he had been advised by the Budget director of the Navy proposal and that he had discussed the construction with the President and

as a result, I believe that it should be re-examined . . .

It is my understanding that one of the arguments used to justify this construction is to maintain labor in our shipyards.

I also understand that while these ships would be of some value in the war against Japan, if that war lasts throughout 1947, they are not regarded as essential.

I appreciate that these ships will also have a post-war value. However, if the ships available to the Navy, now under construction, suffice

[34] Memorandum, January 17, 1945.
[35] Memorandum, February 24, 1945.

for the war against Japan, we should avoid further authorization at this time.

I would appreciate it if you would take immediate steps to defer the construction of these ships until I have had an opportunity to discuss it personally with you.

I am advising the Director of the Budget that I propose to discuss the matter with you and have requested him to withhold approval of the estimate until after our discussion.[36]

The suspicion that the entire point of the Navy program was to have ample postwar supply, a suspicion shared by both Byrnes and Smith, was clearly indicated. The indication that Byrnes had access to some information that the construction was not regarded as essential within the Navy itself, was pointed.

He did not say, as he might have, that by that time he had already obtained an oral admission from Admiral King, that he did not regard the program as necessary. In fact, King insisted that he had not proposed the program, but had submitted it as representing what should be done only if such a program were to be adopted. From discussion with Forrestal, Byrnes learned that the real source was Carl Vinson, chairman of the House Naval Affairs Committee. Forrestal conceded that he did not regard the program as essential but wanted an explanation to offer Representative Vinson, perhaps a letter from the President. All of this was stated in a memorandum Byrnes sent Roosevelt, including the fact that he had already told the head of WPB not to allot materials for the program. Said Byrnes:

When the Budget first protested against the program your statement was, "I *am inclined* to agree with the Navy." You did not make a positive decision.

In view of the expenditure of manpower and material at this time; the fact that many of the ships will not be completed until the end of 1947; that it will require some months to put them in commission; and of the number of enlisted men required to man these ships, I hope you will advise the Secretary that the program should be cancelled. If you have any doubts about it, I hope you will give me an opportunity to talk with you about the matter.[37]

The next day the President made a final decision against the proposed program.

The Secretary of the Navy received compromise approval for

[36] Letter, March 3, 1945.
[37] Memorandum, March 14, 1945.

completion of 12 of the 84 ships—representing 150,000 of the contemplated 644,000 tons—which were claimed to be part of another program and quite necessary. Byrnes wrote Krug, head of WPB, stating, "With the approval of the President, I authorize the allotment of material for the construction of those 12 ships. The President has determined the rest of the program should not be constructed and any outstanding contracts for construction should be cancelled." [38] Byrnes wrote a letter for the President's signature to Forrestal for the latter to use in his explanation to Representative Vinson. Byrnes personally spoke to Vinson and obtained his compliance with the decision. Approximately $1.5 billion had been saved.

KEEPING THE JCS WITHIN THE MILITARY SPHERE

A second incident, running almost contemporaneously with the above, illustrated the way in which OWM insisted that the Joint Chiefs limit their activities to military planning rather than extend themselves to civilian matters. On February 26, 1945 Admiral King wrote to the President and the chairman of the Maritime Commission transmitting recommendations of the Joint Chiefs for additional non-combat ship construction during the last half of 1945. The President referred the recommendation to Byrnes.

The recommendation called for construction of 28 dry cargo ships, of standard and victory types, above previous authorizations. Byrnes was opposed and wrote Admiral Leahy as follows:

the report . . . recommends the construction of 28 cargo ships, in addition to those I have already authorized, although it does not indicate any increase in military requirements.

In my letter of January 11, 1945, I advised the Joint Chiefs of Staff, with the approval of the President, that military shipping within the total tonnage requirements would receive priority and that civilian shipping would be allocated from any remaining tonnage.

Nevertheless, [JCS] fixes a need for additional cargo ships to meet military requirements by assuming that a specific tonnage will be made available for civilian shipping. This is contrary to the principle established in my letter that civilian shipping would be allocated by civilian agencies from the tonnage remaining after legitimate military requirements were fulfilled . . .

The additional 28 cargo ships recommended by the Joint Chiefs of Staff cannot be delivered in 1945. I believe it would be a mistake to

[38] Letter, March 23, 1945.

authorize the construction of these ships until the study which you have
authorized to start April 1 has been completed . . .

Moreover, I would suggest that the Joint Chiefs of Staff can safely
limit their study to a determination of the tonnage required for military
purposes during the remainder of 1945 and throughout 1946. This will
enable the War Shipping Administration to determine the remaining
tonnage available for other than military shipping as well as the necessity for further construction for this purpose . . .[39]

On the same day Byrnes wrote Admiral Land of the Maritime
Commission indicating his disagreement with the program and
asking for his recommendations on future programs. In the
interim, pending the April 1 study by the Joint Chiefs he added,
"I request that you not take any steps to place the additional
construction under contract at this time."[40]

The following month, Admiral Leahy, speaking for JCS, replied
to Byrnes's letter and a basic difference of approach was enunciated.

The Joint Chiefs of Staff note the assurance given in your letter of
11 January and repeated in your letter of 3 March that military shipping needs will receive priority, both as to allocation of ships and repair
facilities, and that civilian shipping will be allocated from any remaining tonnage and facilities.

. . . Civil needs and programs have been continuously in direct
conflict with military needs . . . The Joint Chiefs of Staff, being responsible for the military conduct of the war, are of the opinion they
would be guilty of dereliction of duty in evaluating the adequacy of
shipping for military purposes if they did not take realistic cognizance
of the implications of conflict between civilian and military shipping
demands.[41]

The remainder of the letter defended the actual need for the
ships and claimed an over-all shortage which Byrnes had denied.
It concluded with a statement that although no further study
was necessary "the Joint Chiefs of Staff agree to defer to your
wishes to include the question of the need for the construction
of the 28 dry cargo ships in the study now being undertaken."

The disparity in approach was clear. In effect, OWMR was
directing the military to determine essential military needs. If
these could be substantiated, they would be authorized. The

[39] Letter, March 3, 1945.
[40] Letter, March 3, 1945.
[41] Letter, April 11, 1945. Fred Vinson was now OWMR director and the
letter was addressed to him.

remainder available would be allocated by civilian agencies to civilian use. The JCS were, on the other hand, insisting that since there was a close relationship between civilian allocation and what was considered feasible by the military, they should participate in determining the former, thus perhaps assuring a larger remainder for themselves.

About two weeks later, Fred Vinson, who had succeeded Byrnes, picked up the issue with a long reply to the Admiral. It critically examined and refuted the Joint Chiefs' claims regarding shortages, but, more important, it firmly stated the limitation of their authority and clearly defined areas of responsibility. It left no doubt as to who was the ultimate coördinator.

> When the Joint Chiefs of Staff assert their right to determine purely military requirements for shipping, including civil affairs requirements that are part of the military program, their duty to be reassured as to military priority over civilian requirements, and their obligation to express an opinion with regard to the magnitude of the civilian requirement and the shipping that they think will be available to meet this requirement, I fully agree . . .
> But the final responsibility for determining civilian requirements for shipping and the amount of shipbuilding necessary must rest primarily with the responsible civilian agencies. The responsibility for making final decisions as to the proper balance in the employment of manpower and production resources to obtain the maximum war effort rests with this office . . .[42]

There was apparently no further correspondence from the Joint Chiefs on this issue. There was a tone of finality about Vinson's full statement which may have persuaded them that any further resistance would be met stanchly by OWMR and that they were unlikely to prevail. The position taken by the Joint Chiefs was not devoid of logic, the interrelationship between civilian and military requirements could not be questioned, but it appears clear that both Byrnes and Vinson were affirmatively resisting any move which might extend military intrusion in the conduct of the civilian economy.

THE JPSC AND THE JOINT CHIEFS

Another situation illustrates how OWMR used the Joint Production Survey Committee and reveals that a JCS veto of a Committee recommendation was by no means final.

[42] Letter, April 27, 1945.

In the same March 3 letter which Byrnes had sent to Admiral Land about the cargo ships he questioned the need for 40 additional tankers also requested by the Joint Chiefs. He mentioned that on January 23 he had asked the JPSC to reëxamine requirements for tankers. "I believe you or your staff have had informal advice that the Review Committee finds no need for these tankers." The same day he wrote WPB that he had ordered construction of the tankers deferred.

At the end of March, Byrnes wrote Leahy regarding the tankers, pointing out that the JPSC had said there was no need for them, but that this report was then referred to the Army-Navy Petroleum Board. That Board had previously reported no need for additional tankers, but when the question was raised this time it revised requirements upward, so that a need was indicated.

Of course, requirements which change upward so quickly may in later analysis change downward as quickly. This would indicate that the need for the additional tankers is to support marginal requirements, which are within the probable error of computation. I may point out also that the Joint Logistic Committee recommended their construction only as an insurance to maintain existing shipyards in production . . .

I cannot see how we can need more tankers to defeat Japan than are required now with our forces operating on so many fronts . . .

I ask that you personally consider the cancellation of these tankers. If after you have personally considered it you advise me that you are of the opinion construction should proceed, I will immediately lift suspension. If it is impossible for you to personally consider the question, I ask that you submit it to the Joint Production Survey Committee. You will recall that when this committee was created we agreed that it should be composed of officers of high rank and in whom the Joint Chiefs had such confidence that they could rely and act upon their decisions. One of the Committee's functions certainly was to review such requirements . . .[43]

A few days later Land replied to the Byrnes letter of March 3. He pointed out that when the Joint Chiefs made their request for the tankers on December 30, 1944, "contracts were negotiated and placed immediately." By the time OWMR instructions to desist had arrived, the contracts were already in force for two months. With Byrnes's permission he had held meetings with top persons in government and found PAW, ODT, and Army and Navy in favor of the construction, OWMR against it, and the

[43] Letter, March 31, 1945.

chairman of WPB neutral. Land, therefore, "recommended that this matter be solved by proceeding with the construction of 20 of these tankers and cancellation of 20 . . . An immediate decision is earnestly requested." [44]

The decision facing Vinson, now OWMR director, was difficult. Not only were the contracts let and the Joint Chiefs apparently adamant, but two civilian agencies had vocally joined in support of the military. On April 4 and again on April 12, ODT had written that they had reduced their demands for tank cars due to anticipation of additional water transport and that such additional water transport facilities were needed. Of course, if sufficient military tankers should become available in 1945, that would solve the problem, but the Joint Chiefs thought that was not likely, despite Vinson's opinion. To help stir up opposition, ODT had sent copies of its complaints to PAW, the Chief of Traffic Control in the Army Transportation Service, the Office of Army-Navy Liquidation Commission, the Defense Supplies Corporation, and the War Shipping Administration. Harold Ickes followed on April 13 with a letter in the interests of PAW urging "that there be no reduction in the tanker construction program."

Despite this formidable opposition, Vinson felt that Land's proposal to "split the difference" was unjustified and an apparent victory for the JCS which had refused to comply with the studies of the JPSC. He wrote Land that he had been trying to persuade the Joint Chiefs to settle the matter finally on the basis of the JPSC recommendations.

This effort has not been successful and I appreciate that the request of Justice Byrnes of March 31 to the War Production Board to stop further procurement of components and materials for these forty tankers has not stopped their construction. I appreciate that the present position of the Maritime Commission is, as stated in your letter, embarrassing and untenable and to settle the matter I hereby request that you now cancel contracts for thirty of these tankers forthwith and complete construction of the other ten. It is my opinion that none of these ships is required and certainly none of them is required in connection with military operations, but I appreciate that there have been recent losses and while these do not, I believe, exceed allowances it will, perhaps, make your cancellations easier if the ten of these ships most advanced are allowed to be completed.[45]

[44] Letter, April 7, 1945.
[45] Letter, April 17, 1945.

Vinson then wrote measured letters to ODT and PAW enunciating his decision as final but outlining in great detail his reasons for believing that neither their interests nor military interest would be injured. The letters revealed detailed knowledge of every aspect of the problem and careful study before the decision was made. Vinson reiterated that the Joint Chiefs had rejected the recommendations of their own staff, based upon long study and testimony from all agencies concerned.

More correspondence followed, but the decision remained firm. The JPSC, OWMR's instrument for coördination of strategy and production, had won a victory over its parent organization, the Joint Chiefs of Staff, through strong OWMR support. It is significant that Fred Searls, OWMR representative to the JPSC, wrote most of the above correspondence for Vinson. As to the merits of the debate, not the real concern of this discussion, it appears that within two months, tankers were conceded to be in surplus.

AIR FORCES CUT-BACKS

This type of exchange between the OWMR and the military was not confined to seagoing vessels. In the spring of 1945, Byrnes wrote Leahy he had learned that aircraft production scheduled for post-V-E Day provided no reduction in deliveries to the Navy and only a small reduction to the Army. Pointing to the pressure for consumer goods after the defeat of Germany, Byrnes declared that it would be difficult to convince the public that almost as many aircraft would be needed to defeat Japan as were needed for a two-front war. "If these needs are real, we should be prepared to explain them to the public." Byrnes said he was not equipped to determine the number of aircraft needed to defeat Japan; that was the responsibility of the Joint Chiefs. "However, I do have the responsibility for directing our war economy to meet your expressed requirements, while at the same time protecting our domestic economy to the extent feasible." [46]

Leahy did not answer Byrnes's letter until May. Vinson, now director, found the cut-backs in the AAF program "gratifying." [47] He was not equally satisfied, however, with the status of Navy procurement and, in a letter to Admiral Leahy, maintained that

[46] Letter, March 20, 1945.
[47] Army Air Forces cutbacks during April and May involved 43,792 planes at a value of $7,540,000,000. (OWMR Office Memorandum, May 31, 1945.)

the Navy was statistically concealing its failure to cut back sufficiently.

There is likely to be public criticism of even necessary waste in airplane procurement. Unnecessary waste will add to the criticism. I have discussed this subject generally with the President and feel prepared to insist that the Navy either justify the effective use of its planes in the Japanese war, in proper relationship to the Army Air Forces program and also attrition and obsolescence figures being employed as controls or else make significant cuts in its plane procurement as has now been done by the Army Air Forces.[48]

Two days later Vinson wrote the President asking him to "impress upon the Joint Chiefs of Staff that a review of the aircraft program for the Navy should be a realistic one." He pointed out the Navy's minute cuts in relation to the Army's and insisted that further cuts could be made. However, the tugging and hauling with the Navy did not cease until the end of the war.

UTILIZATION OF EQUIPMENT

A final example illustrates OWMR's attempt to relate military demands to utilization and to look into the latter when it appeared to fall within civilian competence.

In late 1944 the President wrote Byrnes expressing great concern about the manpower shortage in shipyards, expressing his conviction that at least ten more ships a month could be built were it not for such shortages and that the ships were badly needed. He asked Byrnes to look into the matter.[49]

This led to activity on three fronts: a survey of shipping requirements and schedules, a drive for manpower, and inquiry into what was happening to the enormous quantities of ships already available. Here we are concerned with only the last of these items. OWMR soon discovered that ships were failing to return from combat theaters in conformity with reasonable expectation or schedule. Although the generals were demanding more rapid shipments, it was found that large numbers of ships, fully loaded, waited around ports, sometimes for weeks, because of neglect or inability to unload.

The day after the President's memo, Byrnes brought the problem to General Marshall's attention. The General acted promptly

[48] Letter, June 2, 1945.
[49] Memorandum, November 20, 1944.

and indicated that General Somervell, head of Army Service Forces, had already taken cognizance of the problem. Marshall quoted a message sent by Somervell to the Commanding General, European Theater of Operations, which read in part:

Since the early months of 1944 it has been a definitely agreed policy to schedule sailings from the United States to your theater in accordance with the estimated and demonstrated ability of your ports to receive. The number of idle ships in your theater has grown because of your insistent demands for more and more shiploads of supplies, accepting your assurances that there would be a material improvement in discharge capabilities. The world-wide shipping situation is so critical that we cannot accept any increase in the number of idle vessels; rather it is imperative that congestion be relieved and turnaround improved. Because of this, *there is no alternative but to deny your request for more ships in excess of your capacity to unload them until you have restored to useful service a portion of those now immobilized.*[50]

General Marshall commented, "It is apparent from the above quoted message that Somervell is now doing exactly what you had hoped would be done." From then on, there was closer discipline in all theaters on the employment of shipping space. The revelations soon made it clear that the shortage of ships was more apparent than real. Byrnes was soon able to make a lengthy report to the President:

Waste of merchant shipping has been mounting to new peaks. Recently it has caused an artificial appearance of shortage and jeopardized meeting of legitimate demands of the war effort. Too many ships are being used as warehouses. Energetic steps now have been taken to correct the condition and within 60 days it should be remedied . . .
. . . it would seem advisable to delay a decision with regard to the letting of additional contracts until the present study by the Joint Chiefs and the shipping authorities is completed.[51]

The memorandum was full of detailed statistics on delays in turnabouts, the production situation, and the manpower problem. The President was satisfied. The revelations flowing from examination of the use of shipping space were used on future occasions when issues over requirements for additional merchant shipping arose.

[50] Quoted in Memorandum for Byrnes from General G. C. Marshall, November 22, 1944. (Italics from original.)
[51] Memorandum, November 25, 1944.

CONCLUSION

Early in the war Donald Nelson stated his "fundamental concept" that "the war supply organizations should be viewed by all participants as a simple integrated system operating under the general direction of the Chairman of the War Production Board in a unified effort to win the war and not as a group of autonomous or semi-autonomous organizations acting in mere liaison with one another." [52] This was a grand objective, but it was never attained. By 1943 the several agencies were behaving as autonomous units, refusing to accept WPB authority, and relationships were liaison in character. This, in itself made the need of a topside agency such as OWM–OWMR inescapable.

The need for a means of synchronizing strategy and production considerations was equally great. Civilian agencies could not debate strategy with the military. Neither did they generally feel equipped to question the specific needs to fulfill a given strategy. WPB always protested that the military submitted demands without adequate supporting information to make possible critical appraisal. Yet it is doubtful that it would have made much difference if the military had been more generous in dealing with WPB. High officials in WPB pointed out frequently that lacking a merger of strategy and production considerations at the top any attempt to perform an intelligent evaluation of specific demands at a lower level was more or less futile.[53]

Under any circumstances a civilian agency would find it awkward to take an adamant stand against military claims in the midst of war. The risks involved in making a mistake of undersupplying the military were far greater than the risk of oversupply. The military, as self-righteous as any other group of men with great responsibility, did not hesitate to take advantage of this enormous asset.

[52] 77th Cong., 1st Sess., Senate, Special Committee Investigating the National Defense Program, *Hearings*, Pt. 12, April 21, 1942, p. 5077.

[53] A former chairman of the WPB Requirements Committee has been cited as follows: "Gordon stated that military requirements were generally not screened by the Requirements Committee because of lack of definite knowledge of the basic factors employed. He added that Chairman Nelson early decided against doing the war job of calculating military requirements, holding that the task of WPB was one of production and supply." *The Role of the Office of Civilian Requirements in OPM and WPB*, p. 76.

OWM was an imperfect mechanism for synchronizing strategy and production but it had the authority and the structural locus within government to devise techniques for facing this problem and its vigorous steps were on the whole effective.

Limited resources led to active competition among all sectors of the economy and considerable strife in officialdom, most conspicuous when it involved military and civilian authorities. However, the struggle was never a clear-cut fight between the military and non-military. The areas of conflict between the two were inevitably blurred by overlapping interests and responsibilities and the agency line-ups were constantly shifting in the various "battles of Washington." Vigorous earnest men with responsibility for specific programs were reaching into an inadequate pool of resources. Each sought to obtain the largest possible proportion for his own mission and a collision of goals was inevitable.

Whatever merit there may be in the oft-repeated, but questionable, allegation that the military wished to "take over" the economy, the OWM–OWMR experience makes clear that such dominance was not attained. The Army made strong and aggressive representations before the Office, but always bowed to its authority. There was more difficulty with the Navy because the admirals felt confident of fairly constant presidential support. But, despite some sharp differences on the question of "secrecy," the issues with the Navy rarely involved basic controls, but only the volume of particular programs. OWM–OWMR, in its relations with individual branches of the military as well as with the Joint Chiefs of Staff, maintained a clear civilian dominance over all home-front issues.

CHAPTER 5

COÖRDINATING MANPOWER
PROGRAMS

anpower is the ultimate limiting resource of an economy. Our nation was rich in this vital resource. During the defense and early war periods, the labor force was expanded by several millions attracted by high wages and patriotism; unprecedented migration was providing manpower for the swelling centers of war production, and job simplification and training programs helped to meet the enormous demands both for production and the armed forces. Since our reserves appeared more than adequate during these early days, the pleas of manpower officials for stronger measures to establish controls over the labor market went unheeded.

Until the summer of 1943, the manpower problems were largely of a "spot" character, confined to specific issues: shortages of special skills, deficiencies in occupations characterized by low wages and unpleasant work, and in communities overloaded with war contracts. These "bottlenecks," however, were extremely serious. They had to be met when they arose. Unfortunately, the over-all situation, being generally favorable, tended to temper the appearance of emergency and discouraged extraordinary measures. As a result, spot improvisation and indirect measures became the pattern.

By 1944, the local labor shortages had developed into a national crisis. Manpower became the major "bottleneck" in war production. But, by this time, the sense of urgency and fear over the military outcome of the war had diminished, and there was widespread reluctance to undertake any broad new policies of control such as national service. It was believed that such measures were unnecessary and would contribute little to the solution of existing manpower problems. It was urged that voluntary measures be fully explored before compulsion was undertaken. "Totalitarian methods," "forced labor," "civil liberties"—these and similar slogans were generously employed and tended to confuse public thinking as to the nature of the proposals for an over-all manpower program. Debate over the necessity or desirability of national service legislation raged almost incessantly throughout the last two years of the war.

Legislation for manpower control, however well drawn, would have been difficult enough to administer with effectiveness. Labor does not have the mobility of materials; it is not transferable from community to community or plant to plant without a multitude of other adjustments. Special difficulties are created by the problem of increasing hours of work, or arranging new work shifts. Problems of turnover and absenteeism are complicated by their relationship to housing, transportation, inplant facilities for workers, adjustment of shopping hours, child-care and other community facilities.

The concept of a national labor market proved in practice highly elusive, and of not much practical applicability. Rather than one large labor market, there were hundreds of individual labor markets. Throughout the war certain areas had surpluses of labor while others were suffering costly shortages. Some areas faced general shortages for heavy male labor. More than in the case of most great war problems, solutions had to be variable and there had to be great reliance upon local policy and administration.

Finally, the proposals for the mandatory allocation of labor were political dynamite. Few measures could affect so directly the daily lives of the entire working population. The most important economic and political pressure groups in the land were involved. Both labor and management feared the inevitable regulation of labor relations that would come with mandatory work laws.

These factors help to explain why the United States was the only major nation which went through the war without any general legislative authority for labor allocation—except for the military draft. By the same token, manpower was probably the most controversial issue of the war. The complete story of the administration of manpower allocation would furnish a fascinating study of American economic and political institutions. But it cannot be told here. These pages must be confined to high lights selected primarily to illustrate the role played by OWM–OWMR in the manpower picture.

ALLOCATION OF MANPOWER RESPONSIBILITIES

The War Manpower Commission was generally regarded as the central government agency responsible for the administration of manpower. In actual practice authority was widely diffused. When we entered the war there were some twenty-odd agencies with more or less responsibility in the labor supply field. The first major attempt to bring some order into this miscellaneous array came in April 1942 with an executive order creating the War Manpower Commission.[1] WMC was to be primarily a policy-making body empowered to "issue such policy and operating directives as may be necessary" to agencies in the labor supply field. It had few direct operating responsibilities and no line or administrative relationship with the operating agencies. Most significantly, the Selective Service System, whose operations had the most direct effect upon the labor supply in every community, was left completely independent of the Commission. It was a coördinating agency with serious limits upon its sphere of coördination.

To enhance WMC authority and increase its effectiveness, the United States Employment Service and several minor labor supply agencies were transferred to it in September, thus giving the Commission direct operating responsibility.[2] Selective Service was added in December.[3]

The hoped-for unification did not materialize. One month later, the chairman of WMC was induced to transfer all responsibility for agricultural labor supply to the Secretary of Agriculture,[4] thus seriously compromising central management of the nation's manpower program. Nor did the WMC terminate the independent activities of the Civil Service Commission, which recruited for the vastly expanded Federal government, the War Shipping Administration which had the job of supplying labor to the merchant

[1] E.O. 9139, April 18, 1942.
[2] E.O. 9247, September 17, 1942.
[3] E.O. 9279, December 5, 1942.
[4] *War Manpower Commission Release,* January 25, 1943. It was recognized that agricultural interests would support more adequate appropriations for a labor supply program administered by the Department of Agriculture.

fleet, or the Railroad Retirement Board, which conducted an independent employment agency for railroad workers.

The transfer of Selective Service to WMC did not lead to the expected unification of policy and operation. For a variety of reasons Selective Service was never absorbed into the Commission's operations. It always retained its independent and autonomous status. Although its major policy decisions were "cleared" with the chairman of the War Manpower Commission, the 6500 local boards of the Selective Service System continued to operate as before the December executive order.

Highly sensitive to the apparent lack of legal sanctions to enforce its "directives," WMC early determined to depend on support from management and labor. It set up Regional and Area Management-Labor Committees in each of its twelve regions and in most important labor market areas, corresponding to the National Management-Labor Policy Committee required by executive order. These committees turned out to be more than "advisory" and in practice assumed a considerable measure of authority. WMC determined not to impose regulations generally without the consent of these committees, which meant a division of authority and varying impact from place to place.[5]

In addition to the diffusion of the limited manpower authority which existed, some of the most important policies and actions influencing the use of labor were not within WMC jurisdiction at all. Without question the single most effective device for conservation of manpower was the curtailment of certain types of less essential production. Restrictions upon production were entirely within the authority of the War Production Board. Despite the pleas of WMC, it was never the policy of WPB to restrict production because of manpower scarcities.[6] WMC vigorously appealed for a "concentration of production" program for civil-

[5] Although the National Committee had no legal authority and was conceived as merely advisory, it soon began to pass not only on policy matters but on all significant administrative measures, internal structure of the agency, and was even consulted on personnel appointments. In some instances, such as in review of appeals, it carried on operating functions. Rarely had a group of private citizens had as much direct authority in the conduct of the affairs of a government agency.

[6] The closing of the gold mines in October 1942 was the only general curtailment order for nonessential production resulting from manpower pressures. For a comprehensive report, see Maryclaire McCauley, *The Closing of the Gold Mines*, Civilian Production Administration (Special Study No. 9), 1946.

ian items, to reduce the number of plants making a given item, thus obtaining more efficient use of labor and, more important, to remove such production from labor shortage areas to areas of adequate labor supply. WPB was never enthusiastic about the idea, and, after a few abortive and isolated gestures, announced that "concentration" was not feasible.[7]

Since it was recognized that there were severe limits on the extent to which workers could be brought into labor shortage areas, WMC urged vigorously that strong steps be taken to direct the flow of work to where workers where already located. WPB issued a procurement directive designed to accomplish this and the procurement agencies generally sought to place contracts accordingly. The results, however, fell far short of the goal. WMC was never satisfied that a real effort was made to influence the flow of contracts in accordance with labor supply considerations.

In respect to utilization of labor, WMC's vague authority resulted in further controversy. It was always critical of industry's labor demands, claiming they were frequently inflated and reflected wasteful practices and under-utilization. It insisted that to deal adequately with the manpower situation it had to concern itself with the demand for manpower as well as its supply. However, WPB and the procurement agencies resisted WMC's efforts to enter plants for labor utilization studies and any attempts to tailor the stated requirements on the basis of such studies. They claimed this was outside the jurisdiction of WMC which they regarded only—or primarily—as a recruitment agency.

The relative attractiveness of wage rates and earnings obviously played an important role in influencing the movements of labor. WMC urged the War Labor Board to set wages to attract workers to more essential jobs and discourage their leaving such employment. Such a policy would undoubtedly have helped in getting workers for the most critical jobs. But the dangers of abuse were considerable. WLB, therefore, refused to employ its wage controls to influence movement in the labor market. A few exceptions were made, as in the critical case of the foundries, but in general WMC could not look to WLB for direct assistance.

This brief review suggests the inadequacies in the WMC role

[7] Moderate concentration orders were issued for production of stoves, typewriters, and certain farm machinery.

as coördinator of manpower policy and activities. WMC lacked powers even in its own field and it was forced to depend upon the coöperation of other agencies. When such coöperation ran counter to immediate responsibilities of those agencies, WMC had no device for enforcing its directives, nor was there any arbiter to determine whether the WMC interest or the interest of the other agency was more crucial to the war. More than in any other field, labor supply problems were characterized by frequent impasses resulting from lack of, or dispersion of, authority. Thus, establishment of OWM was of special importance in relation to manpower, particularly since labor supply became the most urgent production problem during the latter part of the war.

WEST COAST MANPOWER PROGRAM

In the summer and fall of 1942 a series of voluntary employment stabilization plans were developed in several tight labor communities, such as Baltimore, Louisville, and Detroit. Worked out in agreement with the Management-Labor Committees, these were in effect "anti-pirating" agreements on the part of management and anti-job-jumping agreements on the part of labor. Essential employers agreed not to hire any worker previously engaged in essential work unless he furnished a "statement of availability" from his previous employer or the USES. Regional stabilization plans, covering small towns and rural areas, were also developed. Labor pirating was generally reduced as a result of these programs and more orderly procedures for recruitment and labor stabilization were introduced in many localities. Evasion was, however, easily concealed and, even when revealed, no sanctions were available.

Aside from stabilization of the labor force, an issue arose over where to direct new workers and workers seeking to make a legitimate change of job. Shortly after its creation, WMC requested of WPB a listing, in order of urgency, of all types of production and other economic activity on which WMC could base a labor priority pattern. WPB was unable to provide this on a national basis, and a long controversy arose as to responsibility for establishment of labor priorities. WPB, supported by the armed services, insisted that its clear responsibility for production included establishment of labor priorities which WMC should follow in recruiting and assigning labor. WMC would not compromise and a stalemate continued until late 1943. In the meantime, WMC, with the assistance of other agencies, formulated a general *List of Essential Activities,* as a rough guide to the local USES offices and to workers in general, but the size of the list, its broad inclusive character, precluded its use in relation to priority referrals.

The manpower problem was decidedly confused—with the exception of one or two local areas such as Buffalo, where local authorities simply undertook on their own to rise above Washington's jurisdictional impasse—when a west coast crisis forced action and decision upon the Washington authorities. The agencies involved were in bitter deadlock over policy and locus of authority. In this situation OWM stepped in and provided the necessary leadership to avoid administrative paralysis and set the manpower pattern for the remainder of the war.

The west coast had mushroomed quickly into a key war production center. Twenty-eight per cent of all ship construction was centered in the San Francisco, Portland, Seattle, and Los Angeles shipyards. A substantial portion of all ship repair work was being done there. A large percentage of bomber and fighter plane production was located on the coast. Despite enormous in-migration, this region, relatively undeveloped industrially before the war, was first to experience a general shortage of male workers in all major production centers. This was aggravated by an excessive turnover and absentee rate due to inadequate housing, transportation, child-care, and recreation facilities.

In the summer of 1943 some production schedules were not being met and others were threatened with costly delays. According to a special War Department study, the situation had become so critical that unless "drastic measures" were taken "production [in six leading aircraft plants] will show a decrease in the last six months of 1943, not alone below schedules *but below actual levels reached in the first six months.*" The report also stated that of all the complex problems faced by the industry "the most important, today, is that of MANPOWER." [8]

[8] John D. Hertz and staff, "Manpower Problems in the West Coast Aircraft Industry," August 3–11, 1943. Unpublished report to Hon. Robert P. Patterson, Under-Secretary of War. (Italics from report.)

Thirteen of the 38 shipbuilding yards on the west coast were reported to be behind schedule in June. Transportation was also reported to be in serious trouble. Furthermore, demand was still increasing sharply.

It may be said that there is not a single major production center on the West Coast in which there is not a present labor shortage. More disconcerting even than the problem of obtaining additional employees is the excessive turn-over rate which requires industry on the West Coast to hire four or five times as many workers for replacements as the number needed to attain schedules.[9]

Some steps had already been taken that summer to relieve the situation. Selective Service granted a two-month moratorium on draft calls in the west coast aircraft industry. The procurement agencies, especially the War Department, had imposed vigorous restrictions upon further contract awards in certain coast cities. But the situation continued to deteriorate.

While WMC was being reproached by WPB and the procurement agencies, the former claimed that the armed forces were placing an inordinate number of contracts whose demands could not possibly be met and that WPB was failing in its responsibility to provide WMC with production priorities and to set up reasonable production schedules in relation to labor supply. It also claimed that labor hoarding and poor utilization were rampant and that WPB and the procurement agencies were neither doing anything about it themselves nor allowing WMC to act. WPB claimed Selective Service was making an unreasonably heavy drain on West Coast manpower.

BARUCH-HANCOCK SURVEY

These facts were generally familiar to the director of OWM who assigned his two most distinguised consultants, Bernard M. Baruch and John Hancock, to survey the west coast problem and report to him with recommendations. On August 19, the Baruch-Hancock report was submitted to Byrnes,[10] with a long letter of explanation, as well as a detailed plan worked out by WMC to implement the general recommendations of the report. The letter read in part:

---

[9] Memorandum for War Mobilization Committee meeting, August 26, 1943.
[10] It was made public a month later. *Congressional Record,* September 17, 1943, pp. 7590–7593.

The plan we are proposing strikes at the two basic failures in our manpower program—the lack of any system of labor priorities and the hopelessly unbalanced production demands that have been imposed on the Pacific Coast. These demands for the next six months are so far in excess of the available labor supply that a disastrous breakdown of vital production programs all through the region is threatened—not only of aircraft but shipbuilding, ship repair, canning, mining, lumbering and others.

To bring these demands back into balance and to see that available labor goes where it should, our program calls for establishing a Labor Budget in each critical labor community on the West Coast . . .

On the one side of the Labor Budget, employers would draw upon the available labor on the basis of priorities established in the first instance by the War Production Board [nationally] and applied in each community by a local Labor Priorities Committee headed by an outstanding citizen of the community. The War Manpower Commission would regulate the flow of labor on the basis of these priorities.

On the other side of the Labor Budget, the WPB and other procurement agencies would be responsible for keeping production demands in balance with labor supply. No new contracts would be let in the area unless other production demands were reduced so as to keep the budget in balance.

The report included many other recommendations, including proposals that:

All necessary aircraft workers be deferred;
High school boys working in aircraft plants be retained on a part-time basis after school reopened;
Prevailing cost-plus contracts should be changed, where feasible, to provide an incentive for cost reduction and more efficient use of labor;
All procurement programs on the West Coast be reviewed to cut out any unnecessary requirements;
Less essential industries be curtailed to release workers;
A plan to give reconversion priority to plants and workers with the best war production records be developed in order to check any exodus of workers in anticipation of peace;
Wage adjustments be used to aid manpower allocation;
Occupation be made the basis for draft deferments, rather than family status;
The armed forces should be asked to furlough back to the aircraft plants selected key workers previously drafted;
Deferments of farm workers be tightened; and
Prompt action be taken to improve local housing and transportation conditions, erect additional day-care shelters, adjust shopping hours, and relieve the innumerable other annoyances that come with congestion.

The Baruch-Hancock recommendations largely expressed the position taken by WMC, the agency most under attack. The detailed program, developed by WMC with Baruch endorsement, contained the principle of priority referral to jobs and employment ceilings, already in operation in Buffalo and several other localities.[11] It said, "The War Manpower Commission will be assigned full responsibility for directing and coördinating all phases of the West Coast Manpower Program." A West Coast Production Priorities Committee, under chairmanship of WPB, was to be established. In addition, Area Manpower Priorities Committees, headed by a prominent citizen or a WMC staff member, to be chosen in either case by the appropriate WMC Area Management-Labor Committee, would operate in each important area.

The Production Priorities Committee would

determine relative urgency of production programs on the West Coast, . . . approve and inform the WMC of production schedules or production requirements of major establishments or categories of establishments, . . . review proposals for facilities and for major supply contracts, . . . approve and, through responsible representatives of the agencies concerned, implement a program . . . for redistributing production.

The Area Manpower Committee would list establishments within the area in accordance with urgency of production and need for labor, fix employment ceilings, advise WPB concerning essential production within the area which might be redistributed, and recommend to WMC civilian activities needing adjustment. The Area Management-Labor Committees were to hear appeals from the action of the Manpower Priorities Committees. The program further stated:

The procurement agency will not approve or let contracts for which the War Manpower Commission has not certified that labor can be or will be made available . . . On the basis of recommendations by the West Coast Production Priorities Committee, the War Production Board will exercise its authority over priorities and the allocation of materials to curtail essential civilian production and less essential production on the West Coast in so far as such action will make needed labor available to essential war production.

[11] "West Coast Manpower Program," War Manpower Commission, August 18, 1943 (mimeographed).

Where wage adjustments impeded recruitment or stabilization, representations were to be made through WMC to the War Labor Board and, if necessary, to OES. WMC was to expand its manpower utilization programs and

coordinate the manpower utilization activities of other agencies . . . The War Production Board and the appropriate procurement agencies will use their authority in support of such surveys, and will implement the execution of approved recommendations . . . In determining employment ceilings, Area Manpower Priorities Committees will take into account the effectiveness of labor utilization and the possibilities of meeting additional production requirements in whole or in part by more effective utilization of labor.

All hiring was to be done through USES referrals.

The WMC program was full of controversial points, particularly in regard to centralization of all manpower administration and authority. Byrnes called a meeting of the War Mobilization Committee on August 26 at the White House. Considerable opposition was evident. Members were instructed to review the plan with their agencies and make their recommendations by September 1. Originally the Navy opposed the entire idea. WPB was not averse to the general idea, but felt WMC was usurping its powers.

The War Department expressed the objections of the procurement agencies and WPB when it said:

We believe that there is underlying most, if not all of them [the proposals] a fundamental defect in that there is transferred to the War Manpower Commission and to some extent, to private citizens forming management-labor committees, each of which have no responsibility for the production program, powers which directly control that program. For example, under certain of the suggestions put forward in the memorandum the ultimate control over the placing of contracts would repose in the War Manpower Commission or its agencies. Again, the suggestions that priorities be set, and allocations of labor supply be made, locally in various areas by those who have no responsibility for the production schedules is unsound in principle and unworkable in practice. Our experience thus far in the war has abundantly shown that the allocation of all elements which are necessary to the achievement of the production schedules should be placed in the hands of the agency responsible for that production.

Again the plan seems to approach too closely a transfer of control of labor in the plants to an outside agency by permitting the WMC, the supplier of labor, to determine working practices. We believe that such a step is contrary to fundamental principles of management and would be disruptive of the morale of the industries serving the production agencies.[12]

The letter also attacked the suggestion that war production might be curtailed while civilian occupations might be relatively unchanged. The Acting Secretary of War stated that WPB was working out an alternative plan and decisions should be reserved until this was completed. He ended with an appeal for national service legislation as the only true solution, and stated that the Navy Department and the Maritime Commission had authorized him to say that they were "in general concurrence with the views herein expressed."

OWM refused to permit any delay for purposes of "study." Any proposed changes had to be submitted immediately. Within a day a "modified proposal" was submitted by the Acting Secretary of War "which has the full support of the Navy, Army and Maritime Commission and the personal approval of Mr. C. E. Wilson, Vice-chairman, War Production Board and Chairman of its Production Executive Committee." [13] The opposition plan pushed WMC back to the role WPB and the procurement agencies always felt it should be confined to—recruitment of labor and assignment of such labor to plants in order of priority set by the agencies responsible for production. The WMC role in labor utilization was eliminated and employment ceilings or priorities were not to be related to any such consideration. All control of contracts and production schedules was to remain with the procurement agencies and WPB. However, the opposition had moved toward acceptance of the basic pattern of the Baruch proposals.

THE BYRNES PROGRAM

During the next three days many stormy sessions were held in the OWM offices. The Baruch report was accepted in principle by all, but the WMC implementation was opposed by all except Baruch and Hancock, who took the position that any set of administrative details would be acceptable to them. The problem for OWM was complicated. There were important issues of basic principle, involving the labor utilization authority, the degree of authority to be held by private citizens—the Management-Labor

[12] Letter, John J. McCloy to James F. Byrnes, September 1, 1943.
[13] Letter, John J. McCloy to James F. Byrnes, September 2, 1943.

Committees and the proposed head of the Manpower Priorities Committee—and the degree of control that government should attempt to exercise over the labor market without legislation. There was the ever-present issue of resolving divided government authority and sharp agency competition among powerful units, each of which had some degree of legitimate interest in the problem. There was the touchy but highly essential factor that the agency directly responsible for manpower was distrusted by the others and did not have Byrnes's complete confidence. But, most important, OWM was aware that a precedent-making pattern was being established.

On September 4, 1943, Byrnes announced the West Coast Manpower Program as approved by the War Mobilization Committee. Many of the objections made by WPB and the procurement agencies were evident, and some of the scope desired by WMC was cut down, but by and large it retained the essential features recommended by Baruch and did broaden WMC authority and influence beyond anything it had known before.

The Byrnes program,[14] as it was soon called in Washington, provided for two sets of committees for each of "such West Coast areas as may be deemed necessary by the War Production Board and the War Manpower Commission." The first committee was the Area Production Urgency Committee (APUC), comprised of representatives of the procurement agencies and WMC, and chaired by the WPB representative. This Committee was authorized, in event of persistent shortage of labor, to recommend to the chairman of the WPB Production Executive Committee, adjustments in military procurement programs. "The War Production Board will exercise its control . . . through the Chairman of the Production Executive Committee . . ."

The chairman of APUC, after advice with the Committee, would: determine what production programs were feasible in the area and their relative urgency; inform WMC of approved production schedules or production requirements of establishments or categories of establishments; review proposals for facilities and for major supply contracts and make appropriate recommendations to WPB in the light of prospective availability of manpower;

[14] "West Coast Manpower Program," *White House Press Release*, September 4, 1943; *Congressional Record*, September 17, 1943, pp. 7593–7595.

develop a program for redistributing production from one area to another when manpower factors necessitate it; and recommend to WPB the need for adjustment of civilian production.

The second committee was to be known as the Area Manpower Priorities Committee and would comprise largely the same personnel but be chaired by a WMC appointee, preferably an outstanding citizen of the community or a member of the staff. (The program said nothing about Management-Labor Committee approval.) The committee was advisory to the WMC area director and its functions were to: list establishments, services, or categories of such, according to their urgency, on the basis of determinations submitted by the APUC, and their need for labor; fix employment ceilings and advise the area director thereof; and advise him on civilian activities within the area which might be adjusted.

"On the basis of recommendation by the APUC, the WPB will exercise its authority over priorities and the allocation of materials to adjust civilian production and services, insofar as such action will make needed labor available to essential war production." The USES or other channels approved by it were to be the sole referral agencies in the area and employers were forbidden to hire from any other source and workers were to select employment only from among those jobs they were referred to. WMC would expand its manpower utilization program, but could undertake advice and consultation only "at the request of management of any establishment or the War Production Board." Labor utilization could be taken into account in fixing employment ceilings. Procurement agencies were instructed to encourage the movement of subcontracting out of the area and to cut back production on the west coast at the earliest feasible opportunity. Selective Service was instructed to give special consideration to deferment of essential men.

The program attempted to resolve some old issues. For the first time a system for coördinating manpower activities of related agencies was developed into an administrative pattern. The relationship between WPB and WMC, always confused and in conflict, was reasonably well formulated. Byrnes said, in issuing his report, "Manpower and production cannot be dealt with separately for they are inseparable parts of a single but complicated problem. The West Coast War Manpower Program calls for the closest coöperation between the War Manpower Commission, the War Production Board and the various procurement agencies on a national, a regional and an area basis." A method for establishing manpower priorities, debated without conclusion since early 1942, was now established. It gave WMC authority to set employment ceilings for establishments, to force all hiring to be done only through authorized channels, and ended the freedom of individuals to seek and accept jobs where they wished.[15] It took the first step toward resolving the old conflict as to whether WPB might employ its power over materials allocation to relieve manpower difficulties, a plan which WPB had always fought and did not use even after promulgation of the West Coast Program.

Nationally the program was enthusiastically received. For a short time there was opposition on the west coast for fear that this was a device by Eastern industrial interests to cut down west coast postwar business. There was also considerable opposition from the management-labor committees against "imposition" of the plan without their advice. Local opposition was partly averted by *ex-post facto* consultation and minor administrative revisions.

Committees were established in five selected industrial centers—Seattle, Portland, San Francisco, Los Angeles, and San Diego. Considerable flexibility was allowed, particularly as related to controlled referrals. WPB never did curtail less essential civilian activities, as instructed, nor did WMC succeed in overcoming opposition of the procurement agencies and management to labor utilization services. But recruitment was considerably expedited, labor was channeled more successfully where it was needed, procurement agencies exercised considerably more caution in further contracting for the West Coast.

The program not only survived for the duration of the war but it soon spread in complete or modified form to all shortage areas of the country and "in fact it constituted the main operating program of WMC for the remainder of the war."[16]

[15] Legally, it was highly questionable whether OWM had any more authority to authorize such action by WMC than WMC had in the first instance. But the order was not disputed. Authority is frequently what you make it.

[16] *The United States at War*, p. 439.

OWM provided for adequate follow-up, calling for detailed monthly reports from both WPB and WMC on their respective portions of the program. The Budget Bureau was also asked to "keep in touch with, and report from time to time regarding developments in the several agencies affected by the West Coast production-manpower program to fulfill their responsibilities in the program."

On January 12, 1944, the Bureau made its first report to OWM. It indicated rapid progress in establishment of administrative machinery and development of suitable organization and procedure, although the program had been handicapped by an unfriendly reception in the localities, and such action as contract redistribution could still not be accomplished except against great local resistance. The report continued:

a major contribution of the plan has been the fact that it has brought about a recognition among the procurement agencies of the necessity for adjusting production programs to manpower availability. This recognition retarded the replacement of new demands on the labor markets in the critical areas. Of great importance also is the concept of employment ceilings which has provided an administrative mechanism for limiting demand for manpower; . . .[17]

However, the Bureau felt the real test of the plan remained to be met—the transfer of workers from less essential to more essential activities.[18]

Three months later, when the West Coast Program had been extended to several cities in other parts of the country, the Bureau made another comprehensive report, which concluded: "Although about the same problems persist, it would be correct in general to say that the problems are recognized and that progress is being made in dealing with most of them. Whether those efforts will be completely successful is entirely another question." [19] On that point the Bureau indicated its doubts.

Such doubts were even stronger in OWM. It was recognized

[17] Bureau of Budget, Staff Memorandum, undated. (Transmitted, George M. Graham to Donald Russell, January 12, 1944.)
[18] This was never accomplished. The only all-out effort in this direction was applied in New Bedford, Massachusetts, in the late stages of the war, and failed. National service legislation would have been necessary to carry through such a program with success.
[19] Bureau of the Budget, "Supplementary Report on West Coast Program," Staff Memorandum, April 1, 1944.

that such devices as "controlled referral," "employment ceilings," and "statements of availability" might be circumvented with impunity; since the effectiveness of these devices depended upon community support, it complicated the problem of curtailing less essential production against the opposition of the community; without the curtailment of less essential activities it was difficult to persuade the procurement agencies to remove essential munitions production. OWM took many steps to strengthen the West Coast Program, most conspicuously the directive of August 4, 1944.

DIRECTIVE OF AUGUST 4, 1944

By 1944 manpower was clearly the primary production problem. Almost every important industry was complaining of labor scarcity.

The west coast formula was extended throughout most of the nation. Where the situation was not quite so critical "Modified" Area Production Urgency Committees were established. These committees had all the functions of the full committees except that they could not pass upon new contract awards or undertake to relocate production. In March 1944 the functions of the Area Production Urgency Committees were expanded to include review of all contracts over $50,000 irrespective of labor requirements, although formal approval was not required unless additional labor was needed. In May 1944 WPB prepared a standard clause for all limitation orders designed to prohibit expansion of production in labor shortage areas if it meant interference with any other plant in the area.

By July 1, 1944 WMC had ordered "priority referral," formerly known as "controlled referral," and meaning universal hiring through USES, for male workers in all areas of the country, and employment ceilings applied to all shortage areas. But by the summer of 1944 talk of reconversion was general and "peace jitters" were making the manpower job more complex just at the time it had become tightest.

In the summer of 1944, two sharp conflicts between WPB and WMC, the latter supported by the military, came to a head. First was the question whether non-military or less essential production should be curtailed, even in non-labor shortage areas, in order to make labor available to move into war work, even if it meant moving from one area to another. Donald Nelson opposed such a program, insisting that shutting down of less essential plants did not cause workers to seek war work nor get them to move to critical areas; they would continue to seek work near home and if employment in essential industries was not available they would switch to other less essential work or quit work entirely. WMC and representatives of the military did not agree and considered the situation sufficiently serious to justify drastic action. This later led Nelson to write that "the Army was, quite openly, out to protect war production by the simple means of creating pools of unemployment." [20]

He felt the problem could be handled by the contract clearance procedure which should stop the movement of contracts into areas with inadequate labor. The military and WMC did not oppose Nelson's proposal but considered it inadequate.

The second issue dealt with sanctions. WMC had no power to enforce ceilings on recalcitrant employers or its "statement of availability" procedure on either workers or employers. WMC had long requested WPB to use its priorities power in support of these regulations. Under the firm leadership of John Lord O'Brian, WPB general counsel, the latter always insisted that use of its authority to enforce orders of other agencies would be illegal and impractical. Although the West Coast Program required such steps to be taken, no regulations were issued.

The August 4 directive was designed to resolve both issues.[21] With regard to inter-area recruitment the directive ordered immediate establishment of Area Production Urgency Committees and Manpower Priorities Committees in Groups III and IV labor areas—areas of balanced or surplus labor supply. The APUC committees in these and other areas were "charged with the responsibility of authorizing increased civilian production . . . [but not] until the representative of the War Manpower Commission within the area had certified in writing to the Committee that labor is available for such production without interfer-

[20] *Arsenal of Democracy,* p. 402.
[21] *White House Press Release,* August 4, 1944.

ence with local and inter-regional labor recruiting efforts therein."

This was a twofold blow for WPB. It meant not only that production could be curtailed in one area to relieve labor shortage in another, but it also meant WMC could control rates of expansion or resumption of civilian production. (This subject is covered more fully in Chapter 6.)

Although inter-area and inter-regional recruitment received some stimulation from this order, the attempt to obtain workers for one plant through imposition of ceilings upon another was never successful. Ceilings in themselves could not make available the precise workers needed by other plants; usually the least desirable and least skilled workers were released. Furthermore, release from one plant did not mean that the worker would go where WMC directed.

The sanctions issue was similarly decided in favor of WMC. The directive stated:

> Upon application of the Chairman of the War Manpower Commission, all interested governmental agencies will apply any and all sanctions lawfully available to the Government including allocation of materials, fuel, power and services to ensure compliance with the determinations of the Committee [re employment ceilings].

About six weeks later the first case calling for use of WPB priority power, in accordance with the Byrnes directive, arose. On September 23, Paul McNutt, WMC chairman, requested such action at the Silver States Construction Company of Winslow, Arizona. It happened that no priorities assistance had been granted this company and thus no decision to revoke could be made, but WPB took occasion to review the entire issue. The review, prepared by General Counsel O'Brian, clearly indicated that WPB did not think it proper and did not wish to use this power for other agencies' functions.[22] The directive had referred to "any and all sanctions lawfully available," and O'Brian maintained, "The request now made to use priority to enforce sanctions sharply raises questions as to what if any sanctions are 'lawfully available.'" He described the administrative impediments as well as legal difficulties and expressed doubts whether such penalty could be upheld in court.

[22] Letter, J. A. Krug to James F. Byrnes, October 9, 1944 and Memorandum, John Lord O'Brian to J. A. Krug, October 4, 1944.

WMC and the procurement agencies felt strongly that WPB's adamant position was destroying the effectiveness of the directive. They again brought the issue to OWMR.[23]

Byrnes took a firm stand. The government had to act in time of war and powers had to be tested. He said he was unwilling to ask for voluntary compliance by the many without being prepared to take measures upon the few who were unwilling to cooperate.[24] The wrangle continued into the winter when finally WPB issued Priorities Regulation 26 which held that priorities or allocations granted by WPB could be withdrawn or modified "when the WPB makes a finding that materials or facilities are not being used most effectively for the prosecution of the war as a result of a failure to comply with an employment ceiling or hiring regulation of the War Manpower Commission." [25] The decision remained, however, with WPB. V–E Day came five and a half months later and until that time the power was virtually never used.

In two other points of the directive, WMC authority was extended in one and curtailed in the other. Employment ceilings were ordered in all Groups I and II areas—areas of current or threatened shortage. This merely strengthened an existing WMC regulation and circumvented delays growing out of the appeal procedure by considering the decision of the chairman of the Manpower Priorities Committee immediately effective despite any appeals under way which might ultimately alter the decision. Finally, the directive curtailed a power apparently granted to WMC in the West Coast Program. "If an Area Production Urgency Committee, established in a Group 1 or 2 Labor Area, certifies that the need for production is immediate, the War Manpower Commission will not delay or refuse to proceed with labor referrals in the area on the ground that proper utilization of la-

---

[23] The Under-Secretary of War wrote Byrnes: "It is my recollection that this statement and directive were issued with full knowledge as to certain doubts as to the legal authority of the War Production Board which had been expressed by John Lord O'Brian. Those doubts were resolved in favor of action and our present situation is due simply to the failure of the War Production Board to comply with your directive." (Letter, December 11, 1944.)

[24] *White House Press Release*, December 23, 1944.

[25] WPB Priorities Regulation 26, December 23, 1944. O'Brian resigned three days before this regulation was issued.

bor is not being made." This virtually terminated WMC's long embattled labor utilization program, opposed consistently and successfully by WPB, the procurement agencies, and employers.

COÖRDINATING MILITARY DEFERMENTS
WITH MANPOWER POLICY

The Selective Service System, originally set up in 1940 as an autonomous body, proved to be so firmly entrenched in its autonomy that by the time serious attempts were made to integrate it with other war programs such attempts generally failed. Selective Service lived a life apart, even though its actions had daily influence on virtually all other agencies.

The executive order of December 1942 which placed the System completely under WMC was clear in its intent. Nevertheless, the leadership, authority, and direction of the staff and local Selective Service boards remained virtually untouched. Their work and procedures and, for the most part, their operating policies were uninfluenced by the "merger." McNutt recognized the dangers of any drastic change in controls over SSS and was aware of public support for local administration of the draft boards. Nevertheless, the director of Selective Service resented the merger, and differences were not easily resolved. In December 1943 Congress legislated the divorce of SSS from WMC and thereafter not even the outward forms of coördination remained between the two agencies for mobilizing manpower for the armed forces and for production. Although WMC furnished Selective Service with lists of essential activities and other information to guide it in its occupational deferment policies, the latter acted as it saw fit, until several crises beginning in 1944 caused higher-level intervention.

WPB continually insisted that Selective Service deferment policies should derive from production objectives and that recommendations of WPB officers should play a controlling roll in individual occupational deferment cases. But Selective Service and WPB were as separate as two agencies could be, and the latter had even less influence with SSS than did WMC.

In many respects the Selective Service System was too elusive to come to grips with, even for its own officials. As the law was framed, and under its administrative practices, the System comprised about 6500 autonomous local bodies, which might or might not be guided by general policies.

Even before the great issue arose as to which individuals should be withdrawn from the civilian economy there was, of course, the question of how many—a complex question involving military strategy and industrial war objectives at once. In this question the President saw fit not to give much voice to either WMC or WPB.[26]

THE TYDINGS AMENDMENT

One of the greatest unbalances created in deferment practices resulted from the so-called Tydings Amendment (to the Selective Service Act) of November 1942.[27] The wording of the amendment was not significantly different from existing Selective Service regulations. It provided that essential agricultural workers should not be withdrawn unless satisfactory replacements could be obtained. However, local boards, with support from headquarters, interpreted the intent of the amendment to be virtual universal deferment for agricultural workers. By 1944 this practice reached the proportions of a scandal. While the military made fervent pleas for younger men as combat replacements and such young men, even with highly important and scarce skills, were being called out of industry, agriculture remained a relatively untouchable zone. Industrial workers trying to avoid the draft were transferring to agricultural work for refuge, while agricultural workers could not be persuaded to turn to the higher remuneration of industrial work for fear of losing deferred status.

The matter was touchy. The farm bloc in Congress was known to be stubborn on the issue and opposed any change. When OWMR decided the time had come to meet the problem directly, Byrnes recognized it as a matter on which full presidential support would be required. After discussion with the affected agencies, he obtained the President's approval for his program.

---

[26] In the summer of 1942 the Joint Chiefs of Staff laid plans for peak military personnel strength of 10.8 millions. Both WPB and WMC objected, stating that the residual labor force could not supply armed forces of such magnitude. The President ordered consultation among the three agencies, but then endorsed the Joint Chiefs' plan. The size of the armed forces ultimately exceeded the proposed objective by almost a million and they were adequately supplied.

[27] 77th Cong., 2nd Sess., PL 772, Section 4(k).

On January 2, 1945 Byrnes wrote General Hershey, Director of Selective Service, stating that the Secretaries of War and Navy had advised him that calls to be met in the coming year would exhaust the qualified men in the 18–25 age group at an early date and that Hershey himself had reported the only remaining substantial source of men in this age group was among the 364,000 agricultural deferments.

You have further advised me [Byrnes wrote], that if this group is not available, you must call into the service occupationally deferred men in the next age group, 26 years and older, most of whom are fathers.

The Chairman of the War Production Board, Mr. Krug, advises me that the loss of these men would make it extremely difficult, if not impossible, to meet critical war demands. Moreover, these older men would not meet the expressed needs of the Army and Navy.

He stated that the War Food Administrator had advised that the loss of food production, resulting from induction of the physically qualified men in this age group who did not clearly fall within the scope of the Tydings Amendment, should not result in a critical condition.

The Tydings Amendment to the Selective Service Act does not give the agricultural worker absolute exemption from Selective Service. It was not so intended . . .

I have reported these facts to the President. He has found that the further deferment of all men now deferred in the 18–25 age group because of agricultural occupation is not as essential to the best interests of our war effort as is the urgent and more essential need of the Army and Navy for young men. The President feels in view of existing conditions, agriculture, like our other industries can, with few exceptions, be carried on by those in the older age groups.

The President has authorized me to ask you to take such action in connection with the administration of the Tydings Amendment as may be necessary to provide to the full extent permitted by law for the reclassification and induction of the men agriculturally deferred in the age group 18 through 25.[28]

Hershey promptly ordered a review of all agricultural deferments by local boards and action in accordance with Byrnes's instructions. Although the boards did not generally act with alacrity or enthusiasm, the farm bloc in Congress was soon astir and demanded continued privileged status. In April 1945 they pushed through both houses a joint resolution which was an amend-

[28] *White House Press Release*, January 3, 1945.

ment to the Tydings Amendment and which would, in practical effect, have resulted in the deferment of all registrants engaged in agriculture.

Mr. Vinson, the new OWMR director, used the customary Budget Bureau canvass of agency attitudes and found Mr. Stimson, the War Secretary, strongly recommending a veto.[29] WPB and WMC shared his view. The War Food Administrator thought it should be approved by the President. Hershey submitted a long and equivocal memorandum. Vinson reported fully to President Truman and recommended a veto:

Essentially the problem is to balance the critical needs of agriculture and food production as against the equally critical need of the armed forces for young men. Without doubt, Agriculture has on the whole, received a preferred position in the application of the Selective Service Law. I do not doubt that there was some justification for this preference, and that our food position might be worse if the preference had not been shown. Nevertheless, I doubt extremely whether at this stage of the war we should extend further the special consideration already given to agriculture in the law.[30]

The President vetoed the resolution.

INTER-AGENCY COMMITTEE FOR OCCUPATIONAL
DEFERMENT—1944

From 1944 on, OWM–OWMR became, in effect, the focal point for development of Selective Service policies. The most important single step in coördinating deferment policies was establishment of the Inter-Agency Committee for Occupational Deferment in March 1944. Such a move became practically unavoidable as the controversy over deferment of men under 26 reached the boiling point.

On the one side, industry exerted pressure on WPB to retain those workers under 26 who had already received one or more deferments and were considered crucial. WPB and WMC fought to keep the draft at its lowest possible impact. On the other side, the military was demanding young men as combat replacements and calling for them rapidly since quotas had fallen off sharply

[29] "Under the proposed legislation there not only is nothing to prevent evasion of military service under the guise of farming, but in fact such evasion is affirmatively encouraged." (Letter, Henry L. Stimson to Harold D. Smith, undated—about April 25, 1945.)
[30] Memorandum, April 29, 1945.

in 1943. The Army was in an equivocal position. As the agency demanding men under 26 it could hardly promote generosity in deferments. But as chief procurement agency it was subjected to extreme pressure from contractors to protect their personnel under threat of failure to meet schedules.

Procedures established in the West Coast Program were drawn upon by OWM to deal with this problem. During the period the program was being worked out, conflict had raged over deferment of aircraft workers, the War Department demanding a six-month blanket deferment as opposed to a 60-day interim moratorium, supported by WMC, and granted by SSS. John Hancock, acting for Byrnes, had drawn up an effective settlement:

> In the West Coast manpower program the Selective Service System is arranging to defer and will defer all necessary workers in West Coast airplane plants including their production subcontractors.
>
> The workers in the West Coast airplane plants are divided into two classes: (1) Those currently irreplaceable, and (2) those currently replaceable.
>
> Irreplaceable workers are deferred for a period of six months. They are eligible for additional deferment if they remain irreplaceable to production . . .[31]

The Hancock plan was promptly put in operation. Every west coast aircraft producer and subcontractor was notified that he was to prepare the two lists.

> The appropriate Army or Navy officer in your plant will be asked to assume joint responsibility with you in requests for deferments and to sign such requests jointly with you when he concurs as to the need. He will receive appropriate instructions from his department.
>
> In general terms, your requests for six months' deferments, if concurred in by the Army or Navy officer in your plant, will be sent to the appropriate draft board. If the local draft board does not defer, you are expected to appeal to your appeal board, and there is no induction pending the final settlement of the appeal.[32]

General Hershey sent an official to the coast to see that the plan was understood and accepted. The Army and Navy gave appropriate instructions to their plant representatives. The new pattern for deferments, based on certification of procurement agency representatives, was later extended to other aircraft establishments not on the coast.

[31] *White House Press Release,* October 28, 1943.
[32] Memorandum, John M. Hancock to James F. Byrnes, October 27, 1943.

When in 1944 it became clear that sharp inroads would have to be made on men under 26, and a procedure superior to the catch-as-catch-can methods of local boards, guided only by the WMC *List of Essential Activities,* would have to be found, the west coast procedure was generally adopted. It was decided that men under 26 could be deferred only upon written certification by the State director of Selective Service to the local board. Government agencies, responsible for production or procurement, were to advise the State director regarding the essentiality and deferment of men working in plants in their jurisdiction.

No sooner had the President made this decision than a new dispute arose as to who should determine what industries, activities, or particular plants were to be eligible for this special treatment. The armed services insisted it should be the WPB Production Executive Committee, which determined relative urgencies of production objectives.[33] WMC fought the proposal, arguing that it would mean deferments would be confined to the direct procurement interests of the Army, Navy, and Maritime Commission, to the disastrous neglect of supporting activities such as transportation, scientific development, and other essential services. McNutt proposed that recommendations be submitted by the appropriate agencies to WMC which would "weigh these recommendations from the respective authorities against military and civilian manpower supply and demand, [and] will determine manpower priorities and relate them to deferments. They will then transmit lists of approved plants and programs to the Selective Service System . . ."[34]

After further discussion with OWM, McNutt modified his pro-

[33] "By act of Congress the question is one for the director of Selective Service to decide. To decide it properly, he should have the advice of the agency responsible for war production. That agency is the Production Executive Committee of War Production Board . . . and has on it the men from the war procurement agencies . . . The War Manpower Commission is also represented on the Production Executive Committee . . .

"This advisory job is not one for the War Manpower Commission alone. That agency is not in close touch with the details of war production. It is and should be primarily a recruiting organization. The lists of essential activities and of critical occupations which it has been in the habit of furnishing to Selective Service have never been of any real benefit in determining deferments . . ." (Memorandum, Robert P. Patterson and Frank Knox to the President, March 18, 1944.)

[34] Memorandum, Paul McNutt to the President, March 18, 1944.

posal to call for an inter-agency committee, with WMC as head, to screen and submit to the director of Selective Service recommendations for special consideration of irreplaceable men in approved activities and plants. This proposal was accepted by Byrnes and by the end of March the Inter-Agency Committee on Occupational Deferments had been established. It included the Petroleum Administrator for War, the Solid Fuels Administrator, the Rubber Director, the Director of the Office of Defense Transportation, the War Food Administrator, and the War Shipping Administrator as well as WPB and the large procurement agencies.

Its standards were rigorous. Only production programs specifically approved by the committee were eligible for any deferment consideration and then the man in question had to be certified by his employer, the representative of the government agency with jurisdiction over the plant, and the State director of Selective Service. It meant that decisions on occupational deferment of men under 26 was for all practical purposes removed from the local boards—and a virtual end to such deferments.

INTER-AGENCY COMMITTEE—1945

By the end of 1944, the pool of available men under 26 was virtually dry and attention had to be concentrated on the next age bracket, 26–29. At first OWMR tried to handle this stage through Selective Service. Byrnes called Hershey's attention to the grave concern of the production and procurement agencies regarding the effect on war production caused by withdrawal of men 26–29. He said he had consulted with representatives of the various agencies on measures to minimize the effect. The WMC *List of Essential Activities* had been revised to select the activities deemed most critical. Byrnes continued:

I would appreciate it if you would arrange for this list to be a guide in detemining the men to be selected for the armed services in this age group. I would suggest that consideration be given to the fullest extent practicable to the following order of withdrawals:
1. Registrants not employed in any activities appearing on the Essential Activities List.
2. Registrants whom the Local Boards find to be employed in relatively unimportant jobs in essential activities, and other registrants in such activities who may readily be replaced.
3. Registrants whom the Local Boards find to be employed in rela-

tively unimportant jobs in critical activities, and other registrants in such activities who may readily be replaced.

4. Registrants whom the Local Boards find to be engaged in relatively more important jobs in essential activities.

5. Registrants whom the Local Boards find to be engaged in more important jobs in critical activities.[35]

This approach was not destined to survive. The agencies complained about the activities which had been declared critical and those which had not; they did not trust the judgment of local boards, and they chafed under the uncertainties involved in the entire procedure.

Byrnes reinstituted the inter-agency committee procedure within a month. This time no attempt was made to have the committee in Washington establish which programs and plants would be eligible. The situation had become universally so tight that each case would have to be judged on its merits. In general, each agency was given a quota to cover all plants or activities over which it had jurisdiction, the quota being 30 per cent of the total number of occupationally deferred men in the age groups. The agency could distribute the 30 per cent in whatever way it saw fit among its establishments. Again the procedure was one of certification by the employer, the agency, and the Selective Service System. Although most of the agencies soon complained that they could not live within the 30 per cent, and additional quotas had to be granted to a small number of highly critical activities, in the main this procedure carried through until after V–E Day, when the pressure subsided.

In November 1945, after termination of WMC, OWMR set up a new Inter-Agency Committee on Manpower to review both deferments and requests for release from the armed forces on the basis of industrial need.

MAKESHIFTS IN ABSENCE OF LEGISLATIVE AUTHORITY

In the August 4 directive, Byrnes went about as far as possible without specific legislative authorization. In many instances he invoked authority even when its existence was questionable. In December 1944, to prevent reopening of a Los Angeles race track which would have employed needed manpower, Byrnes asked for

[35] Letter, January 13, 1945. (*White House Press Release,* January 15, 1945.)

a shutdown of all race tracks. Local pressure had forced a decision favorable to the track upon the local WMC director. McNutt was loath to reverse him without assurance that WPB would impose sanctions if an attempt was made to open the track despite denial of a WMC ceiling. WPB gave no such assurance. Finally, Byrnes with oblique reference to the particular incident, settled the matter by announcing,

With the approval of the President, I urge that the management of these tracks take immediate measures to bring present race meets to a close by January 3, 1945 and to refrain from resuming racing from all tracks until war conditions permit . . . I have asked the War Manpower Commission to withdraw all ceiling authorizations. I have also asked the chairman of the War Production Board and the Director of the Office of Defense Transportation to take such steps as fall within their power to prevent the use of critical materials, services and transportation in the operation of these tracks if such steps should prove necessary.[36]

There was some tendency in Washington to mock this type of measure as causing considerable fanfare with virtually no real manpower saving. Byrnes pointed out that race tracks required not only direct labor, but railroad transportation, tires, gasoline, and other important equipment valuable in themselves and with considerable indirect manpower effects. Subsequent reports indicated that the racing ban had even more salutary indirect effects than expected.[37]

The phrasing of the release—it was not a directive or order—indicated some doubt regarding its legal authority, just as in the case of the curfew ordered by OWMR and the request for curtail-

[36] *White House Press Release,* December 23, 1944.

[37] Although the local WMC had claimed that the kind of labor used at race tracks was not useful for war work, press interviews with jockeys and other affected employees indicated most of them intended to take war jobs.

Two months after issuance of the ban, the Federal Communications Commission reported to Byrnes that Western Union had canceled all facilities previously used for collection and distribution of racing information thus reclaiming more than 19,000 miles of leased circuits with more than 700 drops which could now be used for essential purposes. The manpower employed in maintenance and use of these leased circuits was also made available. (Letter, Paul A. Porter to James F. Byrnes, February 21, 1945.)

A survey made during the previous racing season of cars crossing the Delaware River bridge to get to the 50-day meet at Garden State Race Track near Camden, New Jersey, led to an estimate that the ban in this case alone would save approximately 125,000 cars driving 15 miles a day. (Memorandum, Walter Brown to James F. Byrnes, February 26, 1945.)

ment of nonessential travel and cessation of conventions and several other programs designed to save manpower. The general compliance with these "press releases" reflected the status of OWMR and seemed to support the theory that in time of war strict legal authority was not always required. If its source was high enough, if the measure had a reasonable degree of public support, and if the appropriate agency acted with aggressiveness, the effect would be the same.

Nevertheless, OWMR regarded such measures as nothing but makeshift expedients to deal with a basically unsatisfactory condition. In his last report to the President and Congress, Byrnes said:

All of the measures available to the Government were used to coördinate and integrate the work of the several agencies concernd with manpower. Nevertheless, I cannot say that we have had a comprehensive system that works efficiently.

The methods which we have had at our disposal do not permit the withdrawal of sufficient workers from less essential occupations. In large part they apply only to those who have quit or been released from jobs.

They do not place workers in essential jobs in which the work is hard in comparison with the pay received. They do not permit the transfer of workers from loose labor areas to tight areas.

They do not stop workers from quitting the labor market entirely. They do not bring people into the labor market. It is difficult, without direct penalties, to stop some employers from hiring workers without approval or from exceeding established ceilings.[38]

USE OF SELECTIVE SERVICE AS MANPOWER SANCTION

Several attempts were made to make special use of Selective Service as a partial substitute for national service. On February 1, 1943, SSS, at the request of WMC, issued a list of "non-deferable" occupations. Men engaged in such occupations, who were currently enjoying deferred status on the basis of dependency, would be reclassified I–A—available for induction—on April 1, unless they changed occupation. This order was so unpopular that local boards failed to abide by it and it was finally withdrawn in December.

A year later, while discussion of "work-or-fight" bills was raging

[38] James F. Byrnes, *War Production and V–E Day*, Second Report by the Director of War Mobilization and Reconversion, April 1, 1945, pp. 8–9.

in Congress, OWMR sponsored a special drive to use Selective Service to keep men on war jobs and induce more men to accept such jobs, a program which came to be known as Byrnes's "Work-or-Fight Order." [39] The program originated in the fear that concentration of draft calls upon men under 26 was causing older men to leave war work with impunity and would also retard efforts to persuade men in non-war work to make a change. The order stated that Byrnes had requested Selective Service to amend its regulations "to provide for the calling of additional men in the higher age groups into the armed services to replace men released by the Army and Navy to man critical programs." [40]

Byrnes then took steps to see that the Army and Navy did not reject such men after they were called by Selective Service. He wrote the respective Secretaries:

> I have authorized the Selective Service System to call for induction of those men under 38 who leave essential industry, change jobs in essential industry without the authority of local boards,[41] or who do not work in essential industry.
>
> It is possible that this may require the induction of some men in the older age groups into the Armed Services. I believe that if this does result, the Armed Services might well increase their release of men by furlough or otherwise, for placement in essential industries to the extent that such placement is required to sustain war production. Such releases should not be charged against established ceilings for military personnel and your induction calls may be modified accordingly.[42]

This led to an extension of the interpretation of the original order—an extension already widely assumed in the press by local boards. If men the Army could not use were to be inducted and such inductions not charged against Army quotas there appeared to be no reason why 4–F's—the physically unqualified—could not be called as well as the "job-jumpers" over 26. Stimson's reply to Byrnes made this clear:

> the Army will give every coöperation to Selective Service in making effective the "Work or Fight" directive. To that end it will be necessary for us to accept men under thirty-eight (38) for induction who

[39] *OWMR Press Release,* December 9, 1944.

[40] This related to soldiers who were being "furloughed" to help meet critical shortages in specific industries, a practice discussed later.

[41] This created vigorous objection by WMC, which saw its authority over job priorities passing away. A compromise was reached whereby local boards would grant full consideration to WMC recommendations.

[42] Letter, December 19, 1944.

(a) leave essential industry; (b) change jobs in essential industry without the authority of local boards; or (c) who do not work in essential industry, even though not physically qualified for induction under present regulations.

It will be our purpose to process these men back into industry under furlough or otherwise insofar as they are unacceptable for general military service.[43]

The full implication of these regulations was not generally recognized. While the public and Congress debated national manpower legislation, the "Work-or-Fight Order" provided a definite form of national service for males under 38, but with none of the protective provisos regarding working conditions and civil liberties which were contained in the legislation being considered. Under the regulations, any male under 38 not already in essential work or about to leave such work could be drafted and sent to a designated war plant under enlisted reserve status—that is, subject to immediate Army recall. If the man refused to accept such work, he remained in the labor camps which the Army set up.

Fortunately, this twisted version of the Selective Service law was not long or widely applied and less than 50,000 men were affected. Most of them were sent back to industry; the remainder were in camps where the Army had difficulty finding appropriate assignments and where their treatment was not the kindliest, since the measure was consciously punitive. Nevertheless, the order was considered successful by harried officials, repeatedly cornered by manpower crises, and who, in the absence of over-all legislation, appeared to have run out of legitimate devices.[44]

It is also worth nothing that sometime earlier the use of Selec-

[43] Letter, December 23, 1944. Originally the military had objected to the 4–F program. The Army and Navy always resented use of the uniform, and military status, for non-military purposes, feeling it injurious to the morale of the combat soldier. The point is strongly made in a letter to Byrnes from Forrestal, August 4, 1944, in which the latter objected to use of men in uniform for seizure of civilian industries. Patterson also emphasized the point frequently.

[44] The reaction of the New York regional director of WMC was not untypical. "The order itself is good, but by its local implementation, it is somewhat nullified, because the interpretation nowadays of what is essential to the war effort is extremely broad . . . There is no doubt in my mind that psychologically, it was one of the best things we have done lately, and it is unquestionably halting the exodus of many workers from this age group into less essential war work or less essential industry." (Letter, Anna M. Rosenberg to James F. Byrnes, December 30, 1944.)

tive Service was threatened as a wartime strike-breaking measure. In the summer of 1943, when the nation was staggered by its most disastrous wartime strike in the coal mines, and even government seizure had failed to cause the strikers to return, the President wrote the Secretaries of War and Navy asking that the full sanctions of the draft be used against all miners who refused to return to work in a coal mine taken over by the United States.[45] Three weeks later, although the immediate issue had subsided, the President issued a release stating that he would, in the future, use Selective Service to bring coal workers into line if necessary. To make such a program effective he would ask Congress to raise Selective Service age limits to 65 instead of 45. The assumption was that upon being drafted the Army would assign such men back to the mines for duty.

THE ENLISTED RESERVE AS SUBSTITUTE FOR MANPOWER LEGISLATION

The assignment of soldiers to their previous civilian work, usually in enlisted reserve status, was first undertaken during the 1942 crisis in non-ferrous metal mining. About 4300 soldiers were released for work in the mines, which materially but only temporarily improved the situation. A year later the agencies looked to the Army for more soldiers. The War Department was vigorously opposed, but the other agencies declared unanimously that production goals could be met in no other way. This was apparently sufficient to convince OWM which requested the War Department for troops.

OWM also used this device to help meet the west coast emergency. The Baruch-Hancock report recommended that "the armed forces . . . be asked to furlough selected key men, now in the Army, back to the aircraft plants from which they were taken." OWM arranged for WPB to obtain the names of such key men from the manufacturers and to furnish them to the Army and Navy. On receipt of such names the Army and Navy were to determine promptly whether such men could be furloughed. Several thousand soldiers were returned to their old jobs in this way.

In 1944 WMC, supported by WPB, requested release from the

---

[45] Letter, June 3, 1943. In this letter he directed that age deferments for miners 38–45, and physical requirements for all who might be 4–F, be waived.

Army and Navy "of all experienced and qualified foundry work-ers, or for the furloughing for a 90-day period of such workers and for their reassignment to the industry." [46] The request was granted by OWMR.

Army resistance was progressively modified as procurement was threatened by lack of manpower. As time went on many excep-tions were made—for ammunition, rubber tire, cotton duck and aircraft plants, foundries, aluminum sheet mills, and others. In the case of rubber tires, for example, it went so far as to allow soldiers to work in uniform. They remained subject to Army dis-cipline and received regular Army pay in addition to plant wages. As distinguished from the "work-or-fight" draftees, the soldier had to volunteer for such assignments.

Use of the enlisted reserve looked like an easy solution to man-power difficulties. Employers preferred furloughed soldiers; the turnover problem was ended and the men more easily subject to discipline. The liberties of such workers were more limited than those of other workers. But as a technique for solving manpower problems, it was questionable. Had the numbers of men been greater—the volume was quite small—the effect upon soldier morale might have been costly. Furthermore it resulted in a double vulnerability for one portion of the population: physically qualified males, 18–36. Others were free of the hazard of work assignment.

As already indicated, OWM–OWMR and other agencies were never satisfied with such devious devices and never overestimated their effectiveness. From late 1943 to V–E Day, OWM–OWMR advocated national service legislation. The President included appeals for such legislation in his State of the Union messages to the Congress in 1944 and 1945. Byrnes undertook to mobilize and unify before Congress an administration critically divided on the issue, but such legislation was never obtained.[47]

[46] Letter, Paul V. McNutt to James F. Byrnes, October 23, 1944. The let-ter illustrates the integration job required of OWMR. McNutt also requested Byrnes's assistance to (1) get the War Labor Board to expedite foundry wage cases and liberalize policy in granting wage increases; (2) get WPB to reallocate essential foundry work to conserve labor; (3) get OPA to allow higher prices for foundry products to absorb higher wages; (4) assist in importation of West Indies workers for foundries.

[47] The story of the agencies' wrangling *vis-à-vis* Congress on this issue is both interesting and significant. Space considerations make its inclusion here

CONCLUSION

This chapter has dealt only with selected high lights of OWM–OWMR participation in the manpower field. Nothing has been said of such problems as housing and community facilities for war workers, importation of foreign labor, use of prisoners of war, and the less spectacular day-to-day recruiting and placement problems encountered by WMC's local units. The inter-agency struggles on factory inspection to appraise labor utilization, and legislative battles like that over national service legislation, were only mentioned. In all of these matters OWM–OWMR played a strong coördinating and policy-making role. Better than any other one field, manpower problems illustrated the variety and character of OWM–OWMR functions and dramatized the need for such an agency.

Among analysts of government war organization there is a current, perhaps endless, debate as to whether OWM–OWMR would have been essential had the functions of WMC and WPB been encompassed within one agency. It is recalled that before setting up WMC, President Roosevelt offered Donald Nelson the opportunity of incorporating such an agency within WPB. Nelson's former associates have since indicated they thought it a blunder not to have retained authority over manpower planning in WPB.[48]

The close interrelationship between production and manpower is undeniable. It is also true that during its last year most of WPB's activities were largely related to and conditioned by manpower factors over which it had no control. But it is also true that production responsibilities overlap with price controls and purchasing and even strategic planning. It is equally clear that manpower administration overlaps with housing, wage control, transportation, and many other functions allocated to individual agencies. These clear interrelationships, whether in peace or war, always lead to recommendations for combining agencies or functions. During the war there were proposals for all sorts of combinations, some involving three, four, or five large agencies. But for the sake of administrative feasibility, delineations have to be

impractical. The more significant aspects are described in H. M. Somers, *Coördinating the Federal Executive,* 1947, Widener Library, Harvard University (unpublished dissertation).

[48] *Industrial Mobilization for War,* p. 228.

made somewhere and they can never avoid some overlapping.

In the case of manpower there was a special problem. In view of the fact that it was a voluntary program, the coöperation of labor organizations was essential; in a democracy such coöperation would probably have had to be cultivated just as much even if we had had national service legislation. It is doubtful whether labor would have accepted subordination to a production agency, dominated largely by industrialists. (Labor was always unhappy about its relationships in WPB despite two vice-chairmanships under its control.)

Quite likely, had WPB and WMC been combined there would have been less manpower coördinating to be done by a super-body like OWM–OWMR. Similarly, the problems might have been less if Selective Service had been integrated with the central manpower agency. But it would have still left the Army, Navy, Maritime Commission, National Housing Agency, Railroad Retirement Board, National War Labor Board, Federal Works Agency, Civil Service Commission, and many others—all of which were involved in the manpower program—to be coördinated. It is also true that better manpower sanctions might have reduced the conflicts, but there is no doubt that the need for coördination and central policy-making would have remained.

As it was, the last 18 months of the war saw collisions among the agencies which threatened a complete impasse. Only OWM–OWMR made possible any sort of coördination. It did not regard the measures it took as adequate—it kept appealing for legislative authority to the very end—but it made some course of action possible. The net results were probably as successful as the basic situation would allow.

CHAPTER 6

WAR AND INDUSTRIAL
RECONVERSION

*T*he abounding confidence of the American people in the war's outcome and our vast material
resources were reflected in the fact that as early
as 1943 discussion of reconversion and preparation for peace were
already widespread.

The nation did not look forward to the postwar period with
equanimity. The decade preceding the war was associated with
depression. This, plus the knowledge that war prosperity was
based largely on government war contracts, led to considerable
uneasiness about the economic future.

There was general sentiment that the government should prepare for and avoid the possibility of depression. Virtually no
controversy existed over the desirability of early planning for
reconversion. But how much war energy should be diverted to
actual reconversion while the two-front war was still in progress?
How soon should actual measures be taken and how extensive
should such steps be? Here interests and viewpoints clashed vio-
lently. The conflicts reached such bitterness, causing explosive
disruptions within as well as among agencies, that they might
easily have caused great damage to the war programs in 1944 and
1945 had it not been for the existence of OWM–OWMR, a central
office which stood above the contesting agencies and was empowered to resolve their disputes and direct policy.

THE BARUCH-HANCOCK REPORT

Even before we actually entered the war, virtually all agencies
had quietly assigned a small group of persons to draw up some
reconversion principles or postwar programs. This work received
little, if any, attention in the early days. The earliest significant
work appeared in the procurement agencies and in WPB's Procurement Policy Board (originally called the Purchase Policy

Committee) which were concerned with expeditious methods for terminating war contracts. Their concern was immediate since contracts were expiring or being terminated regularly throughout the course of the war, and it was important that financial delays not hamper new war work. But the problem was obviously tied up with methods of handling contract terminations when they would reach enormous volume after the war. Planning was done with an eye to that period.

In March 1943 President Roosevelt recommended to Congress consideration of the postwar plans of the National Resources Planning Board, and the Senate soon established a Committee on Postwar Economic Policy and Planning with Senator George as chairman. A House Committee of the same name, under Representative Colmer, was established ten months later.

As early as April 1, 1943 Chairman Nelson of WPB assigned Ernest Kanzler to study the entire problem of reconversion. Mr. Kanzler submitted a report three months later. In September 1943 Nelson's Bureau of Planning and Statistics undertook a broad study of reconversion problems. This resulted in a preliminary report which was distributed in January 1944. In October 1943 Nelson had asked his operations vice chairman to review all WPB limitation and conservation orders and be ready for their orderly removal in the reconversion process.

On November 5, 1943 the Truman Committee issued a report urging greater attention to problems of contract termination, surplus property disposal, and reconversion. The George Committee reported on November 18 that settlements of canceled contracts were being made without any well-defined over-all policy, that surplus property was being accumulated and disposed of without consideration of its impact upon the national economy, and that piecemeal reconversion was taking place without coördination. It urged development of uniform policy and over-all direction.

Some time before these reports, Justice Byrnes had started work on plans for readjustment of the economy. On October 14, 1943, only three days after he had called together all agency heads "to work out a unified and comprehensive program for aiding discharged veterans," Byrnes again met with these executives to discuss termination of war contracts and disposition of war stocks and plants. The next day the President issued a statement on these problems and indicated that OWM would set up a special unit to deal with war and postwar adjustment problems. After considerable negotiation, Byrnes announced on November 4, 1943 that he had persuaded Bernard M. Baruch to head this unit and "develop unified programs and policies for dealing with war and postwar adjustment problems to be pursued by the various agencies concerned." John M. Hancock, an old associate, was designated Baruch's assistant.

This action received great public approval due to its auspices and Mr. Baruch's reputation. All the agencies hastened to bring their special problems and recommendations to the OWM unit. WPB submitted some 47 studies on reconversion which were under way in different parts of the agency. There appeared to be some issue as to whether reconversion work would be encompassed within WPB or elsewhere, and Nelson wrote Baruch frequently regarding the importance of WPB prestige if it were to retain the services of top men in the organization.[1]

Considerable additional interest was stimulated in anticipation of the Report when the President, in his January 1944 budget message, urged a uniform program for contract termination, disposal of surplus property, and industrial reconversion, and referred to the forthcoming Baruch report.

RECOMMENDATIONS

The Baruch-Hancock Report was made public by Byrnes on February 15, 1944 [2] and immediately received widespread attention from press, industry, and Congress.

The primary recommendations of the Report included:

Creation of a special authority—a "Work Director"—within OWM to give his "entire attention to the problem of bringing jobs to all workers, with emphasis laid upon the returning Servicemen and Servicewomen."

---

[1] J. Carlyle Sitterson, *Development of the Reconversion Policies of the War Production Board, April 1943 to January 1945* (Special Study No. 15), Civilian Production Administration, 1946, p. 28. A vigorous internecine struggle was going on within WPB, involving disagreements over Nelson's reconversion plans, and he feared that the Baruch study might be used to undercut his authority. It turned out he had nothing to fear from the Baruch recommendations.

[2] Bernard M. Baruch and John M. Hancock, *Report on War and Post-War Adjustment Policy*, Senate Document No. 154, 78th Cong., 2nd Sess., February 1944.

". . . quick, fair and final settlement of terminated war contracts through negotiations by contractors and the procurement agencies." A proposal from the Comptroller General that he make advance review of settlements before payment could be final was strongly rejected; it "would quibble the nation into panic." "The review powers of the Comptroller General should be limited to frauds . . ." A complete "financial kit" was prepared to help "settlement teams" arrive at fair settlements based upon clearly stated principles. The big point was rapid freeing of working capital for purchase of materials and for payrolls.

Uniform termination articles in all prime and subcontracts.

"Immediate creation of a Surplus Property Administrator in the Office of War Mobilization . . . with full responsibility and adequate authority for dealing with all aspects of surplus disposal."

Rapid moving out and storing of war materials from plants so as to make room for equipment and materials for civilian production.

Advance planning of contract cancellations—or "cut-backs"—and tightening up of cancellation procedures to assure consideration of interests of all agencies.

". . . not the loosening up that would be the inevitable result of a new super agency cutting across every other agency, but a general tightening up of the entire government machine—both for mobilization and demobilization. The two go hand in hand."

Opposition "to the creation of a new separate Office of Demobilization. Such an agency could hardly avoid coming into conflict with every other war agency and would hinder the prosecution of the war." Lacking war responsibility "it would tend to become a pressure agency seeking to quicken demobilization for its own sake."

"A running conspectus to be maintained by the Office of War Mobilization, of the progress being made by the agencies on the special tasks assigned them."

"Intensification of the fine work, so little known by the public, that has been done in the past seven months by the review boards organized by the Director of War Mobilization, in screening the Services' programs so as to cut out requirements beyond actual needs . . . The cuts already effected by these review boards total many billions."

Preparation of an emergency "X" Day reconversion plan to be used in event of a sudden collapse of Germany.

Complete centralization of program and policy. "The necessary over-all direction in dealing with the many problems of transition is the function of the over-all mobilizing authority—the Office of War Mobilization. The Office of War Mobilization can see both the mobilization and demobilization as one whole, laying out the tasks assigned to each of the operating agencies, eliminating overlappings and conflicts of functions, and making certain that no problems fall undone between the agencies." In regard to the demobilization function, "a small staff set up in the Office of War Mobilization and using the existing agen-

cies, carefully assigning to each its responsibilities and duties and supplying general supervision, can do more than any new great operating
or semi-operating agency that might be created."

Incorporation of these recommendations in legislation. Congress
should clearly set the policies. Executive orders should serve only in
the interim while legislation is being considered.

IMPLEMENTATION

The Report clearly became the official blueprint for government
reconversion activities. A few days after its issuance, the President established the Surplus War Property Administration and
the Retraining and Reëmployment Administration—the "Work
Director" proposed in the Report—both within OWM. The Contract Settlement Act became law on July 1, 1944, setting up an
Office of Contract Settlement. The "G.I. Bill of Rights" was passed
in June 1944. Finally, OWMR was established by law in October
1944.

The war history prepared by the Budget Bureau summarizes
the reconversion roles of the Baruch-Hancock Report and OWM–
OWMR accurately:

> In establishing the Baruch unit to study reconversion, the Office of
> War Mobilization had taken leadership in the Government's planning
> and preparation for reconversion. This function, it and its successor
> agency continued throughout the war and in the reconversion period.
> The President, acting on the Baruch recommendations, assigned to
> OWM the policy-making responsibilities in the fields of surplus prop-
> erty disposal, contract termination, and reëmployment. The administra-
> tive structure, including the constituent agencies which thus developed,
> were transferred by executive order into the legislative organization
> established by Congress with the passage of the War Mobilization act
> of 1944 in October of that year . . .
> From this point on, preparation for peace was largely initiated and
> guided by the new agency. Its requests to the interested Government
> organizations involved for statements of their plans for reconversion
> stimulated such preparations; its actions in resolving stalemates be-
> tween agencies were important steps in furthering action on matters
> relating to the coming era of peace. In its formal quarterly reports to
> Congress and in the frequent statements by its Director before congres-
> sional committees, are described the preparations made for the period
> of transition between victory over Germany and final victory over Japan
> as well as for the larger task of post-war reconstruction.[3]

[3] *The United States at War,* pp. 466–467.

CONTRACT TERMINATION

Concern over prompt settlement of obligations on terminated war contracts had forced itself upon procurement agencies early in the war. The postwar importance of the issue was clearly evident in the fact that a very substantial portion of the nation's industrial assets—involving about half the national product—was tied up in war contracts. Cancellation of any large number of these, accompanied by delay or uncertainty about payments, could easily tie up sufficient resources to start a depression.

WPB's Procurement Policy Board had been struggling to achieve agreement on uniform policies almost from the beginning of the war but, although improvements in the practices of individual procurement agencies were noted, no general agreement had been reached by late 1943, when the problem was already receiving wide attention from industry, the public, and Congress. Consequently on November 12, 1943 the Director of War Mobilization established a Joint Contract Termination Board composed of representatives of War, Navy, and Treasury Departments, the Maritime Commission, the Reconstruction Finance Corporation, and the Foreign Economic Administration, with an OWM representative, Mr. Hancock, as chairman.[4] Three months later, the Baruch-Hancock Report recommended the addition of representatives of the Comptroller General, the Attorney General, and WPB.

It was through the deliberations of this Board that Baruch and Hancock formulated the contract termination recommendations in their Report. However, Byrnes did not wait for the appearance of the Report to give effect to some of the Board's work. One month earlier he directed all procurement agencies to adopt an approved uniform termination article for all fixed-price war supply contracts.

[4] Subject to over-all policy formulation by the Director of War Mobilization, the Board was: (a) "To establish general principles and procedures governing contract termination, . . . binding on the departments . . . (b) To require from each department such reports relating to contract termination settlements as it deems necessary. (c) To develop . . . uniform contract provisions relating to terminations . . . and to make interpretations of such provisions . . . binding on the departments." (Signed agreement by heads of member agencies, November 12, 1943.)

The central theme of the recommendations was speed [5] and finality; undue caution in auditing should not be permitted to create wide unemployment. The Comptroller General, who had asked for a pre-audit, would be confined to post-review for fraud. Trained settlement teams, usually from the original procurement agencies, should make the settlements under policies and formulae developed by the Joint Board.[6] Many provisions were included to assure freeing of working capital.

The principles and provisions of the Contract Settlement Law of July 1944 were in complete accord with the Baruch-Hancock recommendations and the policies developed by the Joint Board. OCS remained technically part of OWMR to the very end, but operated virtually as an independent agency. This agency supervised the handling of many billions of government dollars, distributed over a very large sector of the economy, without incurring even a modicum of criticism. Its job was performed with such rare speed and smoothness that it won almost universal praise.[7] By the end of 1945, 83 per cent of canceled contracts had been settled and about 50 per cent of the total claims involved. By mid-1946 the agency had virtually completed its task. Its successful operation, though in a limited field, represented a too-rare example of how advance planning and preparation can be made to pay dividends.[8]

[5] The Baruch-Hancock Report stated, "On clearance of government property from private plants, we recommend: a deadline of not later than sixty days after the filing of inventory lists, with manufacturers having the right to remove and store property earlier at their own risk." (P. 13.)

[6] Just before the Joint Contract Termination Board went out of business, the chairman announced the formula for settlement of fixed price subcontracts: Full contract price for all completed articles, but nothing for that portion of contract on which work had not begun. On work started, but not completed, payment for actual costs incurred plus a profit margin not to exceed 6 per cent of total costs. ("War Contracts Terminations and Settlements," Office of Contract Settlement, 1946 (dittoed), p. 68.)

[7] In its August 1945 report, the Senate Special Committee Investigating the National Defense Program gave its usual word-lashing to most war agencies but said OCS had acted "speedily and efficiently." See also, 79th Cong., 2nd Sess., House Report 2729, Special Committee on Postwar Economic Policy and Planning, *Final Report,* December 1946, p. 26.

[8] Revelation of apparent fraud in several contract awards and settlements announced by the Comptroller General in August 1949 does not detract from the general evaluation. It was expected that some fraud might be found in post-audit, but it was considered a higher form of economy not to allow pre-auditing to delay reconversion.

SURPLUS PROPERTY DISPOSAL

The Baruch-Hancock Report devoted considerable space to surplus property. It requested immediate designation of a Surplus Property Administrator in OWM and laid down a number of general operating principles. It recognized the enormous complexity of the problem and its potential widespread influence on the economy. Recommending that sound legislation should grow out of experience, it suggested that Congress act only after the Administrator had had time to formulate policy recommendations. The Report advocated the questionable fiscal policy that all profits from surplus disposal should be applied to the national debt, thus earmarking revenue for a specific purpose.

The President promptly set up the Surplus War Property Administration in OWM. He also provided for a Surplus War Property Board of representatives of all affected agencies to advise on policy. Byrnes fought hard but unsuccessfully against establishment of the three-man Surplus Property Board, provided in the Surplus Property Act,[9] passed on the same day as the OWMR Act. Seven months later, when it was clear that surplus property disposal was not proceeding satisfactorily, Congress amended the law to provide for a single administrator. In practice, the surplus property agencies were never integrated within OWM–OWMR and were really independent.

The surplus property path was difficult and rough. It was marked by general disapproval and criticism in contrast to the good fortunes of OCS. The task was more complex, had less previous experience on which the program might be based, and did not have the advantage of clear-cut advance planning. The formal administrative attachment of the Surplus Property Administration to OWMR ended in January 1946 when the President transferred the functions to RFC's War Assets Board, later to become the War Assets Administration.

RECONVERSION OPERATIONS DURING THE WAR

Although the procurement agencies generally objected to any action which might detract from military production while the war was still on, the latter part of 1943 had been marked by a greater tolerance on the part of the military for essential civilian

[9] 78th Cong., 2nd Sess., *PL 457*, October 3, 1944.

production. On July 20, 1943 resumption of production was authorized on ten metal household articles. On November 30, further relaxations were issued on use of copper for hardware and screening, and before the end of that year a program to manufacture two million civilian-use electric flatirons and the cessation of pig-iron allocations were announced. All these modifications were calmly received.

But when Nelson began to lead a fight for postwar reconversion steps, as differentiated from current civilian needs, all proposals for additional civilian supplies were beclouded with suspicion of carrying postwar intentions. In 1944 every proposal for action similar to the 1943 program was met by a storm of protest from the military and almost as frequently from WMC.

WPB's Office of Civilian Requirements labored to avoid the confusion and fought its battles for civilian supply on the basis of essentiality for current war-supporting activities, but it could not overcome the difficulties flowing from the campaign for early reconversion. The other agencies failed to make any distinction between necessary civilian production and Nelson's plans. It is possible that Nelson also experienced some confusion about the two kinds of activity. It was in the midst of the congressional struggle as to whether OCR would be severed from WPB and made independent—a fight hinging on the question of whether civilian supply was given adequate attention in terms of war needs—that Nelson announced his assignment to Ernest Kanzler of a broad study of reconversion problems and policies.

The OWM director had indicated marked concern regarding civilian supply when in June 1943 he wrote Nelson stating that OCR ought

not merely to determine our civilian requirements in the light of the military demands, but also to map out complete plans to deal with and meet those requirements . . . A clear cut and well rounded program should be developed to assure the civilian economy that it is receiving due consideration in the full utilization of our industrial and manpower facilities.

Byrnes asked for a prompt review of all civilian needs and a program for dealing with such needs for the remainder of 1943 and 1944.[10] Although this was a strong endorsement for a vigorous

[10] Memorandum, June 22, 1943.

program of civilian supply, it made no reference to postwar considerations.

Substantial Army cut-backs in late 1943—tanks in September; airplanes, escort vessels and army supply items in October; and a major closing of four aluminum pot lines in December—led Nelson to fire the opening broadsides for early reconversion steps in what he later called a "war within a war" and "the bitterest of all arguments with the Army." [11] He might have said with equal accuracy "the bitterest of arguments with WMC" or "the bitterest of arguments within WPB." In any event, this action set off a chain of violent disagreements which required the constant vigilance of OWM and repeated policy decisions.

The first presentation of Nelson's reconversion policy came at a meeting of the War Production Board on November 30, 1943 when he stated:

Hereafter as manpower, facilities and materials become available in any given area, it shall be the policy of the War Production Board to authorize the production within that area of additional civilian goods, provided such production does not limit production for programs of higher urgency.[12]

WMC Chairman McNutt and the Under-Secretaries of War and Navy were present and did not object. In the light of their later consistent opposition to WPB authorizations, it can only be assumed that they did not believe that any such additional production could be undertaken without limiting more urgent programs, or that they failed to recognize that this was something different from the recurrent civilian supply issue,[13] although Nelson did not make his proposal in terms of *essential* civilian goods but rather *any* civilian goods.

At the next meeting of the Board, Nelson made the trend clearer

[11] *Arsenal of Democracy*, p. 408.

[12] *Minutes of the War Production Board*, Civilian Production Administration, Documentary Publication, No. 4, Government Printing Office, 1946, p. 293.

[13] This view is supported by the fact that only a few days earlier, November 15, the Requirements Committee, on which the military was adequately represented, issued a policy statement: "It will be the policy to produce, or to resume the production of, a sufficient quantity of items the distribution of which is closely controlled to provide for essential uses definitely related to the war effort. This policy will be subject to the availability of materials, critical components and manpower." (Cited in J. Carlyle Sitterson, *op. cit.*, p. 18.)

by asking for opinions on a more liberal policy toward applications for construction of new facilities. War Under-Secretary Patterson objected.[14] At the next meeting, McNutt stated that he doubted that manpower was available to meet any appreciable portion of the demand that would arise under a freer construction policy and that a relaxation of present policies would make it increasingly difficult to persuade idle manpower to move to war production jobs. Navy Under-Secretary Forrestal and Patterson also objected, as did the Deputy Petroleum Administrator, the War Food Administrator, and the chairman of the Maritime Commission, all agreeing that current policies were sufficiently flexible to comprehend any essential new construction, including civilian uses. Nelson went along and the Board made it unanimous that:

The War Production Board's present policies respecting restrictions on new construction and facilities should continue in effect until the probable future course of the war makes it certain that a relaxation will not injure the war effort.[15]

Nevertheless, during this period Nelson's objective of reconversion as such became clear and it ended a short-lived harmony period during which OCR's plea for more essential civilian goods appeared to be receiving sympathetic hearing and was reflected in the development of what was known as the 2021–F procedure for programing civilian supply. With the recognition of a reconversion drive, the military adopted an inflexible opposition, generally supported by WMC, on which it did not yield until 1945. They were strengthened by a report of the WPB Bureau of Planning and Statistics at the end of 1943 which estimated that prospective war output did not indicate any significant volume of resources available for additional non-military production in 1944.

As word got out that reconversion activities were being contemplated, busines leaders began to storm the Washington gates.[16] The agencies opposing reconversion took strong counter-measures. At a meeting of the Production Executive Committee on January 5, Lawrence Appley, WMC deputy director, reported serious labor shortages and declared that little progress would be made in getting the needed manpower as long as manufacturers

[14] *Minutes of the War Production Board*, p. 297.
[15] *Ibid.*, p. 300.
[16] Nelson felt obliged to refute the civilian expansion rumors, which were getting out of hand, at a meeting with business leaders on January 17. (*WPB Press Release*, January 17, 1944.)

in the areas involved contemplated resumption of civilian production. At the January 19 meeting, General Clay, representing Army Service Forces, proposed that PEC take responsibility for determining reconversion policies.[17] At its meeting of February 23, PEC voted the freezing of civilian production to the level of the first quarter of 1944, but this was raised at subsequent meetings.

On March 7, Nelson issued a long policy statement, in the form of a published letter to Senator Francis J. Maloney of Connecticut, in which he indicated that programs for civilian production expansion would be put into effect "whenever the military outlook, and the situation with respect to manpower, materials, and parts indicates the advisability of such action." In April, McNutt wrote Nelson suggesting that WPB take action to give effect to a policy statement adopted by WMC concerning essential civilian production. It provided for utilization of facilities in areas where manpower was most plentiful and stipulated that no additional civilian production should take place in tight labor areas, until enough war production was transferred to other areas.

Meanwhile, at the meeting of April 5, during Nelson's absence, PEC, harassed by labor shortages, unanimously agreed "that no resumption or expansion of civilian production should be effected in any No. I labor area [current shortage] and only to the slightest degree necessary in No. II labor areas [impending shortage]." WPB Staff Memorandum 42 was issued two days later to put this policy into effect. This restrictive measure was immediately met with vigorous protests from OCR, the Smaller War Plants Corporation, and others. When Nelson returned to Washington he immediately revoked the order and on May 9 Wilson issued a substitute which prohibited production expansion in Group I areas unless approved by the Area Production Urgency Committee, where one existed, or otherwise by himself. Expansion in Group II areas was to occur only with the approval of the appropriate WPB vice-chairman. Special exemptions were made for small plants.[18]

Despite restrictive policies and the adamant position of the military, expansion in essential civilian production did take place during this period. The outstanding example was a 50 per cent

[17] Although part of WPB, PEC was under the dominance of Deputy Chairman Wilson rather than Chairman Nelson.
[18] WPB General Administrative Order 2–154, May 9, 1944.

increase in farm equipment. Others included telephones for civilian use, wire garment hangers, steel wool, sanitary ware, commercial nonelectric cooking equipment, dishwashing machinery, and nonelectric water heaters.

THE NELSON RECONVERSION ORDERS

Shortly after the successful landings in France, Nelson announced a concrete plan which brought all the previous pushing and hauling to a head. On June 10, Byrnes asked Nelson to prepare a statement on WPB's reconversion activities, which Byrnes planned to submit to a Senate Committee hearing. Nelson himself was scheduled to appear before a Senate Committee later in the month to describe reconversion activities. These pressures, plus a general loosening of the materials situation, resulted in Nelson again seeking endorsement for a reconversion program from the War Production Board. At the June 13 meeting, following a report from McNutt that manpower stringencies were being aggravated because of a spreading belief that the end of the war was not far off, Nelson proposed a program of experimental models and advanced tooling for peacetime production, which would also permit WPB regional officers to determine locally whether to allow production of specific civilian items and the use of certain materials not under blanket restrictions.[19] General opposition was expressed by Board members, but five days later Nelson made a public release of his reconversion plan.[20]

After stating that war production came first, he expressed his conviction that proper preparation for orderly reconversion would cause management and labor to maintain better all-out war production. He declared that "restrictions which are not essential to war production and which hamper industry's preparations for the reconversion period need to be lifted at once." Four specific steps were to go into effect soon: (1) revocation of WPB orders limiting the use of aluminum and magnesium, to allow unrestricted use of these metals in essential end-products (except in form of castings, foil, or forgings) whenever and wherever manpower was available; (2) permission to any manufacturer to apply for authority to make and test a single model of any product planned for postwar production; (3) provision for any manufacturer to

[19] *Minutes of the War Production Board,* pp. 339–340.
[20] *WPB Press Release,* June 18, 1944.

place unrated orders for tools and machinery for civilian production under conditions that would prevent interference with war production; (4) WPB regional directors, in consultation with WMC, could authorize locally, on an individual basis, manufacturers to produce civilian items on which WPB restrictions might be lifted in the future. The last came to be famous as the "spot authorization" order.

Both Patterson and McNutt put their objections into writing, the first emphasizing that Army production schedules had been slipping during previous months. Although Nelson had instructed his staff to issue the orders on July 1, vigorous objections at the last PEC meeting in June led Wilson, in the absence of Nelson, hospitalized at the time, to delay issuance and take the matter up before a special meeting of the War Production Board on July 4. This meeting aired the entire dispute and indicated that Nelson was not merely isolated so far as the other agencies were concerned but also, within his own agency, he had the articulate support of only his two labor vice-chairmen.[21] His support came largely from the outside—the Senate Special Committee Investigating the National Defense Program and the Senate Small Business Committee.

The War Department reiterated that it was not opposed to advance planning for reconversion. "However, it was the Department's view that the series of orders proposed go beyond planning and, if issued, would seriously interfere with war production." It was claimed that Army items like heavy-duty trucks, tires, heavy artillery ammunition, and steel plate had fallen behind schedule, primarily because of lack of manpower, and that these reconversion steps were incompatible with the new and more stringent manpower controls put into effect by WMC on July 1. The Assistant-Secretary of the Navy concurred. Admiral Land also agreed, emphasized the bad timing and said the Maritime Commission had fallen behind schedule in ship deliveries. McNutt stated that the nub of the issue was:

the issuance of orders would make it extremely difficult, if not impossible, to carry out the manpower program . . . The problem is to get the manpower from loose to tight labor areas. If the prospect of jobs near home closes Group IV areas to further recruitment, programs in

[21] *Industrial Mobilization for War*, p. 804.

the tighter areas will have to be carried forward with the limited labor supply now available.

Wilson replied that

it was upon the assumption that workers cannot be moved in substantial numbers that the Chairman had to a large extent based the four proposed orders. He is most anxious to prevent local unemployment at a time when materials and facilities are available.[22]

After extended debate, McNutt moved a resolution that in view of the chairman's illness and the Board's opinion that "the issuance of the proposed orders at the present time would interfere with war production," they be postponed until Nelson's return. The resolution carried unanimously. When Wilson stated that he had been instructed by Nelson to issue the orders and so could not accept the vote as a guide to his actions, the War and Navy Departments asked for time to appeal to Byrnes.

Nelson returned to face what proved to be his biggest and final fight. Wilson pleaded with him to rescind his instructions. Nelson has stated that he was surprised to find "that an extremely bitter feeling had developed within WPB." But unfortunately he regarded the entire issue as a "long and bitter controversy with the military over control of America's civilian economy" rather than a difference over the timing of reconversion steps, and whether such steps would interfere with the war. He spoke of Wilson and the vice-chairmen of WPB as taking "the Army point of view" and in his later recital of the affair did not mention WMC's opposition.[23] He wrote the President, who turned the matter over to Byrnes who was already reviewing the issue.

After long discussions and a futile attempt to force the agencies to reach an agreement of their own, Byrnes made a decision which in general supported Nelson's position. He authorized issuance of Wilson's proposed orders, but arranged that they be staggered in time and that the spot authorization order be delayed at least a month in order to give WMC time to strengthen its new manpower controls. But recognizing that manpower was the chief bone of contention in the entire issue, Byrnes issued a directive 10 days prior to the spot authorization order which gave WMC power to nullify the order where it deemed necessary.[24] Byrnes

[22] *Minutes of War Production Board*, pp. 341–343.
[23] *Arsenal of Democracy*, pp. 391–416.
[24] Directive of August 4, 1944. See Chapter 5, pp. 154–158.

decided in favor of WMC on the key issue of labor mobility and protected interregional recruitment. Although Byrnes had accepted most of Nelson's reconversion principles, the latter's supporters were disappointed because thereafter the timing of reconversion was no longer exclusively in WPB hands.

As agreed between Byrnes and Nelson, the four reconversion orders were issued about a week apart, starting July 15. The spot authorization order was issued on August 15.

The struggle had been costly. So much bitterness had been generated within and without WPB that it reached the President with a renewed request on the part of the military for Nelson's removal.[25] Only two days after the spot authorization order, the President announced that he was sending Nelson on an important mission to China. About a week later without previous notification to Nelson, Charles Wilson, WPB's second in command, resigned with a stinging attack on Nelson's personal staff and associates.

Relative tranquillity came to WPB with the appointment of J. A. Krug, a former vice-chairman of WPB and friend of Nelson, as the new chairman. Although Krug promptly told a Senate Committee that he was "in complete accord" with Nelson's plans for gradual reconversion, no major discords with the military came during his chairmanship. Krug was reconversion conscious but laid his major emphasis on plans to be applied after the fall of Germany.

THE SPOT AUTHORIZATION ORDER

Since the spot authorization order was merely an "enabling act" and depended upon future decisions in individual cases for effectuation, it proved a source of rancorous contention for most of the remainder of the war. Designed by Nelson as the core of expanding civilian production, it proved something of a boomerang; it had little apparent effect upon reconversion and it may have actually retarded production of essential civilian goods.

Byrnes agreed early in July to issuance of the order on August 15. In the interim, the military reëmphasized that vital munitions schedules were not being met due to manpower shortages. The figures did show such lags but WPB claimed the schedules were not "realistic," and inflated military needs, and that the military was obtaining all reasonable requirements. On August 1, Byrnes

[25] *The United States at War,* p. 488.

called a meeting at the White House to determine the real status of war production. Apparently, he felt that there was sufficient merit to the manpower shortage case, and the WMC argument that production expansion even in localities where labor was plentiful would interfere with recruitment for areas where shortages were acute, so that he issued his August 4 directive which was designed to place safeguards around the forthcoming spot authorization order. In effect, the OWM director accepted Nelson's principle that reconversion steps could be initiated immediately, but inserted an administrative mechanism intended to assure that no war-needed manpower would go into such a program.[26]

The August 4 directive gave administrative power on spot authorizations to the local Area Production Urgency Committees [over which WPB presided], but, no committee was permitted to grant an authorization until the local WMC office had certified in writing that labor was available not only from the local standpoint but also without interference with inter-area and interregional recruitment for war and essential civilian production, thus giving WMC a veto power.

This apparent blow to WPB did not prove serious in practice because, on the whole, the local WMC and WPB officials acted in accord.[27] This development seemed to corroborate a contention of Mr. Patterson's that the authority should be centralized in Washington, since the competition among local communities was such, and pressures of local chambers of commerce so great, that it would be almost impossible for local officials to resist the demands of local businessmen for a "break." [28] Within a few months

[26] See Chapter 5, p. 155.

[27] Although WMC headquarters and its regional directors went on record as strongly disapproving new civilian production and indicated that it did not intend to encourage approvals, the local offices saw the problem differently. "As of January 5, 1945, 5,658 applications had been reported. Of these, 1,301 were denied and 4,357 approved." (Sitterson, *op. cit.*, p. 126.)

[28] For example, the WMC acting director for San Francisco and northern California, testifying before a Senate committee, urged that, after V–E Day, war production in his area be redistributed to other parts of the country so that his area could undertake reconversion simultaneously with other regions. He also asked for prompt pre-V-E Day reconversion steps, despite shortages on the west coast, because otherwise the labor force might migrate to other sections where postwar jobs would be available earlier. (Statement of Sam Kagel, before Senate Committee to Study Problems of American Small Business, San Francisco, July 31 and August 1, 1944.)

some local committees were appealing to Washington to with-draw the entire order since they could not withstand the local pressure involved in turning down applications.

It soon became clear that interpretation of the new order might result in a loss to OCR's essential civilian program. There had been under way, since late 1943, a procedure (2021–F) for civilian production which gave great promise of creating a right of way for essential civilian items. These were to be programed in much the same way as munitions production. The furor over Nelson's plans had already resulted in a failure to distinguish between the war-supporting essential activities which OCR was pushing and straight reconversion production. After the spot authorization order was issued, the questions immediately arose as to what con-stituted civilian production under Byrnes's qualifying directive and whether WMC certification and local authorization procedure were required only for spot authorization production or also for that which had been regularly programed. As finally interpreted, virtually all production subject to direct WPB control was classi-fied as civilian production under the directive and had to run the gantlet of the local procedure. Despite some later special arrange-ments, a blow had been struck at *essential* civilian supply in the drive to avoid indiscriminate expansion of civilian production.

To some degree, reconversion activity had been based on an assumption that the war in Europe would be over during 1944. It was assumed that time for tapering off the military program had arrived. But when a slower pace was set in Europe than had been anticipated, military schedules were stepped up in the fall. With the number of "critical" programs expanding rapidly, considerable doubt arose as to the wisdom of previous reconversion steps. Dur-ing October the director of OWMR flew to Paris to observe the fighting front personally and returned with a graver view of the situation and greater receptivity to military claims.

On October 31, Byrnes held a long meeting with the various agency heads. It dealt with the acute manpower difficulties faced by foundries and in heavy artillery ammunition, heavy trucks, tires, and other military programs. The War and Navy Depart-ments asked for immediate suspension of spot authorization. They also requested retightening of relaxed limitation orders on civilian items and rescheduling of "order boards" of manufacturers which were "choke points" in military programs, in order to insure that such items were given priority over less essential programs. The issue was left unsettled at this meeting.

While Byrnes was reviewing the question the struggle was re-opened at the War Production Board meeting of November 14. After a report by Hiland Batcheller, WPB's Chief of Operations, on the status of critical production programs, which in the light of stepped-up requirements, looked unsatisfactory in several instances, Under-Secretary Patterson deplored the untimeliness of the civilian production trend and noted that "essentiality is not a factor in authorizing production under Priorities Regulation 25 [spot authorization], so that its basis of justification appears to be merely as a 'make work' plan." Observing that the original theory behind the plan was that war production would decline while, in fact, requirements and schedules had risen to new peaks, he recommended that spot authorization be suspended for at least 90 days in Group I and Group II areas. W. Y. Elliott, WPB's vice-chairman for Civilian Requirements, answered with emphasis on the real need for essential civilian supply and recommended even further restrictions on nonessential civilian activities such as night clubs and liquor stores.[29] But this valid distinction was not destined to get full administrative recognition. The WPB chairman turned down the Patterson proposal with a statement that not a single case had been cited where an approved spot authorization application had resulted in interference with military production.[30]

Two days later the OWMR director made a tentative decision in a public letter addressed to WPB, WMC, the Maritime Commission, and the Under-Secretaries of War and Navy.

This letter refers to the two meetings recently held in my office with reference to the deficiences in certain critical programs . . .

It has been suggested that we should completely suspend the operation of the spot authorization procedure in group 1 and group 2 labor market areas and should also completely suspend resumption of the production of civilian supplies. After careful consideration I have determined to defer such drastic action for a reasonable time. If the steps herein directed do not speedily produce the necessary results, I shall not hesitate to take more drastic action.

[29] Elliott had tried to impress upon both Wilson and Byrnes the need for this distinction when the spot authorization order was drafted.
[30] *Minutes of War Production Board*, pp. 364–368.

The decision as to the issuance of spot orders will be made at the local level but the War Production Board will issue directions to regional officials that in any locality where war production is lagging behind schedule because of lack of labor or where there is available skilled labor needed and transferable into regional recruitment, any reconversion requiring labor needed by war plants can not be authorized . . .

Representatives of the War Production Board, the Army, and Navy, and the War Manpower Commission will visit various plants where programs are delayed and apply necessary remedies.[31]

Patterson informed Byrnes that his decision was "a disappointment." "There is nothing new in the steps directed in your letter. They have been tried for months on these lagging programs, but they have not produced the acceleration that is necessary." [32]

With the unexpected temporary turn for the worse in the European War, there was an increasing disinclination to defend reconversion activities. Krug announced that WPB would assume that the war would go on indefinitely.[33] After a hurried meeting with Byrnes on the morning of December 1, it was agreed that a joint declaration, reflecting a keen sense of war urgency, and instructions to all their staffs would be issued by WPB, WMC, and the War and Navy Departments, suspending spot authorization in all Group I areas and in other selected difficult labor markets for a 90-day period. It urged broader use of employment ceilings, WPB material and priority controls, and no authorization of expanded civilian production that required labor of the type needed for war production even in areas where the plan was not specifically suspended.

The inclusive treatment of all civilian production without distinction again brought unsuccessful objection from OCR. Vice-Chairman Elliott took the position that OCR should have the right to designate "must" programs even for Group I areas. He called the problem to Byrnes's personal attention and called the indiscriminate ban on all civilian supply shortsighted and a threat to the war economy.

On January 1, Byrnes officially reported to the President and Congress that he found the reconversion steps taken in 1944 pre-

---

[31] *OWMR Press Release,* November 16, 1944.
[32] Letter, November 18, 1944.
[33] *The United States at War,* p. 489.

mature and incompatible with the conduct of war, and that further steps would be delayed until V–E Day.

We have already made one too early start toward reconversion. During the spring and summer, a wave of optimism swept not only the United States but our allies . . . With the hope of victory in Europe this fall, we went ahead with plans to prepare the country for early reconversion of industry. At the time it seemed the prudent course. Events proved it otherwise . . .[34]

In late January, the suspension of spot authorization was extended to all Group II areas. With the German counter-attack— the "Bulge"—and new anxieties about the war, exclusive attention was given to war production until spring. On April 27, 1945, Krug announced the resumption of spot authorization. This time there was no objection from either the military or WMC. Victory in Europe was only a few days off.

CUT-BACK PROCEDURES

Just as the program of reconversion during war caused confusion between current essential civilian supply and civilian production for postwar reconversion, so the period was beset by the apparently inescapable confusion between handling the current day-to-day cut-backs of military production and the planning for general cut-backs which would be required after V–E and V–J Days. The two, though replete with overlapping considerations, had to be approached differently. Cut-backs and program revisions during war had to be planned primarily to dovetail with other war production or war-supporting civilian production. The general curtailments to come after the war had to be planned primarily with a view toward minimum disruption of the economy and speedy reconversion to peacetime pursuits. This section deals only with the first problem.

Program cut-backs and contract run-outs had been occurring regularly since the beginning of the war and were handled exclusively by the procurement agencies. Until the fall of 1943 they occupied little general attention, since programs were expanding rapidly, and any cut-back was likely to be replaced immediately by another contract. But by November 1943 when war production

[34] James F. Byrnes, *Problems of Mobilization and Reconversion*, First Report of the Director of War Mobilization, January 1, 1945, Government Printing Office, p. 11.

hit its peak, visions of the end of war in Europe were accompanied by considerable talk of reconversion, and possibilities of unemployment were disturbing labor. The problem of appropriate planning of cut-backs began to receive broader attention.

OWM had taken initial steps on this problem by establishing procurement review committees in June 1943 and later, in September 1943, by creating the Joint Production Survey Committee to guide curtailment activities of the procurement agencies. But this was a strictly military unit, except for OWM participation.

By late fall 1943, WPB began to express its obvious concern with such readjustments and demanded that the actions should no longer be within the exclusive domain of the procurement agencies. It was clear that if the volume of cut-backs were to increase, it would be essential to have coördinated activity among the various procurement agencies which had let contracts in the same communities and even the same plants. Labor, through its WPB representatives, demanded a voice in deliberations on the "where" and "how" of cut-backs, in view of the effect on employment.

No intervention by OWM seemed necessary since the situation only required that the agencies concerned work out mutually acceptable machinery. Meetings for that purpose began in November 1943. Cut-back control obviously belonged in WPB, but the deep schism in the agency, brought to a head by the reconversion struggle, resulted in a dispute as to where within the agency authority for handling the problem would be allocated. It caused a stalemate which postponed any decision or action for six months.

Wilson, supported strongly by the military, wanted cut-back authority to rest in PEC, of which he was chairman. Nelson felt that the machinery should be centered in the WPB Program Bureau, more sympathetic to his reconversion views. Despite repeated inter-agency committee studies and recommendations which accentuated the need for action, Nelson could not get himself to render a firm decision. He was unwilling to give the authority to PEC and equally unwilling to bring his dispute with Wilson into the open, since that threatened a breakdown of WPB.[35]

Although Byrnes generally avoided intrusion into internal agency affairs, the delay on cut-back procedures became too seri-

[35] Sitterson, *op. cit.*, pp. 73–76.

ous to overlook. At the close of March 1944, he finally wrote Nelson instructing him to take some action on the problem. Although he avoided any reference to internal WPB difficulties, he asked what progress was being made by WPB in coördinating contract terminations with reconversion programs and said, "I would be glad to consider any suggestion for action on my part that may be in order to give impetus to effective inauguration of the recommendations made in the Baruch-Hancock Report in this regard." [36]

This was in effect an invitation to Nelson to make the decision himself or, if he wished, Byrnes might relieve him of the embarrassment by rendering the decision for him. Nelson was understandably reluctant to have Byrnes settle an internal agency feud. He took neither course. Finally, in May, public furor caused by a conspicuously inept Navy handling of a cut-back at Brewster Aeronautical Corporation forced prompt action. [37] Nelson reluctantly acceded to Wilson and at the end of the month Wilson set up a special PEC staff which, under his direction, was to

inquire into any feature of production, including its scheduling of components, and make available all pertinent information with respect to coördinated adjustments for the resumption, expansion or curtailment of production to the Production Executive Committee and to the Requirements Committee. [38]

Although the new PEC staff clearly was established to gather information and give advice, just what PEC itself was to do about cut-backs and their relationship to resumption of civilian production was left peculiarly unclear. A few days later the OWM director stepped in and issued instructions directly to Wilson.

You are . . . requested to have the Committee, of which you are Chairman, adopt uniform policies for the future cancellation of contracts, giving reasonable notice to management and labor of such cancellations.

The procurement agencies are directed to take prompt action, clear their proposed contract cut-backs and terminations with the Committee

[36] Letter, March 31, 1944.

[37] The cut-back in fighter planes had been made with one week's notice to the management but no plans had been made for substitute work in the plant or moving the workers to other plants. The union dramatized the problem as the workers refused to leave the factory until satisfactory arrangements were made.

[38] WPB General Administrative Order 2–157, May 25, 1944.

set up by you and such cut-backs and terminations shall not be made effective until such clearance is obtained.[39]

The PEC staff's first job was to establish a procedure for advance reporting of cut-backs. In January, Nelson had requested all procurement agencies to file cut-back information with WPB on a uniform basis, but since no machinery existed in WPB for utilizing such information, the reports had served no function. Now the PEC staff, which included representatives of many WPB units, WMC, and the procurement agencies, worked out a detailed plan for reporting and clearance. In a September report to the President on reconversion, Byrnes described the procedure as follows:

> The current procedures for the administration of cut-backs are designed to provide for interim revisions in war requirements. Under these procedures, the procurement agencies determine the allocation of cut-backs among contractors under broad policies developed by the War Production Board [PEC] to secure maximum production. The procurement agencies furnish the War Production Board with advance notice of any cut-back for an item or related groups of items in which the value of the cut-back equals or exceeds $1,000,000 in the current month or any of the next succeeding [six] months.
> As detailed plans are developed, these plans are also reported to the War Production Board. They include information with respect to the facilities involved, the labor employed, the labor area in which the work is located, costs, past production, future requirements, plant capacities, and the selection of facilities for retention and release.
> The staff of the War Production Board [PEC] assigned to the study of cut-backs reviews the detailed proposal and gives clearance or recommends changes which appear desirable . . .
> For cut-backs of over $200,000 but less than $1,000,000 in the current month or any one of the succeeding 3 months, modified information is made available to the War Production Board prior to final determination of the facilities to be cut back.
> As a result of these procedures, the War Production Board, the War Manpower Commission, and the Smaller War Plants Corporation are advised before final notification is given to the contractor so that appropriate arrangements may be made for the use of the facilities for other war purposes or for essential civilian production. This also per-

[39] Letter, June 5, 1944. There was considerable uneasiness in some parts of WPB regarding such unusual direct communication from Byrnes to PEC, a unit within WPB, instead of to Nelson as head of the agency. However, in view of the peculiar developments in WPB during the previous few months, the action was understandable.

mits the development of a program for the utilization of the manpower made available by the cut-back.[40]

Before the month was out, Byrnes supplemented this report with a public letter to the affected agencies instructing them to see that labor was informed in advance, through management, of contemplated cut-backs.

The PEC staff developed certain criteria for allocation of cut-backs when a choice was practically available, but the main effort was concentrated on achieving maximum utilization of resources in continuing war production.

In spite of considerable progress, operations of the PEC staff were found to be unsatisfactory and it was replaced within six months. The reporting machinery proved largely a formality. A high proportion of the cut-backs submitted during the period were non-optional as to locale. The staff was handicapped by lack of knowledge regarding subcontractors. The unexpected prolongation of the war, and the opposition to reconversion meant that cut-backs were utilized almost entirely for war production adjustments. This disappointed advocates of prompt reconversion and made them feel that the review procedure was ineffective. Labor was not satisfied with the arrangements for advance notice. It depended to a large degree upon the coöperation of management which sometimes was averse to following the government's procedures for informing workers.

Mainly, however, the organizational structure proved cumbersome and self-defeating. An excessive number of agencies and persons made up a committee whose meetings resembled a town hall. The large number of cases meant frequent and lengthy sessions which soon resulted in lower-level personnel, without real power, manning the committee.

In November 1944, a Production Readjustment Committee was substituted for the PEC staff. The new committee, by and large, included representatives of the same agencies as had constituted the staff, but the work was broken down by establishing the PRC as a policy-making body and also establishing a Current Production Adjustment Division to serve as an operating unit, as well as three other units for special tasks like V–E adjustments, national

[40] J. F. Byrnes, *Reconversion*, Report to the President from the Director of War Mobilization, September 7, 1944, Government Printing Office, pp. 2–3.

production urgency lists, and coördinating the work of Area Production Urgency Committees. The Current Production Adjustment Division was given the task of handling day-to-day production adjustments resulting from cut-backs. Final responsibility remained with the Production Executive Committee.

Shortly thereafter, OWMR submitted to the new PRC a proposed statement of policy and cut-back regulations. After adopting some PRC suggestions, on January 20, 1945 Byrnes laid down the following policy:

Curtailments . . . or terminations of war contracts shall be integrated and synchronized with the expansion, resumption, or initiation of production, for other war purposes and, to the greatest extent, compatible with the effective prosecution of the war, of production for non-war use. In the planning and application of curtailments and terminations of war contracts, the paramount consideration at all times shall be the retention in war production, to such extent as may be necessary, of facilities with a proven capacity to produce known and contingent future requirements. Subject to this overriding objective, disruption of the national economy should be minimized to the greatest extent practicable, by promoting maximum employment and equalization of the production load among all sections of the country.[41]

The statement also included specific criteria to be followed in selecting facilities to be cut back in accordance with the policy and a regulation that all cut-backs were to be cleared with WPB.

The Byrnes directive caused a flurry of activity in PRC to develop specific procedures to comply with it. In one month the agencies agreed to a full plan which was submitted to and approved by OWMR. It was issued formally on March 5, 1945.[42] It required procurement agencies to report to WPB (Current Production Adjustment Committee), for clearance, all prime contract cut-backs involving over $500,000 in any one of the succeeding twelve months. Certain specific procurement items, particularly those normally in civilian use, were exempt and, of course, there was no control over the sub-contract situation. The directive also established specific policy on the time of notification to contractors prior to a cancellation; in general seven days' notice was required. Elaborate machinery was worked out to provide simultaneous notification to management and labor.

[41] OWMR, "Policies of Contract Curtailment, Non-Renewal and Termination," January 20, 1945.
[42] WPB Directive 40, March 5, 1945.

Although not all the provisions proved to be entirely workable, a vast improvement was noted over the PEC staff period. Clearance itself was largely a formality, but WPB was convinced that the requirement that they submit cut-backs for clearance was an incentive to the procurement agencies to apply the OWMR principles. The simultaneous advance notice to labor and management was too cumbersome for complete success, but was a helpful procedure. The chief drawback, which cannot be overstressed, was lack of control over subcontracts, which were frequently more significant than the prime contracts.

CONCLUSION

For at least a year and a half before the end of the shooting in Europe, a large proportion of the government's attention was devoted to the problem of reconverting the war economy to a peacetime basis without undue disruption and costly delay. Although such foresight deserves full credit, it must also be pointed out that this was a luxury made possible only by unquestioning confidence in the outcome of the war, and a general expectation that it would end at least six months earlier than it did.

Two types of activity were involved: (1) advance planning for the real change-over which would come after victory, and (2) gradual resumption of peacetime enterprise while the war was still in full progress. On some matters, such as financial settlement of canceled contracts and the clearing away of government property, the two considerations overlapped and little fundamental dispute was involved. The agency disagreements dealt largely with locus of authority and procedures. There was also no significant questioning of the desirability of planning for V–E Day.

The sharp policy clashes, with which this chapter has been largely concerned, were over the question of how much, if any, resumption of normal civilian activity we could afford to undertake while the war was still going on. The issues within this dispute were many. The heat engendered caused a greater wave of name-calling in Washington than any other conflict. Nelson's supporters said that the military was engaged in another of its attempts to take over the economy; civilian agencies which agreed with the military were accused of seeking to defer reconversion until "big business" was ready to get in first. On the other hand, Nelson and his followers were accused of being willing to risk prolongation of the war in order to give business interests an early advantage.

These feverish accusations throw almost no light on the real nature of the struggle. "Big business" was represented on both sides of the issue; important civilian war agencies lined up on opposite sides; and within WPB itself top officials were fiercely divided. The agency divisions simply reflected conflicting attitudes growing out of varying responsibilities. The military's single purposed view of expeditious and complete victory before all else clearly set them against early reconversion. WMC's responsibility for supplying war production with adequate manpower, which had become the major "choke point" in war supply, put them squarely on the same side as the military. WPB's major war duty —provision of materials and facilities—was largely solved and it could look to the postwar period with more equanimity than WMC or the procurement agencies. Furthermore, WPB felt that its job involved direct responsibility for the ultimate smooth transition of the economy, a responsibility not equally shared by other agencies. Apart from agency differences, the problem was complex enough to allow for honest divergencies among men of good will, in basic philosophy, in their predictions about the course of the war, and in their appraisal of the blurred "facts."

Here OWM–OWMR was indispensable. It was a healthy thing to have contrary points of view actively presented to public view and consideration. It was not to be expected that the agencies could come to a mutually satisfactory solution through their own negotiations. Nor would it be possible for the President himself to deal adequately with the endless chronology of difficulties arising out of so basically controversial and fluid a set of issues. Only a body charged with over-all policy accountability, with no special responsibility for or identification with any particular phase could make for a balanced consideration of factors. Here was a case where setting of broad policy was not enough. First, the policy had to be fluid and quickly alterable. Second, it was the kind of broad policy which involved daily inter-agency activity and sub-policy making which opened the basic policy to review, interpretation, implementation, or nullification. A constant top-side follow-through was required.

OWM–OWMR, operating with the Baruch-Hancock Report as guide, supplied unquestioned clear leadership in reconversion policy. Its decisions were periodically damned by the disputants, but its leadership never seriously challenged. Some of the plans can be said to have worked out poorly; some were highly successful. The program was changeable, reacting sensitively to military considerations. From a qualified "go ahead" in August 1944 on current reconversion, decisions moved to virtual complete cessation in December, when the "Battle of the Bulge" was at its height, to a reopening of the gates at the end of March 1945. From early 1944 to the end no agency made any policy decisions in the reconversion field without clearing with OWM–OWMR.

CHAPTER 7

THE CONTINUING NEED
FOR PROGRAM COÖRDINATION

*O*ne of the fallacies of our time is the notion that now the war has ended, an era quite different will begin—that we shall be able to return quickly to the 'good old days.' " [1]

This is a comforting illusion and, therefore, popular. Now, four years after victory, it should be clear to all that the size, complexity, pervasiveness, and urgency of government was not a wartime phenomenon. War accelerated the development of big government, but the process goes on in peace and war.

The problem OWM–OWMR was designed to meet, the problem we are equally concerned with today—the need for more effective coördinating machinery at the center of government—was evident long before 1941. The exigencies of war merely dramatized the need to a public and Congress normally indifferent to questions of government machinery except when its inadequacies strike with such immediacy and urgency as to outrage opinion.

While the war job was in some ways larger and more complex, the permanent peacetime job is more difficult in other ways. The war witnessed a vast proliferation of agencies and functions and necessitated unprecedented government controls (not all of which have disappeared) over the industrial life of the nation. But war also created a uniformly accepted singleness of purpose. Basic differences over objectives and direction, which are the marks of democratic society, add to the difficulties of government in times of peace.

Also, witness the growth of new government responsibilities since 1945. The nation has committed itself to a policy of participation in world politics and world economics. We are now en-

[1] S. McKee Rosen, "Introduction," Harold D. Smith, *The Management of Your Government*, Whittlesey House, 1945, p. ix.

gaged for the first time in a peacetime military alliance with eleven nations of western Europe. We are actively engaged in support of, and coöperation with, the economies of vast parts of the world—a practice which in one form or another must continue into the foreseeable future. We strive to influence the political life of most of the world. The administrative implications of this inescapable global role are sweeping. It involves not only great growth in government as a whole, but new and heavy responsibilities which cut across almost every existing agency and regular function of government, including most of the affairs we once liked to think were purely domestic.

. . . so many domestic policies now impinge upon and require reconciliation with international relations. In the future, domestic policy simply cannot be permitted to develop without the check of international consideration, and foreign policy cannot be permitted to develop in a vacuum unrelated to the thousand and one relevant domestic policies. Here is the most compelling new requirement for integration of manifold matters.[2]

The nation is now committed by statute to a permanent policy "to use all practicable means . . . to promote maximum employment, production, and purchasing power."[3] Never before has an American Congress acknowledged so large a degree of continuing peacetime responsibility for the operation of the domestic economy in all its phases. The law states we are now to have an "economic program of the Federal Government."

The development of atomic energy has opened the door to vast expansion of government jurisdiction, whose boundaries are still indeterminate. Aside from its obvious international implications the new energy may ultimately revolutionize industrial and civilian practices. It may replace standardized fuels, such as oil and coal, for many purposes; it could be a new source of electric energy; its manifold uses are hardly explored. By law the sources of this power are and must remain under government control. This places the government in a new relationship to industry, as yet undetermined, but clearly of greater extensiveness than anything we have known before.[4]

---

[2] Paul H. Appleby, "Organizing Around the Head of a Large Federal Department," *Public Administration Review*, vol. 6, Summer 1946, p. 207.

[3] 79th Cong., 2nd Sess., *PL 304*, February 20, 1946.

[4] Section 1(a) of the Atomic Energy Act states: "The effect of the use of atomic energy for civilian purposes upon the social, economic, and politi-

These, and many other specific developments in the direction of additional governmental responsibility, all imply broad varieties of functions involving numerous government agencies. There is no way of compartmentalizing such tasks among particular departments so as to avoid overlapping, diffusion, and interrelationship of activities. As such functions increase, the job of the presidency grows. The situation which faced the President during the war and which graphically called for such an instrument as OWM is in essence perennial, regardless of general government organization.[5] The fundamentals of operative coördination are no different in time of peace than in time of war. In a machine as complex as the Federal government and operating in a highly developed industrial society, the need for central coördination of policies, programs, and operations is constant and pressing.

PREVIOUS DEVELOPMENTS IN STRENGTHENING
PRESIDENTIAL STAFF

For most of our history the President had no staff services. He was a man with a secretary who was presumed to be able to call on the departments for all the help he needed. The distress of recent Presidents at the organizational handicaps to their job was generally answered by studies directed toward more symmetrical grouping of the various Federal agencies.[6]

The first notable landmark in furnishing the President necessary

---

cal structures of today cannot now be determined . . . It is reasonable to anticipate, however, that tapping this new source of energy will cause profound changes in our present way of life. Accordingly, it is hereby declared to be the policy of the people of the United States that, subject at all times to the paramount objective of assuring the common defense and security, the development and utilization of atomic energy shall, so far as practicable, be directed toward improving the public welfare, increasing the standard of living, strengthening free competition in private enterprise, and promoting world peace." (79th Cong., 2nd Sess., PL 585, August 1, 1946.)

[5] "It is a mistake . . . to assume . . . that a need for top level coördination is a mark of poor organization. Rather, it is an index of the extent of specialization and of the consequent division of labor. As a problem, it cannot be avoided in a highly developed society nor in a mature institution . . ." (J. Donald Kingsley, "Top-Level Coördination of Wartime Programs," paper delivered in *Public Administration Lectures Series*, U. S. Department of Agriculture Graduate School, October 1, 1946, MS.)

[6] The most complete report available on reorganization plans in this century is W. Brooke Graves, *Basic Information on the Reorganization of the Executive Branch, 1912–1948*, Legislative Reference Service, Library of Congress, February 1949.

tools for executive management was the Budget and Accounting Act of 1921 (although in a sense the Civil Service Commission was set up as a staff agency to the President). For the first time suitable means were provided by which the President could properly discharge the responsibilities of a manager with regard to the expenditures of the administrative agencies. The President was made responsible for transmitting to Congress a consolidated financial program for the government, and provision was made for a central agency of budgetary and administrative management —the Bureau of the Budget. The head of the Bureau was made directly responsible to the President but he and his agency were formally placed in the Treasury. It was not until 1939 that the Bureau became a formal part of the President's office.

The most significant steps toward developing central coördinating instrumentalities to assist the President came after Franklin D. Roosevelt assumed office in 1933. He started his administration with an apparent intention to make use of the Cabinet, augmented by other agency heads, as a broad coördinating unit. The attempt, as in other instances, was short lived. In July 1933 he established an Executive Council to provide for orderly presentation of business to him and to coördinate inter-agency problems. The Council had no staff or implementing unit and was not effective during its fifteen months of independent existence.

The National Emergency Council was created in November 1933, to coördinate and make more efficient the work of the various government field agencies. In October 1934 the President consolidated the Executive Council and the National Emergency Council under the latter title. It was composed of 34 department and agency heads including all members of the Cabinet, with Donald R. Richberg as executive director. It was an encouraging development and was envisaged as the "center of the whole mechanism of administrative coördination." [7] The director was authorized "to perform the duties vested in the Council," which were impressive:

(a) to provide for the orderly presentation of business to the President; (b) to coördinate inter-agency problems of organization and activity of Federal agencies; (c) to coördinate and make more efficient

[7] W. Y. Elliott, *The Need for Constitutional Reform*, Whittlesey House, 1935, p. 97.

and productive the work of the field agencies of the Federal Government; (d) to coöperate with any Federal agency in performing such activities as the President may direct; and (e) to serve in an advisory capacity to the President . . .[8]

The director could issue rules and regulations "approved by the President" and, on his own, issue additional regulations to supplement or carry out the intent of the President's rules. Such responsibility had to carry with it clear supremacy over the department heads either in the director's own right, by delegation, or through clear understanding that such was the role the President intended. It had to be clear that he was in a better position to know the President's will than any other official and that he spoke for the President and would have his support in a conflict. These conditions did not prevail and Richberg's authority soon declined and his status dimmed rapidly. His offices were not in the White House. Many officials of the administration were known to have more ready access to the President's ear than Richberg. Policies were made and approved by the President without Richberg's knowledge. Department heads found they could ignore him with impunity. While the agency continued to have some formal existence until 1939, it had little significance after its first year.[9]

Other important coördinative beginnings in special fields appeared during this period,[10] including the United States Information Service, set up in March 1934 to serve as a central clearing house for information; the Central Statistical Board, in July 1933, to develop, improve and coördinate Federal and other statistical services; and the National Resources Board, in July 1934, to prepare and present to the President programs for development and use of land, water, and other natural resources.[11]

[8] E.O. 6889–A, October 29, 1934.

[9] It is worth noting that Richberg's regime as "top coördinator" also occurred in an emergency period. The NEC failure has special interest in the light of the latter OWM–OWMR experience. The agency probably deserves more study than it has received.

[10] Roosevelt's early concern with the development of central coördinating bodies and staff assistance may reflect considerably more administrative understanding—perhaps intuition is the word—than he is generally conceded.

[11] The Board was succeeded by the National Resources Committee which later became the National Resources Planning Board. For a critique of the Planning Board, see John D. Millett, *The Process and Organization of Government Planning*, Columbia, 1947.

In 1936 Roosevelt appointed the President's Committee on Administrative Management, whose report he submitted with approval to Congress in January 1937. The most distinguishing feature of the Committee's work was its basic concern with the central control aspects of administrative management. It recognized the President as the pivotal factor in government organization and efficiency. Government organization should be simplified to diminish the complexity of top management. But whatever might be done below, the office at the center, where accountability must reside, must be equipped with the assistance required for a job of indescribable dimensions. The report pleaded, "The President needs help." [12]

Most of the Committee's recommendations were not enacted. But the resulting law, passed in April 1939, did authorize the President to appoint up to six administrative assistants, and the first Reorganization Plan, made possible by the Act, created an Executive Office of the President. It provided for two major staff arms—the Bureau of the Budget and the National Resources Planning Board.

A few months later the President issued a historic order giving organizational form to the Executive Office.[13] Six principal divisions were created: (1) the White House Office, which included the President's secretaries, personal aides, and administrative assistants; (2) Bureau of the Budget; (3) National Resources Planning Board; (4) Liaison Office for Personnel Management; (5) Office of Government Reports; and (6) Office for Emergency Management, a unit to which no attention was paid at the time but which proved to be an important legal convenience during the war.[14] An accompanying statement emphasized that the entire Executive Office "must be molded into a compact organization" and this intention was reflected in the provision that all personnel of these offices should be housed in a single building "close to the White House," a plan not achieved until almost a decade later.

Establishment of the Executive Office of the President is a

[12] The President's Committee on Administrative Management, *Administrative Management in the Government of the United States*, Government Printing Office, 1937, p. 2.

[13] E.O. 8248, September 9, 1939.

[14] For a detailed treatment of the composition of the Executive Office, see F. Morstein Marx, *The President and His Staff Services*, Public Administration Service, 1947.

grand landmark in the administrative history of our government. The chairman of the President's Committee was justified in boasting two years later that the Presidency had been provided with the "first formal piece of machinery to meet its managerial needs" in a century and a half of existence.[15]

Yet, almost as striking as this great stride itself is the gaping omission in both the Report of the Committee and the final structure of the Executive Office. The Committee limited its task to consideration of one large sector of the President's responsibility —administrative management. It concerned itself with personnel management, fiscal management, planning management, and administrative reorganization of the government. Despite the Committee's apparent recognition of the problem, no effective provision was made to assist the President in top program coördination.[16]

Despite the efforts of the Budget Bureau to fill the void, the coming of the war gave early and dramatic evidence of the inadequate organization of the top rung of government. There was widespread demand for an agency for central coördination of programs. OWM was improvised to fill the gap. While OWM– OWMR was not a formal part of the Executive Office, it played the part of the core of that Office during its existence.

Since the war several changes have taken place in the President's Office. The Office of Government Reports has disappeared.[17] The Council of Economic Advisers was added by statute. As this is written, the National Security Resources Board and the National Security Council are being officially added to the Executive Office, although they have had Presidential staff functions from the time of their creation in 1947.[18] In December 1946, as OWMR was assigned to liquidation, the President ap-

[15] Louis Brownlow, "The Executive Office of the President," *Public Administration Review*, vol. 1, No. 2, 1941, p. 101.
[16] Some staff members of the Committee indicated in staff memoranda concern about the omission (for example, W. Y. Elliott, "The President's Role in Administrative Management," 1936, MS.) but the chairman of the Committee told the author that the Committee itself felt it was obliged to overlook the President's other large responsibilities because its assignment was confined to functions of "administrative management," literally interpreted. (Interview with Louis Brownlow, August 21, 1946.) The six administrative assistants were not in a position to effect coördination.
[17] The legal status of this Office is clouded, but the weight of opinion is that it is no longer legally in existence, and that is certainly true in practice.
[18] Reorganization Plan IV of 1949, effective August 19, 1949.

pointed its last director to be Assistant to the President "to continue to aid me in coördinating federal agency programs and policies." [19]

In addition to these formal adjuncts of the President's office, the President has available a variety of other instrumentalities to assist him in his job of formulating and coördinating policy and program. These include emergency coördinating authorities, which he may create from time to time—for example, the National Emergency Council (1933) and OWM (1943); regular agencies endowed with coördinating functions in a limited area, of which the Department of State is the most prominent; special inter-agency committees; special advisory committees such as the President's Committee on Administrative Management (1936) and the President's Commission on Universal Training (1946), which are generally composed of well-known private citizens; Joint Chiefs of Staff, which although an integral part of the National Military Establishment are by law "the principal military advisers to the President"; and a variety of other informal and *ad hoc* arrangements. The Cabinet falls into a special category of presidential help.

These developments of the past two decades are significant indications of the growing recognition and concern over presidential staffing and the necessity for central coördination. Important progress has been made. Yet it remains true today that "Inadequate coördination is the greatest administrative defect in American National Government . . ." [20]

INADEQUACY OF PRESENT UNITS
FOR PROGRAM COÖRDINATION

There are three existing instrumentalities which, it is sometimes claimed, should be able to assume responsibility for program coördination. These are the Bureau of the Budget, the Council of Economic Advisers, and the Cabinet.

BUREAU OF THE BUDGET

The Bureau has had a remarkable development since 1939 and has operated on an enlarged scale with considerable effectiveness. In its work of budgetary control, fiscal management, and

[19] *White House Press Release*, December 12, 1946.

[20] Marshall E. Dimock, "Administrative Efficiency Within a Democratic Polity," *New Horizons in Public Administration*, University of Alabama, 1945, p. 37.

administrative management it has made clear the relationship of these to program development and control and it has made perceptible advances in the field of policy coördination.

At least three important factors contributed conspicuously to the Bureau's expansion into the substantive policy sphere, beyond activities which are clearly part of the budget process. These were the strong leadership of Director Smith, who had a broad and progressive view of the functions of the budget and the role of presidential staff and who enjoyed a close personal relationship with President Roosevelt; the unavoidable overlapping and interrelationships among considerations of budget, administration, and policy formulation; and the fact that the field of programs and policy as such was vacant and available to an agency with imagination and ambition.

The Bureau handled a wide variety of policy and program tasks for President Roosevelt. However, the trend toward an increasing role for the Bureau in this area came to a standstill after 1942. Wartime improvisations to meet the need for central coördination, culminating finally in OWM, reflected doubt that the Bureau could have performed that job. Despite the demise of OWM–OWMR, the Bureau does not appear to have returned to its former role and indications suggest that recently it has taken a more limited view of its job than obtained under Smith.

During the period when the Bureau was emerging from the restricted sphere of narrow concern with the formal aspects of Federal expenditures, some of its supporters adopted a highly defensive attitude against those who did not recognize the inevitable relationships among administration, fiscal control, planning, and policy. However, it is no detraction from the validity of the broad view of the budgetary role to recognize its limitations. These limitations have become clear from experience since 1939 and have been recognized by high Bureau officials. Wayne Coy and Paul Appleby, both recent assistant directors of the Budget, have pointed out that budgetary control and review are important but, after all, particular phases of total programmatic development and coördination.[21] Harold Smith expressed clearly to a

[21] See, Wayne Coy, "Basic Problems," *loc. cit.*, pp. 1124 ff.; Paul H. Appleby, "Organizing Around the Head of a Large Federal Department," *loc. cit.*, pp. 205 ff.; Paul H. Appleby, "Civilian Control of a Department of National Defense," Walgreen Foundation Lecture Series, University of Chicago, 1946, MS.

congressional committee the inability of the Bureau to perform the full staff job required of the Executive Office.[22]

Fiscal control and administrative management are vital elements in total management and coördination. They are and must be closely related to policy development and coördination. But they do not in themselves provide for the latter aspect of the total job. The fiscal device is a fundamental mechanism for control and coördination of a limited type. Innovation in programs and policy is not inherent in the performance of that function. In fact, the tendency is for the more concrete and compelling fiscal task to drive the less tangible policy job into secondary status.[23] It is difficult to conceive that a programmatic development like the West Coast Manpower Program (Chapter 5) could arise out of the budgetary process. The Bureau is properly concerned with control and evaluation of the operations of such a program, but it is wrong to assume that it can also take responsibility for the specialized task of program and policy coördination.

Policy coördination functions require a close and candid relationship between the coördinator and the agencies, with which responsibility for budget and fiscal control may interfere. As officers of the Budget Bureau will testify, the official identified with fiscal control finds his motives suspect. This may be unfair, but it is generally true. Such statements as one made by the Brookings Institution in 1937 reflect a not uncommon view: "Presumably, the prime interest of the Treasury, the Budget Bureau and the General Accounting Office is in the conservation of public funds." [24]

Eleven years later a task force of the Hoover Commission took almost as restricted a view of the budget function and recommended return of the Bureau to the Treasury Department.[25]

In any event, justly or unjustly, such considerations pose enor-

---

[22] 78th Cong., 2nd Sess., House, Special Committee on Postwar Economic Policy and Planning, *Hearings*, March 15—May 3, 1944, pp. 410–411.

[23] "There is a great tendency on the part of budget people to see all policy as budgetary policy or fiscal policy." (Paul H. Appleby, "Organizing Around the Head of a Large Federal Department," *loc. cit.*, p. 210.)

[24] 75th Cong., 1st Sess., *Senate Report No. 1275*, August 16, 1937, p. 17.

[25] John W. Hanes, A. E. Buck, and T. C. Andrews, *Fiscal, Budgeting and Accounting Systems of Federal Government*, Government Printing Office, 1948, pp. 31–32, 39–85. The Commission itself did not adopt the recommendations of its task force.

mous disadvantages to attempts to combine within one unit both policy and program coördinating functions and budgetary responsibility. The Budget Bureau has a fundamental but particular task within a general staff where all tasks are related.[26]

COUNCIL OF ECONOMIC ADVISERS

The functions of the Council of Economic Advisers are to assist the President in preparation of his economic reports to the Congress and to make recommendations to him on economic policy. In taking its pulse count of the nation's economic health it may request information and assistance from other agencies, but it has no advisory, coördinating, or supervisory role in regard to any other agency. The statutory structure of the Council, involving a three-headed board, all requiring Senate confirmation, also practically precludes the possibility that the Council could assume the active political job of day-to-day coördination or programing as an integrated staff arm of the President.[27]

The type of active coördination which was performed by OWM–OWMR and the continuous research and long-range planning envisaged for the Council are both essential in staffing the Presidency, and they are closely related. Effective coördination must be accompanied by some broad plan of direction, and planning itself is futile unless translated into policy activity. Whether the two functions need to be combined within a single unit in the President's Office is, however, disputable. The type of personnel required for these functions differ greatly, the working methods differ, the emphasis and time element differ. An attempt to combine them into one might result in a de-emphasis or neglect of one of the functions, probably the broad type of planning.

But there must be considerable meshing between planning and program coördination, particularly at the Executive Office level. Thus far, the Council has had a rather tenuous relation to the rest of the government and even to other parts of the President's

[26] Despite "the remarkable development of the Bureau of the Budget . . . the rest of the Executive Office remains amorphous and undeveloped, and means are lacking to harmonize policy in major fields." (Arthur W. Macmahon, "The Future Organizational Pattern of the Executive Branch," *American Political Science Review*, December 1944, p. 1181.)

[27] See John D. Millett, *op. cit.*, pp. 159–174, for a critique of the design of the Council. His prophecy of trouble has been borne out by recent developments.

Office and has lived in comparative isolation. The experience of the National Resources Planning Board and economic planning staffs abroad suggests the danger of setting up such units isolated from offices involved in the regular day-to-day operations which may bring the planners' work to life.[28] The Council appears to be on firmer footing than the NRPB and its work has thus far attracted considerable public attention through the President's reports. In fact, the general design of the Council's structure and functions strongly suggests that the primary purpose of its sponsors was to have a medium for calling early public and congressional attention to economic difficulties ahead and thus force-governmental action. Yet, the agency is still too remote from the actual operations of government. Here the catalytic role of a program coördination unit would be highly effective.

At the time of the Council's formation, the Colmer Committee suggested that the proper relationship with OWMR, whose continuation the Committee was requesting, should be that the former make "research studies and conclusions as to long-run policy which would better enable the President and (through its reports) the Congress to frame broad economic policy. The OWMR, on the other hand, has to deal with the integration of immediate economic decisions into this longer run policy."[29]

As already suggested, the present set-up of the Council includes some basic handicaps to its most useful development. The Act of 1946 violated in some important respects the principle that the Executive Office should be a direct staff arm of the President. "It would have been much sounder to rely on the precedent of the Budget and Accounting Act of 1921, under which both the director and assistant director of the Budget Bureau are chosen by the President without need for senatorial confirmation."[30] A single

[28] In Britain, Prime Minister Ramsay MacDonald established an Economic Advisory Council as an "economic general staff" reporting directly to the Prime Minister. It soon lost the interest even of its founder, rarely met and rarely reported. A British authority has pointed out, "if the Prime Minister remembers, these reports are circulated to the Cabinet ministers, by whom they are placed in the wastepaper basket." (W. I. Jennings, "British Organization for Rearmament," *Political Science Quarterly,* December 1938, p. 489.)

[29] 79th Cong., 2d Sess., House, Special Committee on Post-War Economic Policy and Planning, *Eleventh Report,* December 17, 1946, pp. 22–23.

[30] Wayne Coy, "Basic Problems," *loc. cit.,* p. 1132.

head, rather than a council of three (already feuding actively) would be more compatible with the principle of an integrated Executive Office and with the proper performance of staff functions. Furthermore, such detailed legislation itself must be something of a fetter for any flexible use the President may wish to make of his staff.

In any event, whatever the merits of the Council's structure for its present tasks, it is clear that it was not designed for and cannot perform the general function of active program coördination.

THE CABINET

The Cabinet has long been regarded as a policy-making and coördinative instrumentality of the President despite the clear evidence in fact that it rarely serves such a function. It is the uniform judgment of close observers and the testimony of former Cabinet officials that it has not been an effective instrument for formulating policy or for coördination of the executive branch.

The traditional Cabinet, which has no legal standing, consists of the heads of the individual departments, now nine, whose totality does not include a large number of highly important executive agencies. They have no collective responsibility and are not in any sense a single body, except at such moments when the President chooses to call them together. Members report on departmental activities considered to be of interest to the President, but there is rarely any detailed criticism of policies, votes are not taken on issues, and individual department heads are often reluctant to bring up their more intimate problems in front of the others; they await an opportunity to catch the President's ear alone after a meeting. The meetings have been described as "section hands reporting to the boss," and criticism of the "boss" or of each other is not an accepted practice.

The system of departmentalism has become so embedded that individual department heads feel no accountability for over-all policy or the activities of other departments. Cabinet members have reported being "bored" with Cabinet meetings.[31] The segmentalized interests of departments, with their special clienteles, are frequently in conflict with the President's responsibility for the whole public interest, which is considerably more than the

[31] A. W. Macmahon and J. D. Millett, *Federal Administrators*, Columbia, 1939, pp. 5–6.

sum of the interests of the individual departments. Moreover, Presidents have had frequent cause to distrust their Cabinets when they undertook to act as a group.[32]

Awareness of the shortcomings of the Cabinet has led to numerous proposals for Cabinet reform, many of which do violence to the Presidential system.[33] Analogies to the British Cabinet, an entirely different kind of a body, are largely futile, but it is interesting to note that even that body did not attain its highest degree of effectiveness until it developed a secretariat which has served as a connecting link between the developmental work of the permanent ministry staffs and the final formulation of policy by political officers. This provision of a basis for better integration at the top has helped to provide coördination and singleness of purpose throughout the administrative structure.

In this country, in addition to its other handicaps, there exists no machinery to enable this group of busy men, preoccupied with heavy responsibilities, to be a useful collective body. A proposal for vitalizing the work of the Cabinet and bringing it more closely in touch with the Executive Office through the institution of a presidential secretariat is suggested on pp. 222–223.

GROWING RECOGNITION OF THE NEED

Increasing awareness of the many factors which have been discussed—the inescapable trend toward more extensive executive

---

[32] Paul Appleby makes the point that this situation "has led one of the profoundest observers of our government to say privately that the Cabinet members are the President's worst enemies." ("Civilian Control of a Department of National Defense," *loc. cit.*, p. 21.) A White House confidant told the author in 1948, "Truman has had to assert himself as boss recently, and he now makes it clear that he alone makes decisions. For a while, a caucus had developed in the Cabinet which decided on its positions in advance of meeting and presented a united front to the President, and tried to create enormous psychological pressure for the President to follow rather than lead. The President was caught in that for a spell, but he has learned and is now free of it. If given their heads, these fellows will try to become a team independent of him."

[33] The most common are proposals to include leaders of Congress in the Cabinet. See, for example, Edward S. Corwin, *The President—Office and Powers*, New York University, 1948, pp. 353 ff. See also, Herman Finer, "The Hoover Commission Reports—Part I," *Political Science Quarterly*, September 1949, pp. 413 ff., for a strong plea for "a full cabinet system with collective responsibility," an objective which, whatever its merits, seems romantic for any foreseeable future.

responsibilities and their increasing interdependence, the inadequacy of present instrumentalities for policy and program coördination, the frequency of temporary improvisations to fill the gap—has led a growing number of government officials and students of administration to the same conclusion: something new must be added to the President's office.

The Colmer Committee, already extensively quoted on this subject, said, in its final report, that its appraisal of the OWMR experience indicated a continuing need for such a presidential agency.

In the opinion of the committee the experience of this office shows a standing need for a genuine Presidential staff agency to integrate the total policy of the executive branch of the government. Such a staff is essential to secure the proper preparation and execution by separate agencies and departments wherever there is a need for clearance and joint action by several departments on any major issue of policy . . .

The scale of peacetime operations of any modern government involves the necessity of bringing into line general fiscal policy, social objectives, foreign policy, and domestic politics. To accomplish this requires a governmental agency that coördinates not only the major departments but the large numbers of independent regulatory commissions and the many governmental corporations . . .[34]

Wayne Coy, an experienced public administrator who has held important posts in the Executive Office, has called attention to the existing lack of "special facilities designed to capture in each particular matter before the President the best thinking available," a place for the fusion of resources of the executive branch.[35]

Harold Smith, who spent many useful years in the Executive Office, has been quoted by Robert Sherwood as saying that the Office needs "another wing." According to Sherwood that wing meant "a civilian Chief of Staff without much of a staff of his own but with constant access to the President's mind and to all the official intelligence available to that mind—an adviser on policy freed of the special interests and prejudices imposed on any officer who had special responsibility for any one phase of the total government effort."[36]

Don K. Price, another well-known authority, has acknowledged

[34] *Eleventh Report, op. cit.,* p. 22.
[35] Wayne Coy, "Basic Problems," *loc. cit.,* p. 1134.
[36] Robert E. Sherwood, *op. cit.,* pp. 240–241. Sherwood believes Harry Hopkins, during the war years, came closest to filling this role.

the problem and recommended development of an Executive Office secretariat which would deal only with "the main issues of policy." [37]

Professor William Y. Elliott, an experienced administrator, told Congress not long ago:

> It is essential that the President should have, in my judgment, someone who would perform the kind of "Chief of Staff" functions that have been put upon, first, Justice Byrnes, and now upon Judge Vinson in the Office of War Mobilization and Reconversion . . . during the 5 years that I have spent in Washington, the major difficulties which we have encountered have arisen from the lack of adequate staff planning and coördination of policies, quite as much as from the inevitable difficulties of an improvised administration faced with the gigantic problem of war.[38]

Professor John M. Gaus, a well-known authority on administration, has suggested the possibility of a chief of the President's "general staff." [39]

The Hoover Commission, in its first report, gave oblique attention to this problem and recommended that a new "Staff Secretary" be added to the President's Office to prepare for the President "a current summary of the principal issues with which he may have to deal in the near future" and "a current summary of the staff work available on problems that have been assigned to his advisors, his staff agencies, or the heads of departments and agencies." [40]

These are but a few examples of informed and growing concern. All the sources cited see the problem somewhat differently; their proposals vary. But all recognize that the Presidency is not now staffed to cope with some of its major responsibilities, particularly in the area of policy and program coördination.

The need has also been obtaining increasing pragmatic recognition in the Executive Office itself, where the range of respon-

[37] Don K. Price, "Staffing the Presidency," *American Political Science Review*, December 1946, pp. 1165–1167.

[38] William Y. Elliott, "Statement," 79th Cong., 1st Sess., Joint Committee on the Organization of Congress, *Hearings*, March 13 to June 29, 1945, p. 963.

[39] John M. Gaus, *Reflections on Public Administration*, University of Alabama, 1947, p. 47.

[40] Commission on Organization of the Executive Branch of the Government, *General Management of the Executive Branch*, Government Printing Office, February 1949, p. 22.

sibilities falling upon the Assistant to the President has grown conspicuously, and increasing program activities are known to be coördinated through his office.[41] This is, however, merely another improvisation. In long range terms and for most effective conduct of the Presidency, conspicuous and continuing functions require institutional arrangements, which become clearly understood and traditional as part of the presidential office.

PROPOSAL FOR AN OFFICE OF PROGRAM COÖRDINATION

It is proposed that there be added to the Executive Office of the President an Office of Program Coördination whose head would also be Assistant to the President. The basic function of the program coördinator (a happier designation should probably be devised since the word "coördinator" has too often been attached to a man without a job) would be to act for the President in the coördination of day-to-day program and policy operations of the executive branch, in contrast to fiscal management, administrative management, long-range economic planning, and military planning. All of these functions are closely related and must be apportioned among institutional units of the Executive Office, the whole of which should be considered and should act as a unified structure, which it does not today because of lack of organization.

This proposal does not imply a continuation of OWM–OWMR in its early or later form. OWM–OWMR was itself an emergency improvisation suited to a particular time and circumstance. From its experiences are available invaluable lessons for the proposed Office, but it is not in itself the model. In normal times such an Office need not have independent directive powers such as were conferred upon OWM–OWMR; it should not be placed in a position independent of the other vital units of the Executive Office and need not be superior to them; it should not have independent statutory powers giving it a position other than that of a presi-

[41] An interesting development took place in July 1949. After his midyear economic report to Congress, dealing especially with the current growth of unemployment, the President informed his department and agency heads that he wanted to coördinate "Federal programs of direct action or assistance to localities which can be timed and channeled so as to concentrate upon areas where unemployment is heavy . . ." He announced that the Assistant to the President was to assume responsibility for these activities. (*White House Press Release*, July 14, 1949.)

dential agency; and its structure and role should not be legislatively frozen, thus depriving the President of full flexibility in the conduct of his staff and office. While even in its statutory days OWMR did in fact act as presidential staff, the legislation made it quite possible to have behaved in some other fashion.

Nor, at the other extreme, should the program coördinator be the kind of disembodied functionary recommended by the Hoover Commission in the post of Staff Secretary, who would be responsible only for keeping the President "currently informed" and not be "an advisor . . . on any issue of policy" or act for the President in any capacity. The President needs no additional vehicles for assembling information and certainly he should not want it all channeled through one man—even one of such bloodless disinterest as the Commission envisages. He needs help in doing something about the vast quantities of information already available. He needs a man or staff agency to perform essential tasks of an interdepartmental character for him, frequently on the basis of detailed information with which the President ought not to be personally burdened. He needs an office for central control, review, and reconciliation of the myriad particular programs and aspects of programs pursued by individual agencies to keep them consistent with the broad policies of the administration.

The coördinator must be one of the President's closest and most constant advisers and a trusted aide. He should act as the President's eyes and ears in following through on general implementation of administration objectives and in the resolution of conflicts among departments and agencies. In such situations, and in others when the President deems advisable, he should serve as the medium through which the Chief Executive communicates his wishes. He should assist the President by calling special situations to his attention or recommending modifications of programs. He may be employed in any other way which the President finds useful for active and regular coördination of the executive branch.[42]

The President does not ordinarily require a single chief of staff,

[42] This type of office will, of course, blur the conventional demarcation between "staff" and "line" functions. Fortunately, it has been recognized that at the top leadership level a degree of merging of staff and line functions is necessary and desirable. See, for example, Luther Gulick, *Administrative Reflections from World War II*, University of Alabama, 1948, pp. 84–85.

in the literal sense. On the contrary, it is highly desirable that the President be exposed to several staff heads, who approach basic problems from different aspects of presidential responsibility. Ultimate decisions must rest with the President and he should not have to make them from a single recommendation or from facts presented in one fashion; conflicting viewpoints on vital issues must be brought before him by different persons.[43] This protects not only the President's judgments but also his position.

It must be clear to anyone who has observed the Executive Office that here, above all other places, informal arrangements and relationships play a larger role than formal structure. Experience would indicate that the person holding a position like that of the proposed coördinator is soon likely to occupy a position of at least *primus inter pares* among the heads of the various units in the Executive Office. There is the possibility that he may in practice become even more than this. This is something that the President must determine. No rigid structure should be imposed on the President for his own office. He can in practice make the position something more or something less than here indicated, depending upon his own working habits, whom he can get for the job, and perhaps on the political climate of the time. The element of equality among the staff heads in the formal structure is, however, important because it makes possible the direct approach of any unit head to the President without committing an impropriety and assures no untoward insulation of the President from his own staff on important issues.

It has been pointed out that a presidential staff must be composed of two broad classes: "individuals serving the President in an intimate personal way, and units whose chiefs combine an intimate relationship with leadership over systematic staff functions." [44] This important distinction sets off some of the characteristics of the White House Office, which may contain personal staff, political aides, and special temporary assistants, from such systematic organs organizationally related to the rest of the executive branch as is the Bureau of the Budget and as is contemplated for

---

[43] Similarly, the president's staff as a whole must not attempt to shut off department heads from the President. They too report to the President, and the Executive Office should not attempt to exercise a monopoly on counsel.

[44] Paul Appleby, "Civilian Control of a Department of National Defense," *loc. cit.*, p. 28.

the Office of Program Coördination. This distinction was personified in the contrasting services of a Harry Hopkins and a James Byrnes to President Roosevelt: the first an intimate confidant, adviser, and aide with a variety of highly important special assignments but without organizational portfolio; the second and intimate aide charged with top staff functions in a formalized relationship to the executive organization.

In anticipation of crisis periods it appears advisable that the program coördinator carry some formal attachment to both elements of the President's office, which is one reason it has been suggested that he also have the title of Assistant to the President. Wars and other crises have their effect upon the President's office as well as upon the rest of the government's administrative structure. As the last war and other crises have indicated, in emergencies the President may find it convenient or necessary to delegate directive authority of a broad nature to a subordinate in a manner similar to OWM. Instead of creation of additional offices or other improvisations, the logical place for such directive authority is with the Office of Program Coördination. In the event of such a change in a crisis environment, it is not unlikely that the President may desire, or public relations may demand, a new face in such a key position. It should be made easy for the President to bring in a new man as program coördinator (who will have the advantages of an experienced staff), a man whose services he may not be able to obtain except in time of crisis, without appearing to demote or fire the previous occupant. In time of war, Assistant to the President, which would then be a post of personal aide without institutional responsibilities, would still be a big enough job to avoid any loss of face.

The work of the program coördinator would be greatly facilitated if there were appended to his office a presidential secretariat for regular and active use of top inter-agency and Cabinet committees. It is most important that the experience and knowledge of the agency heads be applied, in systematic fashion, to broad policy decisions. The effectiveness of the coördinating unit in the Executive Office will depend in part upon regular joint deliberations of such officials, and the accessibility of their work to the program coördinator. Effective communication involves more than a request for information; it arises out of a working process.

The formal Cabinet is both too large and too small for considering all important issues. Some involve the interests of only a few of its members; other issues involve agencies not identified with the Cabinet at all. Greater effectiveness is to be achieved through development of Cabinet committees (including appropriate heads of other agencies) for consideration of particular fields of policy. These may be standing committees for issues of a continuing nature or *ad hoc* committees for special situations.

Staffing such committees with a skilled presidential secretariat would not only make them more efficient and effective in themselves, but would assure integration of activity with the President's office.[45] Such formalized use of committees with a centralized secretariat should both vitalize the Cabinet and help the President and his program coördinator identify problems requiring action and clarify the issues involved.[46]

SOME GUIDING PRINCIPLES BASED
ON OWM–OWMR EXPERIENCES

The OWM–OWMR experience is rich with practical lessons for the future. Out of the background of trial and error which preceded creation of the agency, out of its life history, its problems and methods, its successes and failures, there emerge some broad guiding principles which should be useful not only to some analogous agency in the event of another holocaust, but also in the development of such a permanent institution as the proposed Office of Program Coördination.

Some of these principles relate to the Office itself, others to the

[45] The Hoover Commission appeared to be taking a very hesitant and short step toward such a secretariat in recommending a "Staff Secretary" for the President to clear information on major problems on which staff work is being done within the President's office or by interdepartmental committees. This appears to be a compromise with the secretariat proposal which was made to the Commission. The Staff Secretary, however, as described by the Commission, would lack a base for performing his job and it appears he would add little to the President's services.

[46] An extremely interesting and important example of the successful operation of a secretariat exists in the Cabinet Food Committee, set up by the President in 1946 with little publicity, primarily because the Departments of State and Agriculture were in disagreement on questions of food shipment abroad. The secretariat was first attached to OWMR and later to the Assistant to the President. The departments and the President's office found it a most useful instrument in giving effectiveness to the Committee.

type of personnel who could occupy the Office successfully. To some extent they are separable. To a large degree, the peculiar functions and role of this kind of office create elements of inseparability. More than in the case of ordinary agencies, the element of personality is crucial.

1. *Institutional Status in the President's Office.* Real coördination on basic issues of policy and program in the executive branch can be achieved only through the office of the Presidency. The personal staff the President requires for such an important and exacting job must have permanent institutional status and must be clearly a presidential arm, accountable only to him.

It is essential that the program coördinator be known to have full presidential confidence and backing; he must be conspicuously an intimate adviser to the President. When he undertakes to speak for the President there should be no doubt that he is doing just that.

Although the permanent establishment of such an Office should probably be recognized by law, it is undesirable that the coördinator have any statutory powers or be accountable to Congress. The President must have complete freedom and flexibility for the proper conduct of his office and all powers of his staff should flow directly from him.

The OWMR statute was a source of considerable controversy. Many students of government pointed to the dubious propriety and wisdom of legislating such broad executive powers to anyone short of the President. It appeared an improper usurpation of executive authority by action of the legislature and threatened an erosion of presidential powers which might mar the cohesiveness and efficiency of the executive branch. No dire consequences did ensue but this may have been in part due to precedents established by OWM as a presidential adjunct.[47]

[47] One writer has claimed that the law did impair effectiveness, although no substantiating evidence is furnished. "As Louis Brownlow has pointed out, this is the first time that Congress has ever created by statute a 'sub-presidential, supradepartmental administrator with authority (so far as transition and reconversion are concerned) over all departments, independent establishments, and agencies in the executive branch of the government,' and with powers in some respects broader than granted to the President himself. Through this act, Congress attempted to participate in administration and curtail the authority of the President by vesting essentially executive functions and powers in one of his assistants. The result was an impairment of

In addition to being an episode in the traditional executive-legislative contest for power, it was also personalized legislation. Many Congressmen were anxious to curb President Roosevelt and take out of his hands as much power as possible over reconversion. Furthermore, they probably would not have approved such an unprecedented law had they not been assured that their popular ex-colleague, "Jimmie" Byrnes, would be appointed director.

In any event, such statutory power for a super-coördinating agency, which must also act as presidential staff, appears at least inadvisable and possibly dangerous.

2. *Jurisdiction Over All Agencies.* The government now contains an impressive array of program coördinating instruments in particular spheres, including inter-agency committees and other devices. These are important and useful; a suggestion has been made in the previous pages for encouraging and strengthening such units through employment of a secretariat. What is needed is the correlation of the work and decisions of all these coördinating bodies of partial jurisdiction whose areas impinge on one another,[48] and an avenue for resolution of conflict and impasse within these lower-level units since they have no final authority. To add one more coördinating unit with limited jurisdiction would be futile. The proposed office's span of jurisdiction, with regard to program coördination, must include all agencies and, in effect, be as broad as the President's,[49] just as the span of the Budget Bureau is all-inclusive in the spheres of administrative management and fiscal control.

This does not involve curtailment of the existing policy-making jurisdiction of any agencies. For example, the Secretary of State is responsible for United States foreign policy and the Secretary of Agriculture for agricultural policy. But should their two departments have difficulty in reconciling divergent views in a

---

the effectiveness of the office, and it has not played the important role in reconversion envisaged by Congress." (Joseph P. Harris, "Wartime Currents and Peacetime Trends," *American Political Science Review*, December 1946, pp. 1146–1147.)

[48] According to one study there were 348 separate interdepartmental units in December 1934. (Mary T. Reynolds, *Interdepartmental Committees in the National Administration*, Columbia, 1939.) Informal estimates indicate the number is far greater now.

[49] The President's limited jurisdiction over the independent regulatory commissions would, of course, also similarly limit the director.

matter such as agricultural exports under a foreign aid program (which has, in fact, occurred), it should be clear that the program coördinator has the task of acting for the President or assisting him in settling such a dispute. Since this is obviously a proper presidential responsibility, it is an appropriate concern of his staff. Responsibilities of department heads are neither altered nor diminished.

OWM–OWMR experience indicated that inclusion of the military within the coördinative jurisdiction may prove most difficult to work out. Yet essentially the problem is no different from that of other departments. Military planning and strategy are the responsibility of the military agencies. But, as was so dramatically clear during the war, and becomes even more apparent during peace, military planning cuts across problems of production and a variety of aspects of the civilian economy. Military affairs cannot be completely autonomous without resulting in military control over all elements of government. The problems of the military have to be reconciled with the interests of the other agencies, and this must be done in the President's office. The recent conflict over peacetime control and development of atomic energy illustrates the impossibility of compartmentalizing "civilian" and "military" jurisdictions.

3. *Restriction of Functions to Top Policy and Program Issues.* The war experience demonstrated clearly that successful central coördination must be completely divorced from any operating or administrative responsibilities. If the central unit is the capstone of an operating organization, it will soon become just another operating agency, however important its operations may be. On the one hand, it loses status; on the other, the pressures and conflicts of operating responsibility result in progressive de-emphasis of the over-all coördinating role. In the competition for the coördinator's attention, immediate operating and organizational problems tend to gain priority over broader issues. Also, accountability for a particular program or set of programs generally proves incompatible with a balanced over-all interest and viewpoint, as Cabinet experience has often revealed.

Furthermore, the Office's topside policy and program responsibility cannot be chopped up by partial transfer to other agencies even when it appears that a single unified program is involved.

The attempt to transfer a portion of OWMR authority (as distinguished from delegation) to the Housing Expediter to carry out the housing program was bad in theory and failed in practice.

Nor should the Office become a holding company encompassing other agencies, even when the responsibilities of those other agencies are also coördinative in character. It proved a mistake to include within OWMR such offices as the Retraining and Reëmployment Administration, the Surplus Property Board, and the Office of Contract Settlement.

It is not implied that one office at the presidential level can be expected to carry out all necessary coördination in the executive branch. In specific areas, lower level coördinating units should, and do, exist. In some instances, a regular line agency may take coördinating responsibility in the field of its special concern, a not uncommon practice. The top coördinator should support and strengthen such lower-level assistance. He should insist upon exhaustion of all lower channels before problems are brought to him, except in gravest emergencies. He should maintain the discipline of "enforcement of cross reference" among agencies. This, furthermore, implies full use of the facilities and talents of all other agencies.[50]

4. *Non-involvement in Normal Functions of Individual Departments.* The coördinator must avoid the two-edged evil of either allowing departments to feel that some of their normal responsibilities—either for administration or policy-making within their regular jurisdiction—have been taken away, or of being drawn into the innumerable detailed problems which they may bring to him to obtain support. By and large, he should take jurisdiction only over issues not susceptible of settlement at the department level—issues which will, in turn, govern hundreds of other detailed decisions down the line—or where inter-agency conflict has caused an impasse. He should not be concerned with development of methods of operation but only with seeing that agencies concerned are following through. Status is soon lost by involvement in minor issues.

On the other hand, these considerations must be balanced

[50] The manner in which OWM–OWMR worked with OES before the summer of 1945 and with the Budget Bureau at certain stages indicates the feasibility and value of such relations.

against the importance of not becoming isolated or detached. Coördination is a continuous development rather than a matter of periodic review or spot adjudication.[51]

The same regard for appropriate functions of other units must apply in the Executive Office itself. This is necessary not only for efficient internal operation, but it must be clear to all departments and agencies who is the person, in the President's office, responsible for a particular problem. Uncertainty will injure all phases of coördination.

5. *Maintenance of Reasonable Control.* If the coördinator's authorized decisions are flouted, he must take prompt and appropriate action either directly or, preferably, through the President.

Top-level coördination should not attempt to eliminate all disputes among agencies, but rather to reduce their volume and magnitude through early delineation of general policy and the provision of a locale for final arbitration. Autocratic rule is of dubious ultimate efficiency. Agencies must be given relatively free rein for debate and for working out their difficulties among themselves, within the broad framework of administration policies. Their conflicts are frequently an excellent source of new ideas, exchange of knowledge, and the revelation of incongruities which may otherwise remain too long submerged. There is danger in discouraging the independent initiative of departments. The Office of Program Coördination should step in only where points of view cannot be reconciled through ordinary exchange or when an agency is clearly acting contrary to the President's policies.

Such a course presents a delicate problem of balance, for reasonable discipline is obviously essential to effective coördination. Without it healthy debate and disagreements may degenerate into the type of feuding which contributes to the too-frequent impression that upper level government officials devote themselves chiefly to internecine warfare. Such discipline does not, however, come primarily from rules and regulations but from status and institutionalization.

[51] ". . . coördination may exist in merely a nominal sense, especially when it is confined to occasional top-level determinations. The President's Committee on Administrative Management pointed out with great clarity that true coördination, being in the nature of a continuing process, must be sustained by the day-by-day work of presidential staff agencies." (Wayne Coy, "Basic Problems," *loc. cit.*, p. 1131.)

Since the coördinator is dealing with departmental heads whose own status it is important to maintain, he should, when basic issues are involved, not give the impression that decisions must be followed simply because they are his but rather that he is reflecting or stating the President's desires. As much as possible he should, in such instances, indicate that he is bringing together all elements in the issue for the President, and assisting him in arriving at a decision, but that the decision is the President's.[52]

6. *Qualifications of the Program Coördinator.* The coördinator must have personal qualities in keeping with his official status. It cannot be emphasized too strongly that paper authority and organizational lines rarely prove adequate in the higher echelons of government. He must not only be a man of highest ability and broad perspective, but should possess independent position and prestige based on wide experience and public respect.[53] A relatively unknown man, no matter how competent, would face difficulties which, while not insuperable, would be an enormous handicap.

The frequently expressed fear that a man in such a position might become a political competitor of the President's and thus undermine the latter's position may present a problem. It suggests the consideration of the office being occupied, if possible, by someone other than a professional politician or a man considered a likely candidate for political office (but certainly not a career civil servant). This will not always be possible, and other considerations may on balance dictate the advisability of a political figure. Nevertheless, as has been pointed out, the authority of the program coördinator depends upon the general recognition of his role as presidential agent. His effectiveness can be brought

[52] Don K. Price wrote the author the following interesting observation: "I think there is no doubt, with respect to major policy or legislative issues, that the OWMR disciplined dissenting agencies much more effectively than did the Bureau of the Budget, chiefly because its procedure was to get hold of them in the earlier stages of policy formation and to deal with them face to face, and incidentally because it had vigorous presidential backing and no competing responsibility for fiscal routine and details."

[53] It is clear that, in considerable degree, Byrnes and Vinson succeeded in obtaining acceptance of their central roles due to the fact that each had great public stature.

to a halt by a few public nods of disapproval from the President. The office is empty of power without presidential backing.[54]

Would the office attract the caliber of man needed? It has been pointed out that in the last two years of OWMR existence there were four different directors. Despite the fact that the office involved broader responsibilities than any Cabinet post, it did not have the long-range status and acceptance to hold the type of man the office demanded, once the crisis stage was over.[55] It was universally regarded as a "war job" and so it was designed. This emphasizes the need for permanent high status institutionalization which is here recommended.

What cannot be avoided is the high vulnerability of such an office. The coördinator will have to "take the rap" for many White House decisions which require a scapegoat. This may ultimately make him "expendable." [56]

7. *Small High-Level Staff.* The Coördinator's staff should be small, probably not exceeding 25 persons, other than clerical help. They should all have high rank, be of recognized high caliber and broad-gauged "generalists" rather than technical specialists. Staff work requiring technical expertness should be assigned to other units of the Executive Office or regular agencies.

There are several dangers in a large staff for such an agency which are clearly revealed in certain phases of OWM–OWMR history. The moment staff expands, a tendency develops to undertake chores not in keeping with the office's status and which tend to erode its influence in matters of top significance. The staff becomes more difficult to keep in tow, and personnel tend to

---

[54] For another point of view, see Don K. Price, "Staffing the Presidency," *loc. cit.*, pp. 1167–1168. Dr. Price says, "The surest way for the President to become a mere constitutional monarch would be to make someone else his prime minister." However, he is referring to a "single aide who is his sole channel of staff advice. A single chief of staff . . ." Since such a role is not recommended here, there may be no real disagreement, although Price is averse to having a man with "political ambitions."

[55] Byrnes, Vinson, and Snyder all preferred the Cabinet posts to which they succeeded.

[56] This is a traditional and necessary function for men close to the President. The story is often told of the headline which became familiar during Theodore Roosevelt's administration, "Loeb Takes Blame," referring to the presidential secretary William Loeb.

branch out in undertakings of their own,[57] using the name of the program coördinator in decisions which others know did not come from the coördinator himself. Moreover, when a technical staff is built up it will tend to duplicate activities of other agencies.

The staff of the Office of Program Coördination must be willingly and patently identified with the President's program. They are political personnel in the high sense of the term. High-policy decision and coördination are the very essence of politics. Policy must remain flexible and subject to change; it must reflect public opinion and the last election; it cannot be fettered by men identified in top-level roles with contrary policies. This need not make the office a haven for patronage. The government has shown that it can attract professionally proven men who do not necessarily want to make government service a career, but wish to be identified with the realization of policies of the administration in power.[58] Knowledge of the operations of government and skill in handling its affairs are too rare to be sacrificed with every spin of the political wheel. Nevertheless, at this high peak in the political hierarchy, this aspect of efficiency may have to bow to democratic necessities. Continuity, highly desirable where feasible, would be maintained in large degree through the suggested presidential secretariat which, while staffed by career civil servants, would work closely with the Office of Program Coördination.

Since the Coördinator must either review or direct the actions of heads of agencies on matters not susceptible of final determination at the departmental level, unusual caution must be exercised regarding delegation of authority to staff members.[59] At the same

---

[57] For an interesting discussion of staff problems see James F. Byrnes, "Statement," 78th Cong., 2nd Sess., Senate, Subcommittee of the Committee on Military Affairs, *Hearings on S. 1730 and S. 1823*, Pt. 7, June 12, 1944, pp. 294–295.

[58] For an interesting discussion of this point see, D. M. Levitan, "The Responsibility of Administrative Officials in a Democratic Society," *Political Science Quarterly*, December 1946, pp. 562 ff.

[59] Early in the life of OWM an experienced student of public administration gave it some sound advice on this point:

"When department and agency heads request a decision from the OWM they expect and should have a firm decision by the Director. Quite apart from the treatment which their position should command, they have a right to demand that decisions of the OWM should really be the considered action of the Director . . . on which they can operate rather than the decision

time, a hard and fast rule of non-delegation cannot be imposed without making the Office an irritating bottleneck. Such an office is sometimes called upon, particularly in times of emergency, to assist agencies which are not in disagreement or questioning policy but merely wish an implementing directive or an affirmation of authority to do something they think needs doing. Such matters may require assistance of the Office of Program Coördination but can be negotiated by personnel other than the coördinator. However, when any real issue is involved the rule of non-delegation should prevail.

A policy of non-delegation would not reduce the importance of the work of the staff. It has the vital task of calling to the coördinator's attention problems which deserve his consideration, collecting information, defining and pointing up issues for him, indicating the factors involved, and helping him arrive at a decision.

The Presidency is today the prime motive force in our constitutional system. Our political and economic evolution and the nature of our party system have focused responsibility upon the President for the origin of major policies and programs and for implementation and effectuation of policies approved by Congress.

It is a matter of grave concern, therefore, that the organization and staffing of the Presidency have failed to keep pace with the evolution of its functions and requirements. There can be nothing

---

of a subordinate which may be reconsidered if and when the issue should happen to come to the attention of the Director.

"Questions that the Director might be willing to delegate to his staff for settlement are not important enough for decision by the OWM . . . The job of the staff ought to be to aid the Director in reaching decisions, not to carve a field in which it can act independently of the Director . . .

"On these sorts of questions [broad political policy], it is difficult enough to establish a sphere of understanding within which the Director can effectively work. Another link of delegation places a strain on the initial delegation to the Director and can be made only at great hazard. It seems to me that we have had enough examples of the disastrous consequences of delegation of decision to subordinates at this high level to settle the issue definitively." (V. O. Key, "The OWM Staff Question," Bureau of the Budget Intra-Office Memorandum, August 16, 1943. Transmitted to OWM.)

This advice was generally followed until 1945, but the policy slackened somewhat thereafter. Evidence indicates that the earlier policy was much more successful.

out national danger in the assignment—or inevitable accretion—of great responsibilities to the President, if we fail to equip him sufficiently with both the authority and the assistance he needs to act responsibly and effectively.[60] We cannot afford to rely on the emergence of "great men" who can meet their responsibilities despite inadequate assistance and organizational equipment. The stakes are too high. While no institutional organization to serve the Presidency can guarantee against the caprices of "personality," discretion and necessity demand that we provide the office with machinery which may minimize the possibility of paralysis at the center of government. To obtain positive coördinated government within the framework of the executive branch, we must supply the tools for effective action at the pivot of government—the President's office.

If we provide the Executive Office with the tools of modern management, obtain a merging of staff and line work within the executive, secure policy cohesion, and fuse planning, policy development and administrative action, we will have taken a long step toward maintaining responsible democratic government. An effective presidential arm for continuous program coördination could contribute substantially to these ends.

[60] "It is not widely enough recognized that the reality of responsible government is dependent upon the ability of the President to control the executive branch." Paul H. Appleby, "The Significance of the Hoover Commission Report," *The Yale Review*, Autumn 1949, p. 8.

INDEX